For Reference

Not to be taken from this room

D1553839

DISCARDED

COLLEGE OF THE SEQUOIAS
LIBRARY

EUROPEAN HISTORICAL DICTIONARIES
Edited by Jon Woronoff

1. *Portugal,* by Douglas L. Wheeler. 1993

Historical Dictionary
of
PORTUGAL

by

DOUGLAS L. WHEELER

European Historical Dictionaries, No. 1

The Scarecrow Press, Inc.
Metuchen, N.J., & London
1993

COLLEGE OF THE SEQUOIAS
LIBRARY

British Library Cataloguing-in-Publication data available

Library of Congress Cataloging-in-Publication Data

Wheeler, Douglas L.
        Historical dictionary of Portugal / by Douglas L.
Wheeler.
                p.   cm. — (European historical dictionaries ; no.
1)
        Includes bibliographical references.
        ISBN 0-8108-2696-8 (alk. paper)
        1. Portugal—History—Dictionaries.   1. Title.
II. Series.
DP535.W44   1993
946.9′003—dc20   93-27030

Copyright © 1993 by Douglas L. Wheeler
Manufactured in the United States of America

Printed on acid-free paper

COLLEGE OF THE SEQUOIAS
LIBRARY

This book is dedicated to the memory of Professor Francis Millet Rogers (1915–1990), late Nancy Clark Smith Professor of Portuguese Language and Literatures, Harvard University, who taught me my first Portuguese language and who made a real difference in launching me on my career in Portuguese Studies.

CONTENTS

ACKNOWLEDGMENTS

In recounting an entire academic career's scholarly debts regarding knowledge of Portugal, where does one begin? My journey of learning on this topic began as a colonial Africanist in Graduate School at Boston University and continued as a member of the first Fulbright Student exchange group in Portugal, 1961–1962. Early on, I was almost overwhelmed with the sheer scale of Portugal's long past. Keeping in mind that the United States as a nation is a little over 200 years old, students will note that as of 1992 Portugal was 852 years old as a nation. There are two scholars in this field to whom I owe a great deal, although I was never formally a student of theirs. These scholars are Professors James Duffy (Brandeis University) and C. R. Boxer (formerly of London University, Yale and Indiana Universities) whose writings on Portugal and her overseas imperial history at the beginnings of my studies on Portugal and Angola caught my attention. Duffy's book *Portuguese Africa* was both a revelation and an inspiration; Duffy's lively writing and trenchant views made dry-as-dust material come alive and put it into contemporary context. While Boxer's many writings on imperial Portugal did not bring events to the present, his witty style and profound research impressed the novice.

I remain grateful, too, to the University of New Hampshire, Durham, for granting me leave from teaching spring term, 1992, in order to complete this project which had begun in earnest in the summer of 1991. I would like to thank the Series Editor, Jon Woronoff, for an early commitment to include a volume on Portugal in the new European Historical Dictionary series. Given the fact that so little Portuguese history is regularly offered in course work in North American colleges and universities and the fact that there are so few up-to-date, general reference works on Portugal's history for the beginning, general reader, it is all the more essential that such a volume as this is now available, even with its inevitable omissions and other shortcomings. When I review my academic career in the Portuguese Studies area, I know that there was little or nothing available to the student or even the traveler or visitor to Portugal who wished to begin to grasp the essentials of Portuguese history, continental and overseas, and to survey the richness of Portuguese civilization. I hope that this volume will fill that gap.

Douglas L. Wheeler

EDITOR'S FOREWORD

Few countries have had a history as extraordinary as Portugal's. A tiny country in a remote corner of southwest Europe, it not only preserved its often threatened independence but conquered a vast, scattered empire. Then, even when other empires succumbed, it fought tenaciously to hold on. This history was sometimes glorious, sometimes shameful, but it could never be ignored. Indeed, at times the past appeared to overwhelm the present. And it is only recently that its people could concentrate on the present and build for the future in a renovated Europe.

It is not easy to grasp the immensity of Portugal's 2,000-year past, but it is necessary if one wants to know where it comes from and where it is heading. Fortunately, this path is clearly marked by our latest historical dictionary. The crucial moments are highlighted in a handy chronology and further elucidated in specific entries. But the recent past and present have pride of place and the future is foreshadowed in other entries and the introduction. These entries cover the most significant persons, places and events as well as essential facets of the economy, society, historical monuments and culture. For those who wish to learn more it is merely necessary to consult the excellent comprehensive bibliography which includes works in English, Portuguese and other European languages.

This volume was written by one of the foremost authorities on Portugal. Douglas L. Wheeler is professor of modern history at the University of New Hampshire, Durham, where he lectures on both Portugal and the former Portuguese territories in Africa. He is also coordinator of the International Conference Group on Portugal and editor of the *Portuguese Studies Review*. Dr. Wheeler, once a Fulbright student in Portugal, returns there for frequent visits. He has written extensively including other books such as *Angola* (with René Pélissier), *Republican Portugal* and *In Search of Modern Portugal* (co-editor with Lawrence Graham).

Jon Woronoff
Series Editor

ACRONYMS AND SPECIAL TERMS

AD	Democratic Alliance (Aliança Democrática)
AR	Assembly of the Republic (Assembleia da República)
Azulejo	Portuguese ceramic (decorative) tile
CADC	Academic Center of Christian Democracy (Centro Académico da Democracia Cristã)
CDS	Social Democratic Center Party (Christian Democrats) (Centro da Democracia Social)
CEP	Portuguese Expeditionary Corps (World War I) (Corpo Expedicionário Português)
COPCON	Operational Command for Continental Portugal (Comando Operacional para Portugal Continental)
Cortes	Representative assembly-council under Monarchy
CR	Council of the Revolution (Conselho da Revolução)
DGS	Directorate-General of Security (Direcção-Geral da Seguridade)
EEC	European Economic Community (or EC)
Estado Novo	"New State" Dictatorship
Fidalgo	Noble, aristocrat
FNLA	National Front for the Liberation of Angola (Frente Nacional para a Libertação de Angola)
FRELIMO	Mozambique Liberation Front (Frente para a Libertação de Moçambique)
FRETILIN	Revolutionary Front of Independent East Timor (Frente Revolucionária do Timor Leste Independente)
GNR	Republican National Guard (Guarda Nacional Republicana)
Golpe	Coup or military insurrection
Golpismo	Tendency for coups or military insurrections
MFA	Armed Forces Movement (Movimento das Forças Armadas)

MPLA	Popular Movement for the Liberation of Angola (Movimento Popular para a Libertação de Angola)
MUD	Movement of Democratic Unity (Movimento da Unidade Democrática)
NATO	North Atlantic Treaty Organization
PAIGC	African Party for the Independence of Guinea and Cape Verde (Partido Africano para a Independência da Guiné e do Cabo Verde)
PC	Centrist Party (Partido Centrista)
PCP	Portuguese Communist Party (Partido Comunista Português)
PIDE	International and State Defense Police (Polícia Internacional e de Defesa do Estado)
PPD	Popular Democratic Party (Partido Popular Democrático)
PR	Reformist Party (Partido Reformista)
PRE	Evolutionist Republican Party (Partido Republicano Evolucionista)
PRP	Portuguese Republican Party ("The Democrats") (Partido Republicano Português)
Pronunciamento	Military coup, insurrection or *golpe*
PS	Socialist Party (Partido Socialista)
PSD	Social Democratic Party (Partido Social Democrático)
PVDE	Vigilance and State Defense Police (Polícia Vigilância e de Defesa do Estado)
UN	National Union (União Nacional)
UNESCO	United Nations Educational, Scientific and Cultural Organization
UNITA	National Union for the Total Independence of Angola (União Nacional para a Independência Total de Angola)
UR	Republican Union Party (União Republicana)

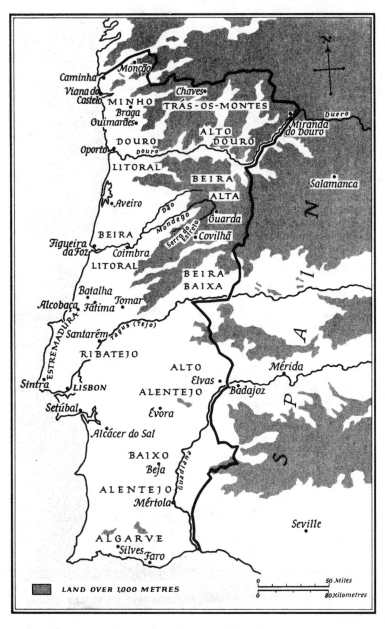

Map of Portugal showing the traditional names of provinces.
Reproduced from Sarah Bradford, *Portugal* (London: Thames &
Hudson, 1973), p. 13, with permission.

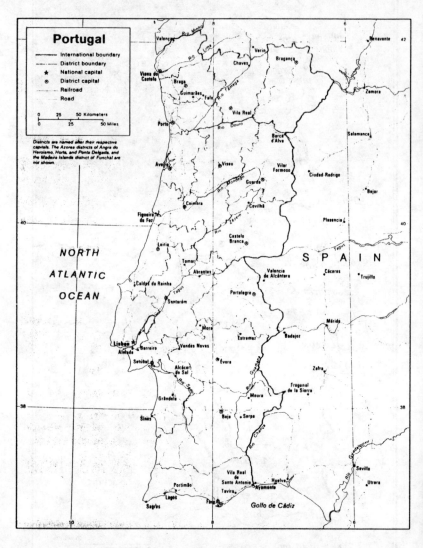

Map showing the current names of Portugal's provinces.

HISTORICAL CHRONOLOGY

15,000–3,000 BC Paleolithic cultures in western Portugal.

400–200 BC   Greek and Carthaginian trade settlements on coast.

202 BC   Roman armies invade ancient Lusitania.

137 BC   Intensive Romanization of Lusitania begins.

410 AD   Germanic tribes—Suevi and Visigoths—begin conquest of Roman Lusitania and Galicia.

714–716   Muslims begin conquest of Visigothic Lusitania.

1034   Christian reconquest frontier reaches Mondego River.

1064   Christians conquer Coimbra.

1139   Burgundian Count Afonso Henriques proclaims himself King of Portugal; birth of Portugal.

1147   With English Crusaders' help, Portuguese conquer Lisbon from Muslims.

1179   Papacy formally recognized Portugal's independence.

1250   Last Muslim city (Silves) falls to Portuguese army.

1384   Aviz Dynasty begins with rule of King João I.

1385   Battle of Aljubarrota, defeat of Castilian invaders with English assistance.

1415	Beginning of overseas expansion as Portugal captures Moroccan city of Ceuta.
1434	Prince Henry the Navigator's ships pass beyond Cape Bojador, West Africa.
1460	Death of Prince Henry. Portuguese reach what is now Senegal, West Africa.
1470s	Portuguese explore West African coast and reach what is now Ghana and Nigeria and begin colonizing islands of São Tomé and Príncipe.
1482–83	Portuguese navigator Diogo Cão reaches mouth of Congo River and Angola.
1488	Navigator Bartolomeu Dias rounds Cape of Good Hope, South Africa, and finds route to Indian Ocean.
1492–93	Columbus' first voyage to West Indies.
1493	Columbus visits Azores and Portugal on return from first voyage; tells of discovery of New World.
1494	Treaty of Tordesillas signed between Portugal and Spain: delimits spheres of conquest with line 370 leagues west of Cape Verde Islands (claimed by Portugal); Portugal's sphere to east of line includes, in effect, Brazil.
1495	King Manuel I and Royal Council decide to continue seeking all-water route around Africa to Asia.
1497–99	Epic voyage of Vasco da Gama from Portugal around Africa to west India, successful completion of sea route to Asia project; Da Gama returns to Portugal with samples of Asian spices.
1500	Bound for India, Navigator Pedro Álvares Cabral "discovers" coast of Brazil and claims for Portugal.

1509	Battle of Diu, India; Portugal's command of Indian Ocean assured for some time with Francisco de Almeida's naval victory over Egyptian and Gujerati fleets.
1510	Afonso de Albuquerque conquers Goa, India; beginning of Portuguese hegemony in south Asia.
1557	Portuguese merchants granted Chinese territory of Macau for trading factory.
1578	Battle of Alcácer-Quivir; Moroccan forces defeat army of King Sebastião of Portugal.
1580	King Phillip II of Spain claims and conquers Portugal; Spanish rule of Portugal, 1580–1640.
1640	December 1. Portuguese Revolution in Lisbon overthrows Spanish rule, restores independence. Beginning of Portugal's Braganza royal dynasty.
1654	Following Dutch invasions and conquest of parts of Brazil and Angola, Dutch expelled by force.
1661	Anglo-Portuguese alliance treaty signed: England pledges to defend Portugal "as if it were England itself." Queen Catherine of Braganza marries England's Charles II.
1668	February. In Portuguese-Spanish peace treaty, Spain recognizes independence of Portugal, thus ending 28-year War of Restoration.
1703	Methuen Treaty signed, key commercial-trade agreement between England and Portugal.
1750	Pombal becomes chief minister of King José I.
1777	Pombal dismissed as chief minister by Queen Maria I.

1791   Portugal and United States establish full diplomatic relations.

1807   November. First Napoleonic invasion; French forces under Junot conquer Portugal. Royal family flees to colony of Brazil and remains until 1821.

1809   Second French invasion of Portugal under General Soult.

1811   Third French invasion of Portugal under General Masséna.

1813   Following British General Wellington's military victories, French forces evacuate Portugal.

1817   Liberal, Constitutional movements against Absolutist Monarchist rule break out in Brazil (Pernambuco) and Portugal (Lisbon, under General Gomes Freire); crushed by Government. British Marshal of Portugal's army, Beresford, rules Portugal.

1820   Liberal insurrection in army officer corps breaks out in Cadiz, Spain, and influences similar movement in Portugal's armed forces.

1821   King João VI returns from Rio de Janeiro, Brazil, and accepts a Constitution; era of Constitutional Monarchy begins. Constitution of 1821 ratified.

1822   September 7. João VI's son, Pedro, proclaims inde pendence of Brazil from Portugal and is named Emperor.

1825   Portugal recognizes sovereign independence of Brazil.

1826   King João VI dies; power struggle for throne ensues between his sons, brothers Pedro and Miguel.

1831–1834   Civil war between Absolutist King Miguel and Constitutionalist Pedro, who abandons throne of Brazil to restore his young daughter Maria to throne of Portugal; Miguel's armed forces defeated by those of Pedro.

1834–1853   Constitutional Monarchy consolidated under rule of Queen Maria II, who dies in 1853.

1853–1871   Regeneration period of economic development and political stability; public works projects sponsored by Minister Fontes Pereira de Melo.

1871–1890   Rotativism period of alternating party governments; achieves political stability and less military intervention in politics and government. Expansion of colonial territory in tropical Africa.

1890   January. Following territorial dispute in central Africa, Britain delivers "Ultimatum" to Portugal demanding withdrawal of Portugal's forces from what is now Malawi and Zimbabwe. Portugal's government, humiliated in accepting demand under threat of a diplomatic break, falls. Beginning of governmental and political instability; Monarchist decline and Republicanism's rise.

1891   Anglo-Portuguese treaties signed relating to delimitation of frontiers in colonial Africa.

1899   Treaty of Windsor; renewal of Anglo-Portuguese defense and friendship alliance.

1903   Triumphal visit of King Edward VII to Portugal.

1906   Politician João Franco supported by King Carlos I in dictatorship to restore order and reform.

1908   February 1. murder by Portuguese anarchists in Lisbon of King Carlos I and his heir apparent, Prince Don Luís. Eighteen year-old King Manuel II, assumes throne.

1910   October 3–5. Following Republican-led military insurrection in armed forces, Monarchy falls and first Portuguese Republic is proclaimed. Beginning of unstable, economically troubled parliamentary Republic form of government.

1915   May. Violent insurrection in Lisbon overturns Government of General Pimenta de Castro; nearly a thousand casualties from several days of armed combat in capital.

1916   March. Following Portugal's honoring ally Britain's request to confiscate German shipping in Portuguese harbors, Germany declares war on Portugal and Portugal enters World War I on Allied side.

1917   Portugal organizes and dispatches Portuguese Expeditionary Corps to fight on the Western front.

April 9. Portuguese forces mauled by German offensive in Battle of Lys. Food rationing and riots in Lisbon. Portuguese military operations in Mozambique against German expedition's invasion from German East Africa.

December 5. Authoritarian, Presidentialist Government under Major Sidónio Pais takes power in Lisbon, following a successful military coup.

1918   November 11. Armistice brings cessation of hostilities on Western front in World War I. Portuguese expeditionary forces stationed in Angola, Mozambique and Flanders begin return trip to Portugal.

December 14. President Sidónio Pais assassinated. Chaotic period of ephemeral civil war ensues.

1919–1921   Excessively unstable political period, including January 1919 abortive effort of Portuguese Monarchists to restore Braganza dynasty to power. Republican forces prevail, but level of public violence, economic distress and deprivation remains high.

1921   October. Political violence attains peak with murder of former Prime Minister and other prominent political figures in Lisbon. Sectors of armed forces and Guarda Nacional Republicana mutinous.

1925   Year of financial and corruption scandals, including Portuguese Bank Note (fraud) case; Military court acquits guilty military insurrectionists and one military judge declares "the country is sick."

1926   May 28. Republic overthrown by military coup or *pronunciamento* and conspiracy among officer corps. Parliament's doors locked and parliament closed for nearly nine years to January 1935. End of parliamentary Republic, Western Europe's most unstable political system in this century, beginning of the Portuguese Dictatorship, after 1930 known as the *Estado Novo*. Officer corps assumes reins of government, initiates military censorship of the press and suppresses opposition.

1927   February. Military dictatorship under General Óscar Carmona crushes failed Republican armed insurrection in Oporto and Lisbon.

1928   April. Military Dictatorship names Professor António de Oliveira Salazar Minister of Finance, with dictatorial powers over budget, to stabilize finances and rebuild economy. Insurrectionism among military elements continues into 1931.

1930   Dr. Salazar named Minister for Colonies and announces balanced budgets. Dictatorship consolidates support by various means including creation of official regime "movement," the

National Union. Salazar engineers a Colonial Act to ensure Lisbon's control of bankrupt African colonies by means of new fiscal controls and centralization of authority.

1932 July. Military Dictatorship names Salazar Premier for first time and cabinet composition undergoes civilianization; academic colleagues and protégés plan conservative reform and rejuvenation of society, polity and economy.

1933 Dictatorship's Constitution ratified by new parliament, the National Assembly; Portugal described in document as "unitary, corporative Republic" and governance influenced by Salazar's stern personality and doctrines such as Integralism, Catholicism and fiscal conservatism.

1936 Violent instability and ensuing Civil War in neighboring Spain, soon internationalized by Fascist and Communist intervention, shake *Estado Novo* regime. Pseudo-Fascist period of regime features creation of imitation Fascist institutions to defend regime from Leftist threats; Portugal institutes "Portuguese Youth" and "Portuguese Legion."

1939 September 3. Premier Salazar declares Portugal's neutrality in World War II.

1943 October. Anglo-Portuguese agreement grants naval and air base facilities to Britain and later to United States for Battle of the Atlantic and Normandy invasion support. Third Reich protests breach of Portugal's neutrality.

1944 June 6. On day of Allies' Normandy invasion, Portugal suspends mining and export of wolfram ore to both sides in war.

1945 May 8. Popular celebrations of Allied victory and Fascist defeat in Lisbon and Oporto coincide with Victory in Europe Day. Following managed elections for Dictatorship's National Assembly in November, regime police, renamed PIDE with increased powers, represses opposition.

1947   Abortive military coup in central Portugal easily crushed by regime. Independence of India and initiation of Indian protests against Portuguese colonial rule in Goa and other enclaves in India.

1949   Portugal becomes founding member of NATO.

1951   Portugal alters Constitution and renames overseas colonies "Overseas Provinces." Portugal and United States sign military base agreements for use of air and naval facilities in Azores Islands and military aid to Lisbon. President Carmona dies in office, succeeded by General Craveiro Lopes (1951–1958).

1958   Air Force General Humberto Delgado, in opposition, challenges dictatorship's handpicked successor to Craveiro Lopes, Admiral Américo Tomás. Delgado rallies coalition of democratic, liberal and Communist opposition but loses rigged election and later flees to exile in Brazil.

1961   January and February. Dictatorship rocked by armed African insurrection in northern Angola, crushed by armed forces. Hijacking of Portuguese ocean liner by ally of Delgado, Captain Henrique Galvão.

April. Salazar defeats attempted military coup and reshuffles cabinet with group of younger figures who seek to reform colonial rule and strengthen the regime's image abroad.

December 18. Indian Army rapidly defeats Portugal's defense force in Goa, Damão and Diu and incorporates Portugal's Indian possessions into Indian Union.

1962   January. Abortive military coup in Beja, Portugal.

1965   February. General Delgado and his Brazilian secretary murdered and secretly buried near Spanish frontier by political police, PIDE.

1968   August and September. Premier Salazar, aged 79, suffers crippling stoke. President Tomás names former cabinet officer Marcello Caetano as Salazar's successor. Caetano institutes modest reforms in Portugal and overseas.

1971   Caetano Government ratifies amended Constitution which allows slight devolution and autonomy to overseas provinces in Africa and Asia. Right-wing loyalists oppose reforms in Portugal.

1974   April 25. Military coup engineered by Armed Forces Movement overthrows Dictatorship and establishes Provisional Government emphasizing democratization, economic development and decolonization. Limited resistance by loyalists. President Tomás and Premier Caetano flown to exile first in Madeira and then in Brazil. General Spínola appointed President.

        September. Revolution moves to Left, as President Spínola, thwarted in his program, resigns.

1975   March. Military coup by conservative forces fails and Leftist response includes nationalization of major portion of economy. Polarization between forces and parties of Left and Right.

        November 25. Military coup by moderate military elements thwarts Leftist forces. Constituent Assembly prepares Constitution. Revolution moves from Left to Center and then Right.

1976   March. Constitution ratified by Assembly of the Republic.

April 25. Second general legislative election gives largest share of seats to Socialists. Former oppositionist lawyer, Mário Soares, elected deputy and named Premier.

1977–1985   Political pendulum of Democratic Portugal moves from Center-Left to Center-Right, as Social Democrats increase hold on Assembly and take office under Premier Cavaco Silva. July 1985 elections give edge to Social Democrats who advocate strong free enterprise measures and revision of Leftist-generated 1976 Constitution, amended modestly in 1982.

1986   January. Portugal joins European Community.

1987   July. General, legislative elections for Assembly give more than 50% to Social Democrats led by Premier Cavaco Silva. For first time, the Republic has a majority government.

1991   July. General, legislative elections for Assembly result in new Social Democrat victory and majority government.

1992   January–July. Portugal holds Chairmanship of European Community.

December. Tariff barriers fall as fully integrated Common Market established in European Community.

INTRODUCTION

Portugal is a small Western European nation with a large, distinctive past replete with both triumph and tragedy. One of the continent's oldest nation-states, Portugal has frontiers which are essentially unchanged since the late 14th century. The country's unique character and 850-year history as an independent state present several curious paradoxes. As of 1974, when much of the remainder of the Portuguese overseas empire was decolonized, Portuguese society appeared to be the most ethnically homogeneous of the two Iberian states and of much of Europe. Yet, Portuguese society had received during two thousand years infusions of other ethnic groups in invasions and immigration: Phoenicians, Greeks, Celts, Romans, Suevi, Visigoths, Muslims (Arab and Berber), Jews, Italians, Flemings, Burgundian French, black Africans and Asians. Indeed, Portugal has been a crossroads, despite its relative isolation in the western corner of the Iberian Peninsula, between the West and North Africa, Tropical Africa, and Asia and America. Since 1974, Portugal's society is no longer as ethnically homogeneous as there has been significant immigration of former subjects from her erstwhile overseas empire.

Other paradoxes should be noted as well. While Portugal is sometimes confused with Spain or things Spanish, its very national independence and national culture depend on being *different* from Spain and Spaniards. Today, Portugal's independence may be taken for granted. Since 1140, except for 1580–1640 when she was ruled by Philippine Spain, Portugal has been a sovereign state. Nevertheless, a recurring theme of the nation's history is cycles of anxiety and despair that its freedom as a nation is at risk. There is a paradox, too, about Portugal's overseas empire(s) which lasted half a millennium (1415–1975): after 1822, when Brazil achieved independence from Portugal, most of the Portuguese who emigrated overseas never set foot in their overseas empire, but preferred to emigrate to Brazil or to other countries in North or South America or Europe where there were established Portuguese overseas communities.

1

Portugal was a world power during the period of 1415–1550, the era of the discoveries, expansion and early empire, and since then the Portuguese have experienced periods of decline, decadence and rejuvenation. Despite the fact that Portugal slipped to the rank of a third or fourth rate power after 1580, Portugal and her people can claim rightfully an unusual number of "firsts" or distinctions which assure their place both in world and in Western history. These distinctions should be kept in mind while acknowledging that for more than 400 years Portugal has generally lagged behind the rest of Western Europe, though not Southern Europe, in social and economic developments and has remained behind even her only neighbor and sometime nemesis, Spain.

Portugal's pioneering role in the discoveries and exploration era of the 15th and 16th centuries is well known. Often noted, too, is the Portuguese role in the art and science of maritime navigation through the efforts of early navigators, map-makers, seamen and fishermen. What is often forgotten is the slender base of resources of this country with a small population largely of rural peasants until recently, a state which occupies but 16% of the Iberian Peninsula. As of 1139–1140, when Portugal emerged first as an independent country, soon to be a unified nation-state, England and France had not achieved this status. The Portuguese were the first state in the Iberian Peninsula to expel the Muslim invaders from their portion of the Peninsula; Portugal had achieved this by 1250, more than 200 years before Castile managed to do the same in her portion of the Peninsula (1492).

Other distinctions may be noted. Portugal conquered the first overseas empire beyond the Mediterranean in the early modern era and established the first plantation system based on slave labor. Portugal's empire was the first to be colonized and the last to be decolonized in the 20th century. With so much of her scattered, seaborne empire dependent upon the safety and seaworthiness of shipping, Portugal was a pioneer in initiating marine insurance, a practice which is taken for granted today. During the time of Pombaline Portugal (1750–1777), Portugal was the first state to organize and to hold an industrial trade fair. In distinctive political and governmental developments, Portugal's record is more mixed and this fact suggests that maintaining a government with a functioning rule of law and a pluralist, representative democracy has not been an easy matter in a country which for so long has been one of the poorest and least educated in the West. Portugal's first

Republic (1910–26), only the third Republic in a largely Monarchist Europe (after France and Switzerland), was Western Europe's most unstable parliamentary system in our century. Finally, the authoritarian *Estado Novo* or "New State" (1926–1974) was the longest surviving authoritarian system in Western Europe's 20th century. When Portugal departed from her overseas empire in 1974–1975, the descendants, in effect, of Prince Henry the Navigator were leaving the West's oldest empire.

Portugal's individuality is based mainly on its long history of distinctiveness, its intense determination to use any means—alliance, diplomacy, defense, trade or empire—to be a sovereign state, independent of Spain, and on a national pride in the Portuguese language. Another master factor in Portuguese affairs deserves mention. The country's politics and government have been influenced not only by intellectual currents from the Atlantic or through Spain from Europe which brought new political ideas and institutions and novel technologies. Given the weight of empire in Portugal's past, it is not surprising that public affairs have been hostage to a degree to what happened in her overseas empire. Most important have been domestic responses to imperial affairs during both imperial and internal crises since 1415 which have continued to the mid-1970s and beyond. One of the most important themes of Portuguese history, and one oddly neglected by not a few histories, is that every major political crisis and fundamental change in the system, in other words, revolution, since 1415 has been intimately connected with a related imperial crisis. The respective dates of these historical crises are: 1437, 1495, 1578–1580, 1640, 1820–1822, 1890, 1910, 1926–1930, 1961 and 1974. The reader will find greater detail on each crisis in historical context in the history section of this Introduction and in relevant Dictionary entries.

PHYSICAL FEATURES

The Republic of Portugal is located on the western edge of the Iberian Peninsula. A major geographical dividing line is the Tagus River: Portugal north of it has an Atlantic orientation; the country to the south of it has a Mediterranean orientation. Geography provides little evidence that Portugal is clearly geographically distinct from Spain and there is no major natural barrier between the two countries along more than 755 miles of the Luso-Spanish frontier. In climate,

Portugal has a number of micro-climates similar to the micro-climates of Galicia, Estremadura and Andalusia in neighboring Spain. North of the Tagus, in general, there is an Atlantic-type climate with higher rainfall, cold winters and some snow in the mountainous areas. South of the Tagus is a more Mediterranean climate, with hot, dry, often rainless summers, and cool, wet winters. Lisbon, the capital, which has a fifth of the country's population living in its region, has an average annual mean temperature in the mid-60°s F (18–19°C).

For a small country with an area of 35,340 square miles (89,000 square kilometers), including the Atlantic archipelagos of the Azores and the Madeiras, which is about the size of the state of Indiana in the United States, Portugal has a remarkable diversity of regional topography and scenery. In some respects, Portugal resembles an island in the Peninsula, embodying a unique fusion of European and non-European cultures, akin to Spain yet apart. Its geography is a study in contrasts from the flat, sandy coastal plain, in some places unusually wide for Europe, to the mountainous Beira districts or provinces north of the Tagus, to the snow-capped mountain range of the Estrela, with its unique ski area, to the rocky, barren, remote Tras-os-Montes district bordering Spain. There are extensive forests in central and northern Portugal which contrast with the flat, almost Kansas-like plains of the wheat belt in the Alentejo district. There is also the unique Algarve district, isolated somewhat from the Alentejo district by a mountain range with a micro-climate and topography and vegetation which resemble closely those of North Africa.

While Portugal is small, just 350 miles (550 kilometers) long and from 80–130 miles (130 to 200 kilometers) wide, it is strategically located on transportation and communication routes between Europe and North Africa, and the Americas and Europe. Geographical location is one key to the long history of Portugal's three overseas empires which stretched once from Morocco to the Moluccas and from lonely Sagres at Cape St. Vincent to Rio de Janeiro, Brazil. It is essential to emphasize the identity of her neighbors: on the north and east she is bounded by Spain her only neighbor and by the Atlantic Ocean on the south and west. Portugal is the western-most country of Western Europe and her shape resembles a face, with Lisbon below the nose, staring into the Atlantic. No part of Portugal touches the Mediterranean and her Atlantic-orientation has been a response in part to turning her back on Castile and Leon (later Spain) and exploring, traveling and trading or working in lands beyond the Peninsula. Portugal was the pioneering nation in the Atlantic-born European discoveries during the Renaissance and her diplomatic and trade relations have been dominated by countries which have been Atlantic powers as well: Spain, England (now Britain), France, Brazil, once her greatest colony, and the United States.

POPULATION AND EMIGRATION

Today Portugal and her Atlantic islands have a population of about 10.3 million people. While ethnic homogeneity has been characteristic of this population in recent history, Portugal's population over the centuries has seen an infusion of non-Portuguese ethnic groups between various parts of Europe, the Middle East and Africa. Between 1500 and 1800, a significant population of black Africans, brought in as slaves, was absorbed in the population. And since 1950, a population of Cape Verdeans, who worked in menial labor, resides in Portugal. With the influx of African, Goan and Timorese refugees and exiles from the empire after 1974, there has been greater ethnic diversity in the Portuguese population.

Population growth is reflected below:

Portugal's Population Since the 16th Century

1527	1,200,000 (estimate only)
1768	2,400,000 (estimate only)
1864	4,287,000 first census
1890	5,049,700
1900	5,423,000
1911	5,960,000
1930	6,826,000
1940	7,185,143
1950	8,510,000
1960	8,889,000
1970	8,668,000 * note: decrease
1980	9,833,000
1992	10,300,000 (estimate)

Traditionally, Portugal is a country with a history of emigration to foreign lands as well as to the overseas empire. During the early centuries of empire, only relatively small numbers of Portuguese emigrated to reside permanently in colonies. But, after the establishment of the second, largely Brazilian empire in the 17th century, greater numbers of Portuguese left to seek their fortunes outside Europe. It was only toward the end of the 19th century, however, that Portuguese emigration became a mass movement, at first, largely to Brazil. While Portuguese-speaking Brazil was by far the most popular destination for the majority of Portuguese emigrants in early modern and modern times, after 1830 the United States and later Venezuela also became common destinations. Portuguese emigration patterns have changed in the 20th century and, as the Portuguese historian and economist Oliveira Martins wrote before the turn of the century, Portuguese emigration rates are a kind of national barometer. Crises and related social, political and economic conditions within Portugal as well as the presence of established emigrant communities in various countries, emigration laws, and the world economy have combined to shape emigration rates and destinations.

After World War II, Brazil no longer remained the favorite destination of the majority of Portuguese emigrants who left Portugal to improve their lives and standards of living. Beginning in the 1950s, and swelling into a massive stream in the 1960s and into the 1970s, most Portuguese emigrated to find work in France and, after the change in US immigration laws in the mid-1960s, a steady stream went to North America, including Canada. The emigration figures below indicate that the most intensive emigration years coincided with excessive political turmoil and severe draft (army conscription) laws during the first Republic (the year 1912 was the high point), that emigration dropped during World Wars I and II and during economic downturns such as the Depression, and that the largest flow of Portuguese emigration in history occurred after the onset of the African colonial wars (1961) and into the 1970s as Portuguese sought emigration as a way to avoid conscription or assignment to Africa.

Despite considerable efforts by Lisbon to divert the stream of emigrants from Brazil or France to the African territories of Angola and Mozambique, this colonization effort failed and most Portuguese who left Portugal preferred the better pay and security of jobs in France and West Germany or in the United States, Venezuela and Brazil, where there were more deeply-rooted Portuguese emigrant communities. As of April 1974, when the military coup in Lisbon signaled the beginning of pressures for the Portuguese settlers to leave Africa, the total number of Portuguese resident in the two larger African territories amounted to about 600,000. In modern times, non-imperial Portuguese emigration has prevailed over imperial emigration and has had a significant impact on Portugal's annual budget (due to emigrants' remittances), on the political system (since emigrants have a degree of absentee voting rights), on investment and business and on culture.

Portuguese Emigration Overseas
(figures rounded off)
Legal emigration, not including illegal emigration.

1887	17,000
1900	ca. 17,000—mainly to Brazil
1910	39,000
1912	88,000—75,000 of these to Brazil
1930	ca. 30,000 (Depression)
1940	ca. 8,800
1950	41,000
1955	57,000
1960	67,000
1965	131,000
1970	209,000

A total of nearly four million Portuguese reside and work outside Portugal as of the early 1990s, or over one third of the country's continental and island population. It has also been said that more Portuguese of Azorean descent reside outside the Azores than in the Azores. The following statistics reflect the pattern of Portuguese emigrant communities in the world outside the mother country.

Overseas Portuguese Communities Population Figures
by Country of Residence
(estimates for 1992):

Brazil	1,000,000
France	650,000
USA	500,000
Canada	400,000
S. Africa	650,000
Venezuela	400,000
West Europe	150,000 (other than France)
Lusophone Africa	50,000
Total:	3,800,000 (estimate)

HISTORY

The history section is organized as follows:

Ancient Lusitania, 2000 BC to 714 AD
Islam, Reconquest and Portugal Created, 714–1140 AD
Reconquest and Burgundian Portugal, 1140–1385
Aviz Dynasty and Portugal's First Overseas Empire, 1385–1580
Portugal under Spanish Rule, 1580–1640
Portugal: Restoration and Second Empire, 1640–1822
Liberalism and Constitutional Monarchy, 1822–1910
First Parliamentary Republic, 1910–1926
New State Dictatorship, 1926–1974
Democratic Portugal, 1974–present

Ancient Lusitania (2000 BC–714 AD)

For several millennia, the history of what is now Portugal in western Iberia was a story of invasion, resistance, counter-invasion, emigration and return emigration. Before Romans described western Iberia or Hispania as "Lusitania," ancient Iberians inhabited the land. Phoenician and Greek trading settlements grew up in the Tagus estuary area and nearby coasts. Beginning around 202 BC, Romans invaded southern Portugal. With Rome's defeat of Carthage, Romans proceeded to conquer and rule the western region north of the Tagus, which they named Roman "Lusitania." In the 4th century AD, as Rome's rule weakened, the area experienced yet another invasion— Germanic tribes, principally the Suevi, who eventually were Christianized. During the 6th century AD, the Suevi kingdom was superseded by yet another Germanic tribe—the Christian Visigoths.

A major turning point in Portugal's history came in 711 as Muslim armies from North Africa, consisting of both Arab and Berber elements, invaded the Iberian peninsula from across the Straits of Gibraltar. They entered what is now Portugal in 714 and proceeded to conquer most of the country except for the far north. For the next half a millennium, Islam and Muslim presence in Portugal left a significant mark upon the politics, government, language and culture of the country.

Islam, Reconquest and Portugal Created, 714–1140 AD

Out of a long frontier struggle between Muslim invaders and Christian communities in the *reconquista* (reconquest) emerged the first dynasty of Portuguese kings (Burgundian) and the independent state of Portugal. Christian forces moved south from what is now the extreme north of Portugal and gradually defeated Muslim forces, besieging and capturing towns under Muslim sway. In the 9th century, as Christian forces slowly made their way southward, Christian elements were dominant only in the area between Minho province and the Douro River; this region became known as *"territorium Portucalense."*

In the 11th century, the advance of the reconquest quickened as local Christian forces were reinforced by fighting, crusading elements from what is now France and England. Christian forces took Montemor (1034), at the Mondego River, Lamego (1058), Viseu (1058) and Coimbra (1064). In 1095, the King of Castile and Leon granted the country of "Portucale," what became northern Portugal, to a Burgundian Count who had emigrated from France. This was the foundation of Portugal. In 1139, a descendant of this Count, Afonso Henriques, proclaimed himself "King of Portugal." He was Portugal's first monarch, the "Founder," and the first of the Burgundian dynasty which ruled until 1385.

The emergence of Portugal in the 12th century as a separate entity in Iberia occurred before the Christian reconquest was completed either in Portugal or in Spain. In the 1140s, the Pope in Rome recognized King Afonso Henriques as monarch of Portugal. In 1147, after a long, bloody siege, Muslim-occupied Lisbon fell to Afonso Henriques' army. Lisbon was the greatest prize of the 500-year war. Assisting this effort were English crusaders on their way to the Holy Land; the first Bishop of Lisbon was an Englishman. When the Portuguese captured Faro and Silves in the Algarve province in 1248–1250, the reconquest was complete, significantly, more than two centuries before Spain completed her reconquest (1492).

Reconquest and Burgundian Portugal (1140–1385)

Two main themes of Portugal's early existence as a nation are the consolidation of control in the independent state and Portugal's defeat of a Castilian threat from the east to its newly-won independence. At the end of this period came the birth of a new royal dynasty (Aviz) which prepared to carry the Christian reconquest beyond continental Portugal across the straits of Gibraltar to North Africa. There was a variety of motives behind these developments. Portugal's independent existence was imperiled by threats from neighboring Iberian states to the north and east. Politics were dominated not only by efforts against the Muslims in Portugal (until 1250) and in nearby southern Spain (until 1492), but also by internecine warfare among the kingdoms of Castile, Leon, Aragon and Portugal. A final comeback of Muslim forces was defeated at the battle of Salado (1340) by allied Castilian and Portuguese forces. In emerging Portugal, the Monarchy gradually gained greater power while it attempted to subordinate or neutralize the nobility and the Church.

The historic and commonplace Portuguese saying, "From Spain, neither a good wind nor a good marriage," was literally played out in diplomacy and war in the late 14th century struggles for mastery in the Peninsula. Larger, more populous Castile was pitted against smaller Portugal. Castile's Juan I intended to force a union between Castile and Portugal during this era of confusion and conflict. In late 1383, Portugal's King Fernando, the last King of the Burgundian dynasty, suddenly died prematurely at age 38 and the Master of Aviz, Portugal's most powerful nobleman, took up the cause of national independence and resistance against Castile's invasion. The Master of Aviz, who became King João I of Portugal, was able to obtain foreign assistance. With the aid of English archers, João's armies defeated the Castilians in the crucial battle of Aljubarrota, on August 14, 1385, a victory which assured Portugal's independence from her Castilian nemesis for several centuries.

Aviz Dynasty and Portugal's First Overseas Empire, 1385–1580

The results of the victory at Aljubarrota, much celebrated in Portugal's art and monuments, and the rise of the Aviz dynasty also helped to establish a new merchant class in Lisbon and Oporto, Portugal's second city. This group supported King João I's program of carrying the reconquest to North Africa since they were interested in expanding Portugal's foreign commerce and tapping into Muslim trade routes and resources in Africa. With the reconquest against the

Muslims completed in Portugal and the Castilian menace thwarted for the moment, the Aviz dynasty launched an era of overseas conquest, exploration and trade. These efforts dominated Portugal's 15th and 16th centuries.

The overseas empire and age of discoveries began with Portugal's bold conquest in 1415 of the Moroccan city of Ceuta. One royal member of the 1415 expedition was young, 21-year-old Prince Henry, later known in history as "Prince Henry the Navigator." His part in the capture of Ceuta won Henry his knighthood and began Portugal's "Marvellous Century" during which the small country was counted as a European and world power of consequence. Henry was the son of King João I and his English Queen, Philippa of Lancaster, but he did not inherit the throne. Instead he spent most of his life, his fortune and that of the wealthy military Order of Christ, on various imperial ventures and on voyages of exploration down the African coast and into the Atlantic. While mythology has surrounded Henry's controversial role in the discoveries, and this role has been exaggerated, there is no doubt that he played a vital part in the initiation of Portugal's first overseas empire and in encouraging exploration. He was naturally curious, had a sense of mission for Portugal and was a strong leader. He also had wealth to expend; at least a third of the African voyages of the time were under his sponsorship. If Prince Henry himself knew little science, significant scientific advances in navigation were made in his day.

What were Portugal's motives for this new imperial effort? The well-worn historical cliché of "God, Glory and Gold" can only partly explain the motivation of a small nation with few natural resources and barely one million people, which was greatly outnumbered by the other powers it confronted. Among Portuguese objectives were the desire to exploit known North African trade routes and resources (gold, wheat, leather, weaponry and other goods which were scarce in Iberia), the need to outflank the Muslim world in the Mediterranean by sailing around Africa, attacking Muslims en route, and the wish to ally with Christian forces beyond Africa. This enterprise also involved a strategy of breaking the Venetian spice monopoly by trading directly with the East by means of discovering and exploiting a sea route around Africa to Asia. Besides the commercial motives, Portugal nurtured a strong crusading sense of Christian mission and various classes in the country saw an opportunity for fame and gain.

By the time of Prince Henry's death in 1460, Portugal had gained control of the Atlantic archipelagos of the Azores and Madeiras, begun to colonize the Cape Verde Islands, failed to conquer the Canary Islands from Castile, captured various cities on Morocco's coast, and explored as far as Senegal, West Africa, down the African coast. By 1488, Bartolomeu Dias had rounded the Cape of Good Hope in South Africa and thereby discovered the way to the Indian Ocean.

Portugal's largely coastal African empire and later her fragile Asian empire brought unexpected wealth but were purchased at a high price. Costs included wars of conquest and defense against rival powers which entailed a loss of skills and population to maintain a scattered empire, to man the far-flung naval and trade fleets and scattered castle-fortresses and to staff her fierce but small armies. Always short of capital, the Monarchy and State became indebted to bankers. There were many defeats beginning in the 16th century at the hands of the larger imperial European states (Spain, France, England and Holland) and many attacks on Portugal and her strung-out empire. Typically, there was also the conflict which arose when a tenuously-held world empire which rarely if every paid its way demanded finance and manpower Portugal herself lacked.

The first 80 years of the glorious imperial era, the golden age of Portugal's imperial power and world influence, was an African phase. During 1415–1488, Portuguese navigators and explorers in small ships, some of them *caravelas* (caravels), explored the treacherous, diseased coasts of Africa from Morocco to South Africa beyond the Cape of Good Hope. By the 1470s, Portuguese had reached the Gulf of Guinea and, in the early 1480s, what is now Angola. Bartolomeu Dias' extraordinary voyage of 1487–1488 to South Africa's coast and the edge of the Indian Ocean convinced Portugal that the best route to Asia's spices and Christians lay south, around the tip of southern Africa. Between 1488 and 1495, there was a hiatus caused in part by domestic conflict in Portugal, discussion of resources available for further conquests beyond Africa in Asia, and serious questions as to Portugal's capacity to reach beyond Africa. In 1495, King Manuel and his council decided to strike for Asia, whatever the consequences. In 1497–1499, Vasco da Gama, under royal orders, made the epic two-year voyage which discovered the sea route to western India (Asia), outflanked Islam and Venice, and began Portugal's Asian empire. Within fifty years Portugal had discovered and begun the exploitation of her largest colony, Brazil, and set up forts and trading posts from the Middle East (Aden and Ormuz), India (Calicut, Goa, etc.), Malacca and Indonesia to Macau in China.

By the 1550s, parts of her largely coastal, maritime, trading post empire from Morocco to the Moluccas was under siege from various hostile forces, including Muslims, Christians, and Hindi. While Moroccan forces expelled the Portuguese from the major coastal cities by 1550, the rival European powers of Castile (Spain), England, France and later Holland began to seize portions of her undermanned, outgunned maritime empire.

In 1580, Phillip II of Spain, whose mother was a Portuguese princess and who had a strong claim to the Portuguese throne, invaded Portugal, claimed the throne and assumed control over the country and, by extension, its African, Asian and American empires. Phillip II filled the power vacuum which appeared in Portugal following the loss of most of Portugal's army and its young, headstrong King Sebastião in a disastrous war in Morocco. Sebastião's death in battle (1578) and the lack of a natural heir to succeed him as well as the weak leadership of the Cardinal who briefly assumed control in Lisbon led to a crisis that Spain's strong monarch exploited. As a result, Portugal lost her independence to Spain for a period of 60 years.

Portugal Under Spanish Rule (1580–1640)

Despite the disastrous nature of Portugal's experience under Spanish rule, "The Babylonian Captivity" gave birth to modern Portuguese nationalism and sense of independence, her second overseas empire, and her modern alliance system with England. Although Spain allowed Portugal's weakened empire some autonomy, Spanish rule in Portugal became increasingly burdensome and unacceptable. Spain's ambitious imperial efforts in Europe and overseas had an impact on the Portuguese as Spain made greater and greater demands on her smaller neighbor for manpower and money. Portugal's culture underwent a controversial Castilianization, while her empire became hostage to Spain's fortunes. New rival powers of England, France and Holland attacked and took parts of Spain's empire and at the same time attacked Portugal's empire as well as the mother country.

Portugal's empire bore the consequences of being attacked by Spain's bitter enemies in what was a form of world war. Portuguese losses were heavy. By 1640, Portugal had lost most of her Moroccan cities as well as Ceylon, the Moluccas and sections of India. With this, Portugal's Asian empire was gravely weakened. Only Goa, Damão, Diu, Bombay, Timor and Macau remained and, in Brazil, Dutch forces occupied the northeast.

On December 1, 1640, long commemorated as a national holiday, Portuguese rebels led by the Duke of Braganza overthrew Spanish domination and took advantage of Spanish weakness following a more serious rebellion in Catalonia. Portugal regained national independence from Spain, but at a price: dependence on foreign assistance to maintain her independence in the form of the renewal of the Alliance with England.

Restoration and Second Empire (1640–1822)

Foreign affairs and empire dominated the Restoration era and aftermath, and Portugal again briefly enjoyed greater European power and prestige. The Anglo-Portuguese Alliance was renewed and strengthened in treaties of 1642, 1654 and 1661 and Portugal's independence from Spain was underwritten by English pledges and armed assistance. In a Luso-Spanish treaty of 1668, Spain recognized Portugal's independence. Portugal's alliance with England was a marriage of convenience and necessity between two nations with important religious, cultural and social differences. In return for legal, diplomatic and trade privileges as well as the use during war and peace of Portugal's great Lisbon harbor and colonial ports for England's navy, England pledged to protect Portugal and her scattered empire from any attack. The previously-cited 17th century alliance treaties were renewed later in the Treaty of Windsor, signed in London in 1899. On at least ten different occasions after 1640 and during the next two centuries, England was central in helping prevent or repel foreign invasions of her ally, Portugal.

Portugal's second empire (1640–1822) was largely Brazil-oriented. Portuguese colonization, exploitation of wealth and emigration focused on Portuguese America and imperial revenues came chiefly from Brazil. Between 1670 and 1740, Portugal's royalty and nobility grew wealthier on funds which derived from Brazilian gold, diamonds, sugar, tobacco and other crops, an enterprise supported by the Atlantic slave trade and the supply of African slave labor from West Africa and Angola. From what survived the terrible Lisbon earthquake of 1755, visitors today can see where much of that wealth was invested: Portugal's rich legacy of monumental architecture. Meanwhile, the African slave trade took a toll in Angola and West Africa.

In continental Portugal, Absolutist Monarchy dominated politics and government and there was a struggle for position and power between the Monarchy and other institutions such as the Church and nobility. King José I's chief minister, known in history usually as the Marquis of Pombal (ruled: 1750–1777), sharply suppressed the nobility, the Church (including the Inquisition, now a weak institution) and expelled the Jesuits. Pombal also made an effort to reduce economic dependence on England, the oldest ally. But his successes did not last much beyond his disputed time in office.

Beginning in the late 18th century, the European-wide impact of the French Revolution and the rise of Napoleon placed Portugal in a vulnerable position. With the Monarchy ineffectively led by an insane Queen (Maria I) and her indecisive Regent son (João VI), Portugal again became the focus of foreign ambition and aggression. With England unable to provide decisive assistance in time, France—with Spain's consent—invaded Portugal in 1807. As Napoleon's army under General Junot entered Lisbon meeting no resistance, Portugal's royal family fled on a British fleet to Brazil where it remained in exile until 1821. In the meantime, Portugal's overseas empire was again under threat. There was a power vacuum as the monarch was absent, foreign armies were present and new political notions of Liberalism and Constitutional Monarchy were exciting various groups of citizens.

Again, England came to the rescue, this time in the form of the armies of the Duke of Wellington. Three successive French invasions of Portugal were defeated and expelled, and Wellington succeeded in carrying the war against Napoleon across the Portuguese frontier into Spain. The presence of the English army, the new French-born ideas and the political vacuum combined to create revolutionary conditions. The French invasions and the Peninsular wars, where Portuguese armed forces played a key role, marked the beginning of a new era in politics.

Liberalism and Constitutional Monarchy (1822–1910)

During 1807–1822, foreign invasions, war and civil strife over conflicting political ideas gravely damaged Portugal's commerce, economy and novice industry. The next terrible blow was the loss of Brazil in 1822, the jewel in the imperial crown. Portugal's very independence seemed to be at risk. In vain, Portugal sought to resist Brazilian independence by force, but in 1825 it formally acknowledged Brazilian independence by treaty.

The country's slow recovery from the destructive French invasions and the "war of independence" was complicated by civil strife over the form of Constitutional Monarchy which suited Portugal. After struggles over these issues between 1820 and 1834, Portugal's moderate Constitutional Monarchy settled somewhat uncertainly into a new political, social and economic order which featured a new upper middle class based on land ownership and commerce; a Catholic Church which though still important lived with reduced privileges and property; a largely African (third) empire to which Lisbon and Oporto devoted increasing spiritual and material resources starting with the liberal imperial plans of 1836 and 1851 and continuing with the work of institutions like the Lisbon Society of Geography (estab. 1875); a mass of rural peasants whose bonds to the land weakened after 1850 and who began to emigrate in increasing numbers to Brazil and North America, if not to the empire; and a Monarchy whose Constitution (Charter of 1826) lent it strong political powers in order to exert a moderating influence between the feuding executive and legislative branches of government.

Chronic military intervention in national politics began in 19th century Portugal. Such intervention, usually commencing with coups or *pronunciamentos* (military revolts), was a shortcut to the spoils of political office and could reflect popular discontent as well as the power of personalities. An early example of this was the 1817 *golpe* (coup) attempt of General Gomes Freire against British military rule in Portugal before the return of King João VI from Brazil. Except for a more stable period from 1851 to 1880, military intervention in politics, or the threat thereof, became a feature of the Constitutional Monarchy's political life and it continued into the first Republic and the subsequent Dictatorship.

Beginning with the Regeneration period (1851–1880), Portugal experienced greater political stability and economic progress. Military intervention in politics virtually ceased, industrialization and construction of railroads, roads and bridges proceeded, two political parties (Regenerators and Historicals) worked out a system of rotation in power and leading intellectuals sparked a cultural revival in several fields. In 19th century literature, there was a new golden age led by such figures as Alexandre Herculano (historian), Eça de Queirós (novelist), Almeida Garrett (playwright and essayist), Antero de Quental (poet) and Joaquim Oliveira Martins (historian and social scientist). In her third overseas empire, Portugal attempted to replace the slave trade and slavery with legitimate economic activities, reform the administration and expand Portuguese holdings beyond coastal footholds deep into the African hinterlands in West, West Central and East Africa. After 1841, to some extent, and especially after 1870, colonial affairs, combined with intense nationalism, pressures for economic profit in Africa, sentiment for national revival, and the drift of European affairs would make or break Lisbon governments.

Beginning with the political crisis which arose out of the "English Ultimatum" affair of January 1890, the Monarchy became discredited and identified with the poorly functioning political system, political parties splintered and Republicanism found more supporters. Portugal participated in the "Scramble for Africa," expanded its African holdings, but failed to annex territory connecting Angola and Mozambique. A growing foreign debt and State bankruptcy as of the early 1890s damaged the Constitutional Monarchy's reputation, despite the efforts of King Carlos in diplomacy, the renewal of the Alliance in the Windsor Treaty of 1899 and the successful if bloody colonial wars in the empire (1880–1897). Republicanism proclaimed that Portugal's weak economy and poor society were due to two historic institutions: the Monarchy and the (Catholic) Church. A Republic, its stalwarts claimed, would bring greater individual liberty, efficient, if more decentralized government and stronger colonial program while stripping the Church of its role in both society and education.

As the Monarchy lost support and Republicans became more aggressive, violence increased in politics. King Carlos I and his heir Luís were murdered in Lisbon by anarchist-Republicans on February 1, 1908. Following a military and civil insurrection and fighting between Monarchist and Republican forces, on October 5, 1910, King Manuel II fled Portugal and a Republic was proclaimed.

First Parliamentary Republic (1910–1926)

Portugal's first attempt at democracy, the First Republic, was the most unstable, turbulent parliamentary republic in the history of

20th century Western Europe. During a little under 16 years of the Republic, there were 45 governments, a number of legislatures that did not complete normal terms, military coups and only one President who completed his four-year term in office. Portuguese society was poorly prepared for this political experiment. Among the deadly legacies of the Monarchy were a huge public debt, a largely rural, apolitical and illiterate peasant population, conflict over the causes of the country's misfortunes and lack of experience with a pluralist, democratic system.

The Republic had some talented leadership but lacked popular, institutional and economic support. The 1911 Republican Constitution established only a limited democracy, as only a small portion of the adult male citizenry was eligible to vote. In a country where the majority was Catholic, the Republic passed harshly anti-clerical laws and its institutions and supporters persecuted both the Church and its adherents. During its brief, disjointed life, the First Republic drafted important reform plans in economic, social and educational affairs, actively promoted development in the empire and pursued a liberal, generous foreign policy. Following British requests for Portugal's assistance in World War I, Portugal entered the war on the Allied side in March 1916 and sent armies to Flanders and Portuguese Africa. Portugal's intervention in that conflict, however, was too costly in many respects and the ultimate failure of the Republic in part may be ascribed to Portugal's World War I activities.

Unfortunately for the Republic, its time coincided with new threats to Portugal's African possessions: World War I, social and political demands from various classes which could not be reconciled, excessive military intervention in politics and, in particular, the worst economic and financial crisis Portugal had experienced since the 16th and 17th centuries. After the original Portuguese Republican Party (PRP, also known as the "Democrats") splintered into three warring groups in 1912, no true multiparty system emerged. The Democrats, except for only one or two elections, held an iron monopoly of electoral power and political corruption became a major issue. As right-wing dictatorships elsewhere in Europe began to take power in Italy (1922), neighboring Spain (1923) and Greece (1925), what scant popular support remained for the Republic collapsed. Backed by a right-wing coalition of landowners from Alentejo, clergy, Coimbra University faculty and students, Catholic organizations and big business, career military officers led by General Gomes da Costa executed a coup on May 28, 1926, turned out the last Republican government and established a Military Dictatorship.

New State Dictatorship (1926–1974)

During the Military Dictatorship phase of the authoritarian period (1926–32), professional military officers, largely from the army, governed and administered Portugal and held key cabinet posts but soon discovered that the military possessed no magic formula that could readily solve the problems inherited from the first Republic. Especially during the years 1926–1931, the Military Dictatorship, even with its political repression of Republican activities and institutions (military censorship of the Press, political police action and closure of the Republic's rowdy parliament), was characterized by similar weaknesses: personalism and factionalism, military coups and political instability, including civil strife and loss of life, State debt and bankruptcy and a weak economy. "Barracks parliamentarism" was not an acceptable alternative even to the "Nightmare Republic."

Led by General Óscar Carmona, who had replaced and sent into exile General Gomes da Costa, the Military Dictatorship turned to a civilian expert in finance and economics to break the budget impasse and bring coherence to the disorganized system. Appointed Minister of Finance on April 27, 1928, Coimbra University Law School Professor of Economics António de Oliveira Salazar (1889–1970) first reformed finance, helped balance the budget and then turned to other concerns as he garnered extraordinary governing powers. In 1930, he was appointed interim head of another key ministry (Colonies) and within a few years had become, in effect, a civilian dictator who, with the military hierarchy's support, provided the Dictatorship with coherence, a program and a set of policies.

For nearly forty years after he was appointed the first civilian Premier of the Dictatorship in 1932, Salazar's personality dominated the system. Unlike Fascist dictators elsewhere in Europe, Salazar was directly appointed by the army but was never endorsed by a popular political party, street militia or voter base. The scholarly, reclusive Coimbra University Professor built up what became known after 1932 as the *Estado Novo* ("New State"), which at the time of its overthrow by another military coup in 1974 was the longest surviving authoritarian regime in Western Europe. The system of Salazar and the largely academic and technocratic ruling group he gathered in his cabinets was based on Lisbon's central bureaucracy (*"Estado"* or administrative State) which was supported by the President of the Republic—always a senior career military officer Gen. Oscar Carmona (1928–1951), Gen. Craveiro Lopes (1951–58) and Admiral Américo Tómaz (1958–1974)—and various forces built up under the system. These included a rubber-stamp legislature or "National Assembly" (1935–1974) and a political police known under various names PVDE (1932–1945), PIDE (1945–1969) and DGS (1969–1974). Other defenders of the regime's security were the National Republican Guard, a kind of second army, the Portuguese Legion (1936–1974) and the Portuguese Youth [Movement] (1936–1974). In addition to censorship of the media, theater and books, there was political repression and a deliberate policy of de-politicization. All political parties except for the approved movement of regime loyalists, the *"União Nácional"* or "National Union" (1930–1974), were banned and the regime's basic survival strategy was a no-risk Statism.

The most vigorous and more popular period of the Dictatorship was 1932–1944, when the basic structures were established. Never monolithic or entirely the work of one person (Salazar), the New State Dictatorship was constructed with the assistance of several dozen top associates of the Coimbra Professor who were mainly academics from law schools, some technocrats with specialized skills and a handful of trusted career military officers. The Dictatorship's 1933 Constitution declared Portugal to be a "unitary, corporative Republic," and pressures to restore the Monarchy were neutralized. While some of the regime's followers were Fascists and pseudo-Fascists, many more were conservative Catholics, Integralists, Nationalists and Monarchists of different varieties and even some reactionary Republicans. If the Dictatorship was authoritarian, it was not totalitarian and, unlike Fascism in Mussolini's Italy or Hitler's Germany, it usually employed the minimum of terror necessary to defeat what remained a largely fractious, incoherent opposition.

With the tumultuous Second Republic and the subsequent Civil War in nearby Spain, the regime felt threatened and reinforced its defenses. During what Salazar rightly perceived as a time of foreign policy crisis for Portugal (1936–45), he assumed control of the Ministry of Foreign Affairs. From there, four basic objectives were pursued: supporting the Nationalist rebels of General Franco in the Spanish Civil War (1936–1939) and concluding defense treaties with a triumphant Franco; ensuring that General Franco in an exhausted Spain did not enter World War II on the Axis side, maintaining Portuguese neutrality in World War II with a post-1942 tilt toward the Allies, including granting Britain and the United States use of bases in the Azores Islands; and preserving and protecting Portugal's Atlantic Islands and its extensive, if poor, overseas empire in Africa and Asia.

During the middle years of the Dictatorship (1944–1958), many key Salazar associates in government either died or resigned, there was greater social unrest in the form of unprecedented strikes and clandestine Communist activities, intensified opposition and new threatening international pressures on Portugal's overseas empire. During the earlier phase of the Cold War (1947–1960), Portugal became a steadfast if weak member of the U.S.-dominated NATO alliance and, in 1955, with American support, Portugal joined the United Nations. Colonial affairs remained a central concern of the regime. As of 1939, Portugal was the third largest colonial power in the world and possessed territories in tropical Africa (Angola, Mozambique, Guinea-Bissau and São Tomé and Príncipe Islands) and the remnants of her 16th century empire in Asia (Goa, Damão, Diu, East Timor and Macau). Beginning in the early 1950s, following the independence of India in 1947, Portugal resisted Indian pressures to decolonize Portuguese India and used police forces to discourage internal opposition in her Asian and African colonies.

The later years of the Salazar-dominated dictatorship (1958–1968) witnessed the aging of the increasingly isolated but feared Premier and new threats both at home and overseas. While the regime easily overcame the brief oppositionist threat from rival Presidential candidate, General Humberto Delgado, in the spring of 1958, new developments in the African and Asian empires imperiled the Lisbon-based system. In February 1961, oppositionists hijacked the Portuguese ocean liner *Santa Maria* and, in following weeks, African insurgents in northern Angola, though they failed to expel the Portuguese, gained world-wide media attention, discredited the Dictatorship and began the 13-year colonial war. After thwarting a dissident military coup against his continued leadership, Salazar and his ruling group mobilized military repression in Angola and attempted to develop the African colonies at a faster pace in order to ensure Portuguese sovereignty. Meanwhile, the other European colonial powers (England, France, Belgium and Spain) rapidly granted political independence to their African territories.

At the time of Salazar's removal from power in September 1968, following a stroke, Portugal's overseas efforts appeared to be successful. President Tomás appointed Dr. Marcello Caetano as Salazar's successor in the Premiership. While maintaining the Dictatorship's basic structures, and continuing the regime's essential colonial policy, Caetano attempted wider reforms in colonial administration and some devolution of power from Lisbon as well as more freedom of expression in Lisbon. Still, a great deal of the budget was devoted to supporting the wars in Africa. Meanwhile in Asia, Portuguese India had fallen when the Indian Army invaded in December 1961. The loss of Goa was a psychological blow and of the Asian empire only East Timor and Macau remained.

The Caetano years (1968–1974) were but a hiatus between the waning Salazar era and something new. There was greater political freedom and rapid economic growth (5–6% annually to late 1973), but Caetano's Government was unable to reform the old system thoroughly and refused to consider revolutionary methods either at home or in the empire. In the end, revolution came from junior officers of the professional military who organized the Armed Forces Movement. It was this group of several hundred officers, mainly in the army and navy, which engineered a largely bloodless coup in Lisbon on April 25, 1974. Their unexpected action brought down the 48-year-old dictatorship.

Democratic Portugal (1974–present)

Following successful military operations of the Armed Forces Movement against the Caetano government, Portugal experienced what became known as the "Revolution of Carnations." It so happened that during the rainy week of the military action, Lisbon flower shops were featuring carnations and the revolutionaries and their parties adopted the *red* carnations as the most common symbol of the event as well as of the new freedom from dictatorship. The Armed Forces Movements (MFA), whose leaders at first were mostly little known majors and captains, proclaimed a three-fold program of change for the new Portugal: democracy; decolonization of the overseas empire, after ending the colonial wars; and developing a backward economy in the spirit of opportunity and equality. During the first nineteen months after the coup, there was civil strife, some anarchy and a power struggle. With the passing of the old regime, public euphoria burst forth as the new Provisional Government proclaimed the freedoms of speech, press and assembly and abolished censorship, the political police, the Portuguese Legion, Portuguese Youth and other regime units, including the National Union. Scores of political parties were born and joined the senior political party, the Portuguese Community Party (PCP), and the Socialist Party (PS), founded shortly before the coup.

Portugal's unusual Revolution of 1974–1975 went through several phases. There was an attempt to take control by radical Leftists, including the PCP and its allies. This was thwarted in time by moderate officers in the army as well as by two political parties' efforts: the Socialists and the Social Democrats (PPD, later PSD). The first phase was from April to September 1974. Provisional President General Spínola, whose 1974 book *Portugal and the Future* had helped prepare public opinion for the coup, met irresistible Leftist pressures. After Spínola's efforts to avoid rapid decolonization of the African empire failed, he resigned in September 1974. During the second phase, from September 1974–March 1975, radical military officers gained control, but a coup attempt by General Spínola and his supporters in Lisbon in March 1975 failed and Spínola fled to Spain.

In the next phase of the Revolution, March–November 1975, a strong Leftist reaction followed. Farm workers occupied and "nationalized" 2.5 million acres of farmland in the Alentejo province and radicals in the Provisional Government ordered the nationalization of Portuguese banks (foreign banks were exempted), utilities and major industries, or about 60% of the economic system. There were power struggles among various political parties—a total of 50 emerged—and in the streets there was civil strife among labor, military and law enforcement groups. A Constituent Assembly, elected on April 25, 1975, in Portugal's first free elections since 1926, drafted a democratic Constitution. A Council of the Revolution (CR), briefly a revolutionary military watchdog committee, was entrenched in the government (1976–1982) under the Constitution, until a later revision. During the chaotic year of 1975, about 30 persons were killed in political frays while unstable provisional governments came and went. On November 25, 1975, moderate military forces led by Colonel Ramalho Eanes, who later was twice elected President of the Republic (1976 and 1981), defeated radical, Leftist military groups' revolutionary conspiracies.

In the meantime, Portugal's scattered overseas empire experienced a precipitous and unprepared decolonization. One by one the former colonies were granted and accepted independence—Guinea-Bissau (September 1974), Cape Verde Islands (July 1975) and Mozambique (July 1975). Portugal offered to turn over Macau to the People's Republic of China, but the offer was refused then and later negotiations led to the establishment of a reversion date of 1999. But in two former colonies, the process of decolonization had tragic results.

In Angola, decolonization negotiations were greatly complicated by the fact that there were three rival nationalist movements in a struggle for power. The January 1975 Alvor Agreement signed by Portugal and these three parties was not effectively implemented. A bloody civil war broke out in Angola in the spring of 1975 and, when Portuguese armed forces withdrew and declared that Angola was independent on November 11, 1975, the bloodshed only increased. Meanwhile, most of the white Portuguese settlers from Angola and Mozambique fled during the course of 1975. Together with African refugees, more than 600,000 of these *retornados* ("returned ones") went by ship and air to Portugal and thousands more to Namibia, South Africa, Brazil, Canada and the United States.

The second major decolonization disaster was in Portugal's colony of East Timor in the Indonesian archipelago. Portugal's capacity to supervise and control a peaceful transition to independence in this isolated, neglected colony was limited by the strength of giant Indonesia, distance from Lisbon and Portugal's revolutionary disorder and Portugal's inability to defend Timor. In November 1975, before Portugal granted independence and as Timorese nationalists fought for hegemony, Indonesia's armed forces invaded, conquered and annexed East Timor. The East Timor question still remains a contentious international issue in the United Nations as well as in Lisbon and Jakarta.

After several free elections and record voter turnouts between April 25, 1975 and June 1976, civil war was averted and Portugal entered a difficult period of adjustment to the new situation. The Armed Forces Movement was dissolved and the military were removed from governing structures and returned to the barracks. The 1976

Constitution was revised several times as of 1982 and 1989 in order to re-emphasize the principle of free enterprise in the economy while much of the large, nationalized sector was privatized. In June 1976, General Ramalho Eanes was elected the first constitutional President of the Republic (five year term) and he appointed Socialist leader Dr. Mário Soares as Prime Minister of the first constitutional Government. During 1976 to 1985, Portugal's new system featured a weak economy and finances, labor unrest, administrative and political instability. The difficult transition was eased in part by the strong currency and gold reserves inherited from the Dictatorship, but Lisbon seemed unable to cope with high unemployment, new debt, the complex impact of the refugees from Africa, world recession and the agitation of political parties. Four major parties emerged from all the maelstrom of 1974–75, except for the Communist Party, all newly founded. They were, from left to right, the Communists, the Socialists which managed to dominate governments and the legislature but not win a majority in the Assembly of the Republic, the Social Democrats (PSD) and the Christian Democrats (CDS). During this period, the annual growth rate was low (1–2%) and the nationalized sector of the economy stagnated.

Enhanced economic growth, greater political stability and more effective central government ("The State") as of 1985, and especially 1987, were due to several developments. In 1977, Portugal applied for membership in the European Community (EC). In January 1986, with Spain, Portugal was granted membership and economic and financial progress in the intervening years has been significantly influenced by the comparatively large investment, loans, technology, advice and other assistance from the EC. Low unemployment, high annual growth rates (5%), and moderate inflation have also been induced by the new political and administrative stability in Lisbon. Led by Prime Minister Cavaco Silva, an economist who was trained abroad, the Social Democrats' strong organization, management and electoral support since 1985 have assisted in encouraging economic recovery and development. In 1985, the Social Democrats turned the Socialists out of office and won the general election, though they did not have an absolute majority of Assembly seats. In the elections of 1987 and 1991, however, the PSD was returned to power with clear majorities of over 50% of the vote.

The new Democratic Portugal, despite the complex economic, social and educational problems it had to address and solve, many of them decades in the making, could face the 21st century with reasonable assurance if not full confidence. While more than a third of the Portuguese people resided and worked abroad, Portugal no longer bore the crushing burden of an unmanageable, restive empire and its relations with the new Lusophone African states were improved. Portuguese citizens enjoyed full civil and human rights and culture was flourishing with the new freedoms. International support for the new democracy and for economic development was on a scale unknown in the country's long history. While its precise relationship with the European Community and with individual countries remained the subject of negotiation, Portugal was much less isolated and more hopeful of promising changes than at any time in this century.

PORTUGUESE SOCIETY AND ECONOMY

Even in post-1974 Portugal, the past always seems present in a nation with a history of great duration. An American documentary film on Portugal in the late 1970s described this ancient country as "a Past in Search of a Future." With Portugal fully involved in the dynamic European Community, the country is now living "a Present in Search of a Future." For, despite the progress of the years since the mid-1970s, Portugal's economy and society have a long way to go in many different problem areas before they can claim to be on a par with the development found even in Spain, much less the remainder of Western Europe.

As Portugal struggles to move from underdevelopment, especially in many rural areas beyond the coast, to development, it must also keep in mind the perils of too rapid modern development which can damage two of its most precious assets: its scenery and environment. The growth and future prosperity of the economy will depend not only on overseas Portuguese communities' remittances in funds and investment, but also on the degree to which the government and the private sector can flourish while remaining stewards of clean air, soil, water and other finite resources on which the tourism industry depends and on which Portugal's world image as a unique place to visit rests. With a multitude of scenic historic buildings where the visitor can see history in tile and stone, this distinctive country is a kind of museum-state.

As world attention is diverted to Eastern Europe and the former Soviet Union, little Portugal is often forgotten or taken for granted as a member of the European Community. But its progress during more than a decade since the Captains' coup in 1974 has been steady. Still, the pressing social, educational and economic problems of Portugal are too entrenched for simple, quick solutions and they cannot be overcome in merely a decade, or two, or even three. Consider just the general statistics of comparison with the remainder of the present European Community. While Portugal has passed Greece in per capita annual income and has had a higher growth rate than the average member, in all the social and educational indicators Portugal remains the weakest and least developed. There is 20% illiteracy; fully 40% of Portuguese homes do not have running water or modern plumbing; there is a severe housing shortage; there is also a tragic health crisis and the medical system is in need of reform. These facts are indicative of a society which badly requires an improved educational system at all levels and whose lack of resources restricts public access to secondary and higher educational levels. While new roads, highways and bridges have been built, many hospitals are sub-standard and social security pensions are inadequate. In addition, there is a growing gap between the rich and the poor.

Statistics on employment in Portugal are deceptive. Portugal boasts one of the lowest unemployment rates in the EC, but it is public knowledge that there is a good deal of under-employment in various sectors and that the bloated State bureaucracy is not only inefficient but a drain on the public purse. Furthermore, one explanation of the low unemployment rate is the existence of continued, widespread Portuguese emigration to work abroad. Many of the overseas Portuguese retain Portuguese citizenship, visit Portugal regularly, send money home and expect to play a larger role in Portuguese society as well as in politics in the future. This massive pool of about four million Portuguese abroad, some of whom if they resided permanently in Portugal would be unemployed or under-employed and consuming public services, represents at least indirectly relief for the unemployment situation. Portugal, then, is a relatively poor country which for over a century has produced more people than it has produced jobs. This was and is a fact of life in Portuguese society old and new. Whatever the causes behind this large emigration factor, a master factor in Portugal's modern history, emigration is a question which is both traditional and contemporary and every government since the late Braganza monarchy has had to address it.

Democratic Portugal is enjoying the new cultural, social and political freedoms. It has benefited extensively from membership in the European Community since 1986 and, whatever public doubts there may be about the price to be paid, it is likely that no Portuguese Government in the near future can afford to sever this connection. That said, as the tariff and worker movement walls come down in 1993 and thereafter, sectors of Portugal's still undeveloped economy and society will suffer adverse effects. Strikes of about-to-be-laid-off Customs House workers in Lisbon are only a harbinger of the future indications of the price to be paid for EC membership. Over the coming years, the new Portugal must make its own way and decide how best to meet its own special needs while cooperating with and participating in the EC, the United Nations, whatever evolves out of NATO, and other international organizations.

THE DICTIONARY

AFONSO I, KING. See HENRIQUES, KING AFONSO.

AFONSO III, KING (reign: 1246–1279). Member of the Burgundian dynasty and King of Portugal who completed the *Reconquista* (Reconquest) of Portugal's territory from the Muslim invaders. Afonso's reign featured a number of important measures: imposing greater unity on the kingdom; establishing the power of the throne over the Church (q.v.); and shifting Portugal's capital from Coimbra to Lisbon (qq.v.). Afonso III was the father of future King Dinis (q.v.), who ruled Portugal from 1279 to 1325.

AJUDÁ, FORTRESS OF ST. JOHN THE BAPTIST OF. Tiny colonial enclave of only a few acres, Portugal's Fortress of St. John the Baptist of Ajudá was a Portuguese possession in the West African country of Dahomey (renamed Benin) from the 17th century. Ordered built by the Captain-General of São Tomé in 1680, the stone fortress was close to the shore of the Gulf of Guinea. Portugal's fragile sovereignty over this historic site was ended in 1961 when the government of independent Dahomey forcibly occupied the place. Before this process of unilateral decolonization was carried out, the Portuguese official in charge of the Fortress set fire to the interior of his bungalow nearby and drove to the airport. Intransigence against all decolonization pressures was the Dictatorship's response even in the strange case of Ajudá.

AJUDA, PALACE OF. Massive Ajuda Palace, in Ajuda section of Lisbon (q.v.), incredibly never finished, is the largest former royal residence in the capital. Like so many other Portuguese palaces now open to the public or in current government use, it is actually a "working palace-museum," containing countless treasures within its royal walls. Ajuda Palace was built beginning in 1802 to replace a wooden palace close by which had burned down. Construction endured throughout the remainder of the 19th century. Neoclassical in style, Ajuda Palace retains a somewhat forbidding, cold look, but the interior is dominated by a rich mixture of 19th century Portuguese art which includes many paintings, tapestries, ceramics and statuary. Ajuda also features an important library, one documentary key to the history of the century during which the Palace was built, with rare manuscripts and books as part of contemporary government records.

ALBUQUERQUE, AFONSO DE (1462?–1515). One of the greatest conquistadores of Portugal's Asian empire in its early phase and, in effect, the founder of the nation's Asian empire. Initially serving the King in Portugal's Moroccan conquests, Albuquerque first went to India (q.v.) in 1503 and during the period 1503–1515 he extended Portugal's maritime empire from the west coast of India to Malacca and made efforts to take various port-cities in Arabia including Aden and Ormuz. Among his ambitious schemes was the plan to carry a crusade to the Muslims in Arabia and capture the holy city of Mecca. Known as the most capable of Portugal's early empire builders, Albuquerque was a man of many talents: soldier, sailor, administrator, statesman, diplomat and strategist. Poorly rewarded for his Herculean efforts on behalf of King Manuel I (q.v.), Albuquerque was humiliated when he witnessed the arrival of a new Governor, appointed without his knowledge by the King. Exhausted and mortally ill from his campaigns, he died in Goa, Portuguese India, on December 16, 1515.

ALBUQUERQUE, JOAQUIM MOUSINHO DE (1855–1902). Portugal's most celebrated colonial soldier of the modern era, Governor and conqueror of the Gaza state in Mozambique (q.v.). A career army officer with noble lineage, "Mousinho," as he became known in his generation, later helped to shape Portugal's administration and policies in Mozambique, following army service in India. He served largely as a soldier involved in so-called "pacification" campaigns in Mozambique (1890–

1895) and then as an administrator, where he acted as Royal Commissioner and Governor-General of Mozambique from 1896 to 1898.

After he first visited Africa in 1890, the year of the English "ultimatum" (q.v.), the principal part of his career would be devoted to Portuguese Africa and he was to become a noted authority on African affairs and policies. Appointed Governor of the District of Lourenço Marques (today, Maputo) in late 1890, he returned to Portugal in 1892 and then became part of the most famous military expedition to Portuguese Africa of the modern era, the 1895 force sent to Mozambique to conquer the African state of Gaza, in southern Mozambique. Albuquerque distinguished himself in this bloody campaign; at the battle of Coolela, on November 7, 1895, Portuguese forces using the novel machine gun defeated and slaughtered the army of Gaza King Gungunyane. Following his appointment as Military Governor of the Gaza district, Albuquerque grew impatient with the failure of his superiors to give the coup d'grace to the Gaza kingdom by killing or capturing its leader, Gungunyane, who had escaped after the battle of Coolela. With a small force, Mousinho raided his refuge at Chaimite, Mozambique and captured Gungunyane who did not resist (January 1896).

These bold deeds in the 1895 campaign and the surprise kidnapping of Mozambique's most powerful African leader made Albuquerque a hero in Portugal and a colonial celebrity in several other European states. Among the honors showered upon this unusual soldier was the 1896 double appointment as Governor-General and Royal Commissioner of Mozambique colony. His service as chief administrator of Portugal's second most important African territory during 1896–1898 was significant but frustrating. His efforts at sweeping reforms, rejuvenation and decentralization of authority and power were noble but made little impact at the time. He resigned in anger after his failure to move the Lisbon colonial bureaucracy and returned to a restless, relatively inactive life in Portugal. Unable to adjust to dull garrison duty, after he completed his masterful colonial report-memoir on his African service (*Moçambique, 1896–1898*), Albuquerque in vain sought new challenges. Briefly he served as Tutor to Prince Luís, heir apparent of King Carlos I (q.v.), but his efforts to volunteer as an officer in wars in South Africa and China failed.

His idea of a military dictatorship to reform a lagging Constitutional Monarchy rejected both by his patron, King Carlos, and by much of the political system, Lieutenant Colonel Mousinho de Albuquerque found life too painful to bear. On January 8, 1902, while on a Lisbon tram, Albuquerque committed suicide with his own pistol. His importance for future colonial policy in Africa was manifest as Portugal made efforts to decentralize and reform administration until 1930. After 1930, his personal legend as a brave colonial soldier who was an epitome of patriotism grew and was exploited by the Dictatorship led by Salazar (q.v.). Mousinho de Albuquerque was adopted by this regime between 1930 and 1960 as the military-colonial patron-saint of the regime and as an example to Portuguese youth. The name of the place where he surprised Gungunyane, Chaimite, was adopted as the name of an armored car used by the Portuguese army in its post-1961 campaigns in Africa. *See* CARLOS I, KING; GENERATION OF 1895.

ALCÁCER-QUIVIR, BATTLE OF (August 4, 1579). Known to history also as "The Battle of the Three Kings," this event helped weaken Portugal, deprive the country of a non-Castilian legitimate male heir and led to her loss of independence. The site of the battle, known in Arabic as Alcazar-el-Kebr, is southwest of Arzila, Morocco, some 20 miles (50 kilometers) from Tangier. It was here that the Portuguese armed forces under the command of the foolhardy young King, 24-year-old Sebastião of Aviz (q.v.), were defeated and dispersed by Muslim forces under the Sharif of Morocco. More than 8,000 Portuguese died, including the King whose body was apparently buried in Alcácer. About 15,000 of the Portuguese and their allied forces became prisoners in Morocco and few managed to escape to Portuguese forts on the coast. As a result of the disappearance of Sebastião and the defeat of an important part of the country's defense forces, Portugal was more vulnerable to Spanish power than since the late 14th century.

In Morocco and in Portugal, rumors grew into legends concerning the fate of the young King. The cult and mythology of Sebastianism (q.v.) arose out of the initial uncertainty concerning the monarch's fate and the tragic decline and defeat of Portugal. "Sebastianism" featured myths that the King had survived, would return on a foggy morning to Portugal to drive out the Spanish invaders and to restore Portugal to its former greatness. A vast literature in poetry, stories, novels, songs and folklore grew around the sentiment of "Sebastianism." Beginning in the late 16th century in Portugal, persons posing as the returned Sebastian, there to save Portugal, began to appear. *See* SEBASTIANISM; SEBASTIÃO I.

ALCOBAÇA, MONASTERY OF. Located in Alcobaça, Leiria district, this is Portugal's largest church and premier religious monument in Gothic style. Alcobaça was established by the first Portuguese King, Afonso Henriques (q.v.), in the 12th century. According to tradition, its foundation followed the King's wish after the conquest of the town of Santarém from the Moors. The King chose Cistercian monks, recently arrived from France, to oversee the project and to administer the establishment. Construction of what became a Cistercian Abbey and Church began only in 1178. After many delays, the Church was finally completed and dedicated in 1252, though parts of the building were unfinished. The massive structure is in the shape of a Latin cross and the naves are over 60 feet high. Various Portuguese kings and their families are buried in Alcobaça; here also are the famous tombs of the ill-fated Dona Inês de Castro and King Pedro I (qq.v.). Among 18th century visitors and travelers who made the beauty and wonder of Alcobaça famous in England and elsewhere was the wealthy English eccentric and writer, William Beckford, whose 1835 account of his visits to Alcobaça, in effect, put Portugal on the map of English travelers henceforth.

ALJUBARROTA, BATTLE OF (August 14, 1385). The battle which helped ensure the independence of Portugal from Spain (q.v.) for nearly two centuries, presented João I of Aviz (q.v.) as a formidable political figure and assisted John of Gaunt as claimant of Castile's throne. Against a larger Castilian force under Juan of Castile, Portuguese and English forces under commanders such as Nun'Alvares Pereira, the Portuguese chief officer, triumphed. The result of the battle was to strengthen Portugal's independence and political unity as the Monarchy and various classes began to prepare for overseas expansion into the Atlantic and to Africa. Socially, a consequence was the weakening of certain landed classes, which had backed the Castilians, and the rise of Lisbon and Oporto (qq.v.) merchant classes, backers of João of Aviz. In order to commemorate the famous victory of 1385 at Aljubarrota, King João I ordered the construction of a monastery at Batalha. *See* BATALHA, MONASTERY OF.

ALMEIDA, ANTÓNIO JOSÉ DE (1866–1929). Leading political figure in the First Republic, stalwart of Republican politics and the only President of the Republic to serve a full term of office during that political experience (1910–26). Like a number of the leading political figures of his generation, Almeida was educated at Coimbra University's (q.v.) medical school and was a staunch Republican opponent of the Monarchy. Almeida was reputedly the finest speaker and debater of the Republican leaders. When the Provisional Government was named following the Republican Revolution of October 5, 1910, Almeida was included. Compared to Afonso Costa (q.v.), a moderate Republican, Almeida was involved in the fragmenting of the Republican Party (PRP) in 1911–1912 and formed an alternate Republican Party, the Evolutionist Republican Party (PRE) or Evolutionists. Almeida headed one government as Prime Minister (1916–1917), but rapidly became exhausted and disillusioned by the First Republic's unstable, ineffective politics and government. After the assassination of Sidónio Pais (q.v.) in late 1918 and the failed right-wing revolution of 1919, Almeida declared himself non-partisan and his party, the PRE, was dissolved. Loyal to the idea of the Republic, however, Almeida wished to serve in some capacity. Due to his image of being above the political fray, he was elected by the Congress as President of the Republic and served his full term (1919–1923). Prematurely aged by the experience, he withdrew from politics and died in Lisbon in 1929. *See* POLITICAL PARTIES.

ALMEIDA, FRANCISCO DE (1450?–1510). One of the most notable conquistadores and empire-builders of Portugal's early Asian empire and the first Viceroy of Portuguese India. Having served the Catholic Kings in the Granada campaigns, Almeida was also a skilled navigator-sailor. In 1505, King Manuel I (q.v.) dispatched Almeida to India (q.v.) as the first Viceroy, with a fleet of 21 ships and about 1500 soldiers. A ferocious and cruel fighter, Almeida fought his way up the coast of East Africa and along the west coast of India. In early February 1509, Almeida's fleet annihilated a Muslim fleet in the harbor of Diu (q.v.), ensuring Portugal's naval supremacy in the Indian Ocean for more than a century, one of the more decisive naval engagements in world maritime history. Having served as Viceroy successfully during 1506–1509 when replaced by Afonso de Albuquerque (q.v.), under orders from King Manuel, Almeida obstinately refused to step down. Orders from Portugal arrived in a fleet in India in October 1509 and Almeida was forced to accept the fact of his dismissal. On his return to Portugal, when landing near the Cape of Good Hope, Almeida was killed in a skirmish with Africans. *See* DIU, BATTLE OF.

ALVOR, AGREEMENT OF. The ill-fated Alvor Agreement was signed in Alvor, Algarve province, in January 1975. The purpose of the Agreement was to facilitate the peaceful, lawful decolonization of Portugal's former colony of Angola (q.v.). The conference which worked out and signed this instrument was hosted by Portugal's Provisional Government, backed by the Armed Forces Movement (q.v.) which had overthrown the Dictatorship on April 25, 1974, and which had called for rapid decolonization of Portugal's African colonies after a truce in the colonial war. Decolonization negotiations proceeded fairly smoothly in the other African territories, but in Angola rather than one African nationalist movement or party three were struggling for power. They were the National Front for the Liberation of Angola (FNLA), led by Holden Roberto; the Popular Movement for the Liberation of Angola (MPLA), led by Agostinho Neto who had trained as a physician in Portugal; and the National Union for the Total Independence of Angola (UNITA), led by Jonas Savimbi. By the Alvor Agreement, which was signed by four parties: Portugal, FNLA, MPLA and UNITA, the decolonization process would be realized in several stages, ending in November 1975, following free elections with the three nationalist parties participating, Portugal overseeing the elections and the new Army of Angola comprised of elements of the three African parties' armies which had fought Portuguese forces off and on since 1961.

Portugal's government in Lisbon and its government and forces in Angola attempted, but failed, to put the Alvor Agreement into full effect. A civil war broke out in the spring of 1975 in Angola among the three nationalist forces, eventually with the FNLA and UNITA entering an alliance against the MPLA. No all-Angola army was ever constituted and a power struggle among the three armed movements ensued. The MPLA won control of the Luanda region. As the Portuguese forces and Commissioner withdrew, Portugal did not hand over power to any one group. On November 11, 1975, with the Alvor Agreement a dead letter and no elections having been organized, the MPLA declared the independence of Angola and the civil war continued. Angola's independent beginnings were unique in African history: the colonial power suddenly withdrew without handing over power officially to a nationalist party, but "to the people of Angola," and Angola was born as a free state embroiled in a bloody civil war which was to last to the early 1990s. *See* ANGOLA.

ANGLO-PORTUGUESE ALLIANCE. The world's oldest diplomatic connection and alliance, an enduring arrangement between two very different nations and peoples, with important practical consequences in the domestic and foreign affairs of both England (q.v.) and Portugal. The history of this remarkable alliance which has had commercial and trade, political, foreign policy, cultural and imperial aspects, can be outlined in part with a list of the main alliance treaties after the first treaty of commerce and friendship signed between the monarchs of England and Portugal in 1373: 1386—Treaty of Windsor (q.v.), 1654, 1661, 1703—Methuen Treaty (q.v.), 1810, 1899—Treaty signed at Windsor also.

Common interests in the defense of the nation and its overseas empire (in the case of Portugal, after 1415; in the case of England, after 1650) were partly based on characteristics and common enemies both countries shared. Even in the late Middle Ages, England and Portugal faced common enemies: large continental countries which threatened the interests and sovereignty of both, especially France and Spain (qq.v.). In this sense, the Anglo-Portuguese Alliance has always been a defensive alliance in which each ally would assist the other when necessary against its enemies. In the case of Portugal, that enemy invariably was Spain (or component states thereof, such as Castile and Leon) and sometimes France (i.e. when Napoleon's armies invaded and conquered Portugal as of late 1807). In the case of England (after 1707, Britain), that foe was often France and sometimes Spain as well.

Beginning in the late 14th century, England and Portugal forged this unusual relationship, formalized with several treaties which came into direct use during a series of dynastic, imperial, naval and commercial conflicts between 1373 and 1961, the historic period when the Anglo-Portuguese Alliance had its most practical political significance. The relative world power and importance of each ally has varied over the centuries. During the period 1373–1580, the allies were similar in respective ranking in European affairs and during the period 1480–1550, if anything, Portugal was a greater world power with a more important navy than England. During 1580–1810, Portugal fell to a third rank European power status and, during 1810–1914, England was perhaps the premier world power. During 1914–1961, England's world position slipped while Portugal made a slow recovery but remained a third or fourth rank power.

The commercial-trade elements of the alliance has always involved an exchange of goods between two seafaring, maritime peoples with different religions and political systems but complementary economies. The 1703 Methuen Treaty established a trade link which endured for centuries and bore greater advantages for England than for Portugal, though Portugal derived benefits: English woolens for Portuguese wines, especially Port (q.v.), other agricultural produce and fish. Since the signing of the Methuen Treaty, there has been a vigorous debate both in politics and in historical scholarship as to how much each nation benefited economically from the arrangement in which Portugal eventually became dependent upon England and the extent to which Portugal became a kind of economic colony of Britain during the period from 1703–1910.

There is a vast literature on the Alliance, much of it in

Portuguese and by Portuguese writers, which is one expression of the development of modern Portuguese nationalism. During the most active phase of the Alliance, from 1650–1945, there is no doubt but that the core of the mutual interests of the allies amounted to the proposition that Portugal's independence as a nation in Iberia and the integrity of its overseas empire, the third largest among the colonial powers as of 1914, were defended by England, who in turn benefited from the use by the Royal Navy of Portugal's home and colonial ports in times of war and peace. A curious impact on Portuguese language and popular usage had also come about and endured through the impact of dealings with the English allies. The idiom in Portuguese, "*é para inglês ver*," means literally "it is for the Englishman to see," but figuratively it really means, "it is merely for show."

The practical defense side of the Alliance was effectively dead by the end of World War II, but perhaps the most definitive indication of the end of the political significance of an Alliance which still continues in other spheres occurred in December 1961, when the army of the Indian Union invaded Portugal's colonial enclaves in western India, Goa, Damão and Diu (q.v.). While both nations were now NATO allies, their interests clashed when it came to imperial and Commonwealth conflicts and policies. Portugal asked Britain for military assistance in the use of British bases against the army of Britain's largest former colony, India. But Portugal was, in effect, refused assistance by her oldest ally. If the Alliance continues in the 1990s, its essence is historical, nostalgic, commercial and cultural. *See* CATHERINE OF BRAGANZA; ENGLAND; METHUEN, TREATY OF; PORT WINE; WINDSOR, TREATIES OF.

ANGOLA (AND ENCLAVE OF CABINDA). From 1575 to 1975, Angola was a colony of Portugal. Located in west-central Africa, this colony has been one of the largest, most strategically located and richest in mineral and agricultural resources in the continent. At first Portugal's colonial impact was largely coastal, but after 1700 it became more active in the interior. By international treaties signed between 1885 and 1906, Angola's frontiers with what are now Zaire, Zambia, Congo-Brazzaville and Namibia were established. The colony's area was 481,000 square miles (1,246,700 square kilometers), Portugal's largest colonial territory after the independence of Brazil (q.v.). In Portugal's third empire, Angola was the colony with the greatest potential.

The Atlantic slave trade had a massive impact on the history, society, economy and demography of Angola. For centuries, Angola's population played a subordinate role in the economy of Portugal's Brazil-centered empire. Angola's population losses to the slave trade were among the highest in Africa and its economy became, to a large extent, hostage to the Brazilian plantation-based economic system. Even after Brazil's independence in 1822, Brazilian economic interests and capitalists were influential in Angola; it was only after Brazil banned the slave trade in 1850 that the heavy slave traffic to former Portuguese America began to wind down. Although slavery in Angola was abolished, in theory, in the 1870s, it continued in various forms and it was not until the early 1960s that its offspring, forced labor, was finally ended.

Portugal's economic exploitation of Angola went through different stages. During the era of the Atlantic slave trade, ca. 1575–1850, when many of Angola's slaves were shipped to Brazil, Angola's economy was subordinated to Brazil's and to Portugal's. Ambitious Lisbon projects followed when Portugal attempted to replace the illegal slave trade, long the principal income source for the Government of Angola, with legitimate trade, mining and agriculture. The main exports were dyes, copper, rubber, coffee, cotton and sisal. In the 1940s and 1950s, petroleum emerged as an export with real potential. Due to the demand of the World War II belligerents for Angola's raw materials, the economy experienced an impetus and soon other articles such as diamonds, iron ore and manganese found new customers. Angola's economy, on an unprecedented scale, showed significant development which was encouraged by Lisbon. Portugal's colonization schemes, sending white settlers to farm in Angola, began in earnest after 1945, though such plans had been nearly a century in the making. Angola's white population grew from about 40,000 in 1940 to nearly 330,000 settlers in 1974, when the military coup occurred in Portugal.

In the early months of 1961, a war of African insurgency broke out in northern Angola. Portugal dispatched armed forces to suppress resistance and the African insurgents were confined to areas on the borders of northern and eastern Angola at least until the 1966–1967 period. The 13-year colonial war had a telling impact on both Angola and Portugal. When the Armed Forces Movement (q.v.) overthrew the Dictatorship on April 25, 1974, the war in Angola had reached a stalemate and the major African nationalist parties (MPLA, FNLA and UNITA) had made only modest inroads in the northern fringes and in central and eastern Angola, while there was no armed activity in the main cities and towns.

After a truce was called between Portugal and the three African parties, negotiations began to organize the decolonization process. Despite difficult maneuvering among the parties, Portugal, the MPLA, FNLA and UNITA signed the Alvor Agreement (q.v.) of January 1975, whereby Portugal would oversee a transition government, create an all-Angola army and supervise national elections to be held in November 1975. With the outbreak of a bloody civil war among the three African parties and their armies, the Alvor Agreement could not be put into effect. Fighting raged between March and November 1975. Unable to prevent the civil war or to insist that free elections be held, Portugal's officials and armed forces withdrew on November 11, 1975. Rather than handing over power to one party, they transmitted sovereignty to the people of Angola. Angola's civil war continued into the early 1990s. *See* ALVOR AGREEMENT; EMPIRE.

ARMED FORCES MOVEMENT/MOVIMENTO DAS FORÇAS ARMADAS (MFA). The organization of career military who overthrew the *Estado Novo* (q.v.) dictatorship in a virtually bloodless military coup or *pronunciamento* (q.v.) on April 25, 1974. This organization began as a clandestine group of junior career officers, largely from the Army, but later including Air Force and Navy officers, who had a series of secret meetings in Évora and other cities beginning in the summer and fall of 1973. The general grievances of these officers, who tended to be junior officers in their 30s and 40s with the ranks of lieutenant, captain and major, centered on the colonial wars in Portugal's African empire. By 1973 these conflicts were more than a decade old and in two of the wars, namely Guinea-Bissau and

Mozambique (qq.v.), the Portuguese forces were taking heavy losses and losing ground. The catalyst for organizing a formal professional protest at first was not political but professional and corporate: a July 1973 law passed by the Caetano (q.v.) Government which responded to a shortage of officer candidates in the African wars by lowering the professional qualifications for officer candidates for militia officers, something deeply resented by the career officers. But the MFA then organized the military coup of 1974 that met little resistance. *See* TWENTY-FIFTH OF APRIL; CARVALHO, OTELO SARAIVA DE; CAPTAINS, MOVEMENT OF THE.

AZORES ISLANDS. Atlantic archipelago of nine islands: Terceira, São Miguel, Santa Maria, Corvo, Graciosa, São Jorge, Faial, Pico and Flores. This autonomous region of Portugal is 5,821 square miles (2,247 square kilometers) in area. First settled in the 1420s by Portuguese and Flemish colonists, the economy of the archipelago passed through various phases.

The Azores' main crops in four phases were: (1) 15th and 16th centuries: wheat and sugar; (2) 17th century: woods; (3) 18th and 19th centuries: oranges; (4) 20th century: cattle, dairy products, tobacco and pineapples.

The location some 900 miles (1900 kilometers) west of Portugal and over 1100 miles (2400 kilometers) from the eastern coast of the United States (q.v.), and on major sea and trade routes, influenced the islands' development. Major themes of their history are: isolation, North American influence, neglect by Portugal and emigration to North America. As of the 19th century, large numbers of Azoreans emigrated to the United States. By the last quarter of the 20th century, statistics suggested, more people of Azorean descent lived in North America than inhabited the still sparely settled islands. Beginning in World War I, when the U.S. Navy maintained a base at Ponta Delgada, São Miguel island, the Azores' society and economy have been influenced by foreign military base activity. In World War II (1943), British forces used an air base (Lajes) on Terceira island, under an agreement with Portugal, and thereafter the United States made a similar arrangement at Santa Maria. From 1951 on, the U.S. administered an air base at Lajes, Terceira, under NATO auspices. With that, American assistance and military base funds have played an important role in the archipelago's still largely unindustrialized economy.

Since the 1960s, several Azorean independence movements have emerged as well as other groups which advocate that the islands become part of the United States. Such movements have been encouraged by the islands' isolation, a troubled economy and the fact that Portugal has never made developing the islands a major priority. After the fall of the Dictatorship in 1974, the Democratic Portugal organized new efforts to assist the Azores and, in the 1976 Constitution, the Azores were declared an Autonomous Region of Portugal with greater rights of self-government and management. In the 1990s, emigration from the Azores to both the United States and Canada continued, though not at the pace of the earlier periods. At the same time, hundreds of thousands of overseas Portuguese from the Azores Islands resided in the eastern United States, California and Canada. *See* INTRODUCTION, POPULATION AND EMIGRATION.

AZULEJO. Portuguese glazed tile(s) used to decorate walls, fountains, tables and other household furniture. The word comes from the Arabic word *"azuleij"* ("slippery" or "ornamental tile"). These tiles have a variety of glazed and painted decorations from geometric to anthropomorphic and are rectangular or square in shape. Influenced both by Arabic tiles and Dutch tiles (after 1600), the Portuguese *azulejo* changed its decorative motif over the centuries. While early tiles featured only geometric decoration patterns, in the 17th and 18th centuries the classic blue and white decorations which portray individuals or animals or hunting scenes became typical. Since before the 16th century, *azulejos* have decorated the interior and exterior walls and furniture of Portuguese houses, palaces, villas, castles, chapels and churches as well as many public buildings. Next to mosaic sidewalks in towns and cities and gilt wood altars in churches, the *azulejo* art is the most typical Portuguese decor in all sections of the country.

- B -

BACALHAU (CODFISH). Since the 15th century, codfish has been the favorite national dish of the Portuguese. Voyages of the

navigator Corte-Real to Newfoundland, North America, late in
that century, aroused the Portuguese interest in consuming
codfish, particularly in its dried form. For centuries thereafter,
Portuguese codfishing fleets visited the Newfoundland banks
and returned with their precious catches. During periods when
Portugal's economic fortunes were low and when the necessary
shipping was unavailable, the Portuguese arranged to have
English fishermen obtain codfish. After 1835, an annual
Portuguese codfish fleet visited Newfoundland again. Oddly
enough, despite the traditional codfish fleet system, the national
fleet usually acquired only 10–15% of the codfish required and
the remainder was supplied by England (q.v.), Sweden and
Norway. Although the Portuguese codfish fleet ceased to
operate some years ago, codfish remains as popular as ever and is
increasingly expensive.

BATALHA, MONASTERY OF. A prime example of Portuguese
Gothic architecture, Batalha Monastery was ordered built by
King João I (q.v.) of Aviz in gratitude for his victory over the
army of Castile at the battle of Aljubarrota (1385) (q.v.).
Located at the town of Batalha, Leiria district, Batalha's style
was influenced by earlier constructions including Alcobaça
Monastery (q.v.), which is not far away. Begun in 1387–1388,
much of it was completed by the middle of the 15th century,
but there were later works on it as well. The so-called
"Imperfect Chapels" remain unfinished to this day. This
Monastery-Church includes the Royal Tomb in the Chapel of
the Founder, the double tomb of King João I and Queen Filippa
of Lancaster, the parents of Prince Henry the Navigator (qq.v.).
Batalha is formally known as the "Monastery of Santa Maria of
Victory" in Portugal, but in Britain the building is usually
referred to as the Battle Abbey. Batalha also contains Portugal's
Tombs of the Unknown Soldiers, from World War I, where two
soldiers—one killed in Europe and one killed in Africa—with
unknown identities were buried. Members of the armed forces
perpetually guard the site within Batalha Monastery. *See*
ALJUBARROTA.

BEJA, CITY OF. District and city in former Alentejo province, with
about 20,000 population. Its Roman name was *"Pax Julia"* and

it is located about 85 miles (190 kilometers) southwest of Lisbon (q.v.), in a wheat-growing section of the country. Beja is in the heart of the *latifundia* (q.v.) region, the large landed estates of the south which in part were expropriated or nationalized by farm workers during the Revolution of 1974–1975 (q.v.) and in the subsequent agrarian reform movements. Beja's industries feature olive oil, pottery, textiles and leather. Since the 1970s, it is the capital of the district. On New Year's Day 1962, Beja was the scene of an attempted revolutionary action of oppositionist General Humberto Delgado's (q.v.) followers, at the Infantry Regiment No. 3's barracks in Beja, an effort which collapsed and resulted in the arrest of Delgado's followers and death by a stray bullet of Under Secretary of State of the Army, Lt. Col. Jaime Fonseca. Traditionally, Beja is an area with a relatively strong vote for the Portuguese Communist Party. *See* LATIFUNDIA; PROVINCES, PORTUGAL'S HISTORIC.

BELÉM, NATIONAL PALACE OF. Since 1911, Belém Palace in western Lisbon is the official residence of the President of the Republic. This 18th century pink palace is a superb historical legacy in itself and represents an important part of the country's monumental patrimony. Ordered built by King João V (q.v.) in 1726, Belém Palace was altered during the course of the 19th century. Intricate interior decorations and art and elaborate gardens enhance the palace's delicate image. Belém Palace was the preferred residence of Queen Maria II (reigned: 1834–1853) as well as of King Carlos I (qq.v.) and Queen Amélia (reigned: 1889–1908). The annex to Belém Palace, once the royal riding ring and stables, is currently the National Museum of Coaches. *See* CASTLES, PORTUGUESE.

BELÉM, TOWER OF. Built during the country's early imperial age when Portugal was a world maritime power, the Tower of Belém (*Torre do Belém*) in Lisbon (q.v.) was constructed as a defense against maritime attack in the Tagus River (q.v.). This historic stone tower, one of Portugal's most perfect Manueline-style monument-treasures, was begun in 1515 by order of King Manuel I (qq.v.). The first architect was the military architect Francisco Arruda and the Tower was built in the River Tagus.

With changes in tides, time and the shoreline since, the Belém Tower today rests firmly on the Belém shoreline. The Tower was built to accommodate a garrison, a prison and artillery to ward off pirates and other raiders coming from the Atlantic up the Tagus River. Eclectic in architectural style, the Tower's styles include Roman-Gothic, Manueline, with touches of Venetian and Moroccan influence. Located not far from massive Jerónimos (q.v.) convent, the Tower is square and is surrounded by a polygonal bulwark as well as walls facing the Tagus. Centuries after its use in defense had ceased, the Tower in its restored state became a memorable symbol of Portugal's Age of Discoveries and Expansion as well as a much-photographed icon in tourist literature. See JERÓNIMOS, MONASTERY OF; CASTLES, PORTUGUESE.

BRAGA, CITY OF. City and capital of Braga district in the Minho province, northwest Portugal. The population is about 60,000. As a city in Roman-ruled Lusitania (q.v.) its name was "Bracara Augusta." Historic sites include Roman ruins and a 12th century cathedral. The city had an important traditional role in the Catholic Church (q.v.) and in medieval Christianity. More recently, Braga was noted as the place where General Gomes da Costa on May 28, 1926, made his initial pronunciamento (q.v.) of military rebellion against the parliamentary First Republic, and where the "march on Lisbon" by rebel military units began. See GOMES DA COSTA, MANUEL DE OLIVEIRA.

BRAZIL. Former Portuguese colony (ca. 1500–1822) once described on old maps as "Portuguese America." Until 1822, the colony of Brazil was Portugal's largest, richest and most populous colonial territory and held the greatest number of overseas Portuguese. Indeed, until 1974, long after Brazil had ceased being a Portuguese colony, the largest number of overseas Portuguese continued to reside in Brazil.

Discovered in 1500 by Pedro Álvares Cabral (q.v.), Brazil experienced significant coastal colonization by Portugal only after 1550. As Portugal's world power and colonial position in North Africa and Asia entered a decline, Brazil began to receive the lion's share of her imperial attention and soon the empire was dominated by Brazil. While Portuguese colonization and civilization had an essential impact on the complex making of Brazil, this fact must be put into perspective. Besides other European immigrants (Italian, German, etc.) and Asian (Japanese), two other civilizations or groups of civilizations helped to construct Brazil: The Amerindians who inhabited the land before 1500 and black Africans who were shipped to Brazil's coast as slaves during more than three centuries mainly from west and central Africa. There is a long history of Portuguese military operations to defend Brazil against internal rebellions as well as other colonial intruders. The French, for example, attacked Brazil several times. But it was the Dutch who provided the greatest threat when they held northeast Brazil from 1624–1654, until they were expelled by Portuguese and colonial forces.

Until the 17th century, Portuguese colonization was largely coastal. By the 18th century, Portuguese groups began to penetrate deep into the hinterland, including an area rich in minerals, Minas Gerais ("General Mines"). Lisbon extracted the greatest wealth from Brazil during the "golden age" of mining of gold and diamonds from 1670–1750. But hefty profits for the King also came from Brazilian sugar, tobacco, cotton, Brazil woods and coffee. By the time of Brazil's independence, declared in 1822, Portuguese America had become far more powerful and rich than the mother country, Portugal. Only a few years before the break, Brazil had been declared a Kingdom, in theory on a par with Portugal. A major factor behind the Brazilian independence movement was the impact of the residence of the Portuguese royal family and court in Brazil from 1808 to 1821.

What is the Portuguese legacy to Brazil after more than 300 years of colonization? Of the many facets which could be cited, perhaps three are worthy of mention here: the Portuguese language (Brazil is the only Latin American country which has Portuguese as the official language); Portuguese political and administrative customs; and a large community, mostly in coastal Brazil, of overseas Portuguese. *See* EMPIRE, PORTUGUESE OVERSEAS; FREYRE, GILBERTO; LUSO-TROPICALISM.

BUÇACO, BATTLE OF. An important battle in what is known as the Peninsular Wars in European history and the Wars of Independence in Portuguese history. In the third invasion by

French (q.v.) forces under Emperor Napoleon, Marshal Masséna entered Portugal from Spain in August 1810. The allied forces under the Duke of Wellington (q.v.) were comprised of English (q.v.) and Portuguese troops. Masséna marched from Guarda and moved to attack across the hills of Buçaco to Coimbra (q.v.). Wellington's forces blocked the way to Coimbra and Lisbon (q.v.) and held an advantageous position. Against the advice of his council, Masséna decided to take the offensive. The battle of Buçaco commenced in the morning of September 27, 1810, and the French were defeated with considerable losses. The site of the battle in the woods and hills of Buçaco is marked by a commemorative obelisk, not far from the elegant Hotel-Palace of Buçaco, built originally for the last Braganza monarchs. *See* WELLINGTON, DUKE OF.

BUÇACO, FOREST AND MOUNTAIN OF. On the boundary between Coimbra and Viseu districts, the Buçaco (former spelling: Bussaco or Busaco) forest and mountain (ca. 1,795 feet or 8,400 meters high), were the site of a famous Peninsular War victory of Wellington (q.v.) over the French forces under Masséna on September 27, 1810. A monument remains to attest to this defeat of Napoleon. Not far from this spot is the Hotel-Palace of Buçaco, completed just before the Monarchy was overthrown in the Revolution of October 5, 1910. In Portuguese tradition, it is said that the Royal family wished to build, in effect, the last royal palace of the dynasty, but could not afford the cost of such a construction and eventually converted the palace into a hotel open to the public. This magnificent palace structure is now run as a hotel and combines various architectural styles, from Edwardian dining rooms and a billiards room to neo-Gothic, Arabic and neo-Manueline Rococo. Off the beaten track in the lovely Buçaco forest area, the Hotel-Palace remains a recent historic monument and it is said that before it was completed the last reigning Braganza King, Manuel II (1908–1910) (q.v.), on more than one occasion met his French paramour there. *See* MANUEL II, KING; WELLINGTON, DUKE OF.

BULLFIGHTING. Until soccer (*futebol*) assumed that role in the 20th century, bullfighting was perhaps Portugal's most popular national sport. Portugal's variation of this blood sport which is also pursued in Spain and a number of Latin American countries as well as occasionally the United States, differs from that found in neighboring Spain. The contemporary Portuguese bullfight emphasizes pageantry, spectacle, horsemanship and bull-jumping during a typical "program" of six bulls.

The Portuguese participants wear 18th century costumes, including plumed three-cornered hats, silk breeches and buckled shoes and boots, and the bulls are not killed in the arena. In the early stages of each "fight," the bull is taunted and harassed by participants on foot or on horses. In the final stage of each bull's appearance, the bull is challenged to charge by a group of seven men called *forcados,* who proceed to incite the bull to charge the first man in front of the lined-up row of six other men. The object is to jump on the bull's head, hold the horns and stop the bull's forward progress. Even though the bull's horns are cut and padded and horses wear padding, injuries to persons and horses do occur. In Portuguese tradition, it is said that the bull-jumping activity goes back to the ancient Phoenician or even Minoan customs of bull-jumping as a popular sport.

In recent years, bullfight audiences have decreased in number while soccer has increasingly drawn greater crowds. During the 18th century, when killing the bull was part of the Portuguese bullfight, during one series of incidents a number of aristocratic bullfighters died in the arena. The government of the day thereafter banned killing the bull and made such an act against the law. *Matadores* who killed the bull in the fight then were fined. The traditional bullfight season in Portugal runs from May into October each year. It was customary during the Dictatorship that after the bullfight the bulls, though not killed in the bullring, were slaughtered soon afterward and the meat donated to feed the poor. The supply of horses and bulls for this blood sport remains a business of some consequence in the Ribatejo district, north of the Tagus, the "cowboy" and cattle section of central Portugal.

- C -

CABRAL, PEDRO ÁLVARES (1467?–1520?). Portuguese noble-man whose fleet discovered Brazil (q.v.) for Portugal in 1500.

Born in Belmonte, Portugal, Cabral was a *fidalgo* (q.v.) in the court of King João II and he married a niece of the conquistador, Afonso de Albuquerque (q.v.). Except for his nobility, it is not known why King Manuel I (q.v.) selected Cabral to command a fleet to voyage to India (q.v.) to follow up Da Gama's (q.v.) pioneering journey. Cabral's fleet contained 13 ships and as many as 1500 crew members and departed the Tagus on March 9, 1500. The fleet's pilots and mariners executed the voyage skillfully with the intention of reaching India directly, but winds and currents carried them further west than was intended and, on April 22, 1500, they sighted land and later named the country the land of "Vera Cruz" (the True Cross), followed by "Santa Cruz" (Holy Cross), and finally *"Brazil,"* after the wood which was the country's first main product. Cabral landed and claimed the land for Portugal. Much of the detail of this discovery is described in a celebrated account of Pedro Vaz da Caminha. Cabral's fleet continued to Calicut, India, where the Portuguese began to carve out a trade empire by means of war, alliance and trade. He returned to Portugal, his ships laden with Asian wealth. Cabral refused to accept the command of another India fleet in 1502 and apparently did not venture to sea again. His tomb is in the Church of Graça, Santarém.

CAETANO, MARCELLO JOSÉ DAS NEVES ALVES (1906–1980). Marcello Caetano as the last Premier of the *Estado Novo* (q.v.) Dictatorship was both the heir and successor of Dr. Salazar (q.v.). In a sense, Caetano was one of the founders and sustainers of this unusual political system and, at various crucial stages of its long life, Caetano's contribution was as important as Salazar's.

Born in Lisbon (q.v.) in 1906 to a middle class family, Caetano was a member of the student generation which rebelled against the unstable parliamentary First Republic and sought answers to Portugal's legion of troubles in conservative ideologies such as Integralism, Catholic reformism and the Italian Fascist model. One of the most brilliant students at the University of Lisbon's Law School, Caetano soon became directly involved in government service in various ministries, including Salazar's Ministry of Finance. When Caetano was not teaching full-time at the Law School in Lisbon and influencing new generations of students who became critical of the regime Caetano helped construct, he was in important government posts and working on challenging assignments. In the 1930s, he participated in reforms in the Ministry of Finance, in the writing of the 1933 Constitution, the new Civil Code, of which he was in part the author, and in the construction of the Corporative (q.v.) system which sought to control labor-management relations and other aspects of social engineering. In a regime largely directed by academics from Coimbra (q.v.) and Lisbon Universities' Law Schools, Caetano was the leading expert on constitutional law, administrative law, political science and colonial law. A prolific writer as both a political scientist and historian, Caetano was the author of the standard political science, administrative law and history of law texts, works which remained in print and in use among students long after his exile and death.

After his apprenticeship service in a number of ministries, Caetano rose steadily in the system. At age 38, he was named Minister for the Colonies (1944–1947) and unlike many predecessors, he "went to see for himself"and made important research visits to Portugal's African territories. In 1955–1958, Caetano served in the number three position in the regime in the Ministry of the Presidency of the Council (Premier's Office) and left office for full-time academic work in part because of his disagreements with Salazar and others on regime policy and failures to reform at the desired pace. In 1956 and 1957, Caetano briefly served as interim Minister of Communications and of Foreign Affairs.

Caetano's opportunity to take Salazar's place and to challenge even more conservative forces in the system came in the 1960s. Portugal's most prominent Law Professor had a public falling out with the regime in March 1962, when he resigned as Rector of Lisbon University following a clash between rebellious students and the PIDE (q.v.), the political police. When students opposing the regime organized strikes on the University of Lisbon campus, Caetano resigned his Rectorship after the police invaded the campus, beat up and arrested some students, without asking permission to enter University premises from University authorities.

When Salazar became incapacitated in September 1968, President Américo Tomás (q.v.) named Caetano Prime Minister.

Caetano's tasks were formidable: in the midst of remarkable economic growth in Portugal, continued heavy emigration of Portuguese to France (q.v.) and other countries and the costly colonial wars in three African colonies, namely Angola, Guinea-Bissau and Mozambique (qq.v.), how could the regime engineer essential social and political reforms, win the wars in Africa and move toward meaningful political reforms? Caetano supported moderately important reforms in his first two years in office (1968–1970) as well as the drafting of Constitutional Revisions in 1971 which allowed a slight liberalization of the dictatorship, gave the opposition more room for activity and decentralized authority in the overseas provinces (colonies). Always aware of the complexity of Portugal's colonial problems and of the ongoing wars, Caetano made several visits to Africa as Premier and sought to implement reforms in social and economic affairs while maintaining the expensive, divisive military effort, Portugal's largest armed forces mobilization in her history.

Opposed by intransigent right-wing forces in various sectors in both Portugal and Africa, Caetano's modest "opening" of 1968–1970 soon narrowed. Conservative forces in the military, police, civil service and private sectors opposed key political reforms, including greater democratization, while pursuing the military solution to the African crisis and personal wealth. A significant perspective on Caetano's failed program of reforms, which could not prevent the advent of a creeping revolution in society, are two key developments in the 1961–1974 era of colonial wars: despite Lisbon's efforts, the greater part of Portuguese emigration and capital investment during this period were directed not to the African colonies but to Europe, North America and Brazil.

Prime Minister Caetano, discouraged by events and by opposition to his reforms from the so-called "Rheumatic Brigade" of superannuated regime loyalists, attempted to resign his office, but President Tomás convinced him to remain. The publication and public reception of African Hero-General António Spínola's (q.v.) best-selling book, *Portugal e O Futuro* (Portugal and The Future) in February 1974 convinced the surprised Caetano that a coup and revolution were imminent. When the virtually bloodless, smoothly operating military coup was successful on April 25, 1974, Caetano surrendered to the

COLLEGE OF THE SEQUOIAS
LIBRARY

Armed Forces Movement (q.v.) in Lisbon and was flown to Madeira Island and later to exile in Brazil (qq.v.), where he remained for the rest of his life. In his Brazilian exile, Caetano was active writing important memoirs and histories of the *Estado Novo* from his vantage point, teaching law at a private university in Rio de Janeiro, and carrying on a lively correspondence with persons in Portugal. He died at age 74, in 1980, in Brazil.

CAMACHO, MANUEL BRITO (1862–1934). A leading political figure of the First Republic, leader-founder of a principal pre-1919 party and High Commissioner of Portuguese East Africa in the 1920s. Brito Camacho was trained as a medical doctor, but became noteworthy first as the editor of a fighting Republican newspaper, *A Luta* (The Struggle) which played a role in the Republican propaganda era in the years before the October 5, 1910 Republican revolution. Camacho became one of the principal Republican leaders during 1906–1912 and, when he dissented from the radical line of the Portuguese Republican Party (PRP), he split from that party and formed his own Republican Union (UR) party which lasted from 1912 to 1918.

A major policy issue for Camacho and his UR followers was opposition to Portugal's active intervention in World War I on the Allied side. When Portugal did enter the war in March 1916, Camacho lent his political influence through his newspaper and his following to opposition to the PRP's policy of war intervention. Camacho played an important role in the preparation of political and military support for Sidónio Pais' (q.v.) December 1917 coup which succeeded in overthrowing the PRP and ousting Afonso Costa (q.v.). After the assassination of Sidónio Pais and the brief civil war of early 1919, Brito Camacho withdrew from domestic politics and sought rest and escape abroad. In a brief but important period (1921–1923), Camacho served as the Republic's High Commissioner in Mozambique (q.v.). He spent much of the remainder of his life in research and writing. *See* POLITICAL PARTIES.

CAMÕES, LUÍS DE (1525?–1579?). Portugal's national epic poet of the Discoveries era and author of the most celebrated piece of national literature, Luís de Camões' lifespan marked both

COLLEGE OF THE SEQUOIAS
LIBRARY

the high tide and ebbing of Portuguese imperial power. Educated at the University of Coimbra, Camões for much of his life, most of which remains largely unknown, was an adventurer overseas. He served as a soldier in Morocco, as Portugal began to lose its hold on parts of Morocco, and was later imprisoned. After his release, he shipped out to Portuguese India, to Goa, where he served the King. He lived in Goa, Macau and Mozambique (qq.v.), and his Eastern years left a permanent mark on his mind and soul. Upon his return to Portugal, he continued writing as a poet and in 1572 his most famous work, better known and more quoted than any other piece of the nation's literature, *Os Lusíadas* (The Lusiads) was published in Lisbon. Whatever the reception of his epic poem, the story of the great Vasco da Gama's (q.v.) voyage to India (1497–1499) within the context of the history of Portugal, Camões cannot have gained a great deal from its publication. It is said that he fell into poverty, that a servant or friend of his was forced to beg for food for Camões and that when he died he was in misery. In Portuguese tradition, it is also recounted that before he died he was informed of the disastrous battle of Alcácer-Quivir (q.v.) in 1578 and the resulting loss of the King, his army and any defenses remaining to Portugal. Camões, the story goes, exclaimed, "I die with the Fatherland!"

CAPE VERDE ISLANDS, ARCHIPELAGO OF THE. Consisting of ten main islands (Santiago, Maio, Boa Vista, Sal, Fogo, São Vicente, São Nicolau, Brava, Santo Antão and Santa Luzia), the archipelago was sighted first by the Venetian navigator in Portuguese service, Alvise de Cá da Mosto in the late 1450s. The Islands' area is about 1,557 square miles (4,030 square kilometers). Prince Henry the Navigator (q.v.) gave the task of colonizing the islands to another Italian, the Genovese Antonio da Noli. Actual settlement, nevertheless, began only in 1463 under King Afonso V. Captain-Donataries were granted charters to colonize and, in 1550, the city of Praia was established on the island of Santiago and became a principal center of activity. Slaves from West Africa were brought to work the islands' plantations and millet and coconut trees were introduced as staple foods. Following attacks on the islands by French pirates, Portugal created the post of Governor of Cape Verde in 1592.

Until the middle of the 18th century and the reign of King José I, these islands were governed by the private captaincies. Thereafter, they were ruled directly by Portugal's representatives.

Due to their geography, topography and climate, the Cape Verde islands lack good soil for agriculture or minerals and frequently suffer long, periodic droughts. The result of this and until recently sparse Portuguese investment has been that the islands have one of the poorest economies in the world.˙ Emigration to work abroad has often been the only alternative for survival. As a result, large overseas communities of Cape Verdeans reside and work in the United States (especially in the eastern states of Rhode Island and Massachusetts) and in Portugal. In July 1975, Portugal granted independence to the Cape Verde Islands, now a Republic.

CAPTAINS, MOVEMENT OF THE. An informal name for the Armed Forces Movement (MFA), the organization of career military officers which organized the overthrow of the Dictatorship on April 25, 1974. A significant portion of the Army officers of the MFA were Captains who had fought in Portugal's African colonial wars in the 1960s and 1970s. Some historians noted parallels between the Captains' movement of 1973–1974 and the movement of "Young Lieutenants" of May 28, 1926, which bloodlessly overthrew the first parliamentary Republic (1910–1926). *See* ARMED FORCES MOVEMENT; CARVALHO, OTELO SARAIVA DE; TWENTY-EIGHTH OF MAY; TWENTY-FIFTH OF APRIL.

CARLOS I, KING (1863–1908). The second to last reigning King of Portugal and second to last of the Braganza dynasty to rule. Born in 1863, the son of King Luís I (q.v.), Carlos was well-educated and became an accomplished sailor as well as an artist of maritime scenes in oil paintings. A selection of his paintings remain on display in various museums and halls. His reign began in 1889, when his father died, and was immediately marked by controversy and conflict. In January 1890, the Monarchy was weakened and Carlos' authority placed in question in the crisis of the "English Ultimatum" (q.v.). Portugal's oldest ally, England (q.v.), threatened an end to the

517-year-old alliance and hostilities over the question of territorial expansion in the "Scramble for Africa." While Carlos was a talented diplomat, who managed to repair the damaged Anglo-Portuguese alliance and to promote other foreign policy initiatives, his reign was marked by the failure of Monarchist politics, the weakening Monarchy and rising Republicanism. As Monarchist politics became more unstable and corrupt, the Republic opposition grew stronger and more violent. Carlos' appointment of the dictatorial João Franco Government in 1907 and Franco's measures of January 1908 repressing the opposition were, in effect, the King's death warrants. While returning from a royal trip to the Alentejo on February 1, 1908, King Carlos and his heir apparent, Prince Luís, were shot in their open carriage in Lisbon by *carbonária* (anarchist Republicans). Though their two murderers were killed by guards on the spot, the official investigation of their murder was never completed.

CARLOTA JOAQUINA, QUEEN (1775–1830). Daughter of King Carlos IV of Spain (q.v.), she was born in Aranjuez, Spain, and was married at the tender age of ten to João, son and heir of Queen Maria I (q.v.). When Dom José, the eldest son of Queen Maria I died in 1788, Carlota Joaquina, who had become an unpopular Spaniard living in alien Portugal, was named Princess-Heiress. Always in conflict with her well-meaning but indecisive husband, João, Carlota became the leader of an extreme reactionary court party and was frequently in conflict with her more malleable husband. When the royal family fled to Brazil (q.v.) in 1808 to escape the French army of invasion, she accompanied them and remained in Brazil until she returned to Portugal with her husband in 1821.

From that time on, Carlota Joaquina was never far from the center of political conflicts and controversy as the Portuguese political system was caught in the grip of a violent struggle between the forces of Constitutionalism and Absolutism. After returning from Brazil, she refused to swear allegiance to the new constitution presented to her husband, King João VI, and was placed under house arrest. She was a power behind the throne of her son, Dom Miguel (q.v.), as he proclaimed himself an Absolutist King, threw out the Constitution and prepared to rule the country in 1828. Before the civil war called "The War of the Brothers" (q.v.) (Dom Miguel vs. Dom Pedro, both her sons) was concluded with Pedro's military victory in 1834, Carlota Joaquina died and thus did not have to witness Dom Miguel's defeat and permanent exile. *See* WAR OF THE BROTHERS.

CARMONA, ANTÓNIO ÓSCAR DE FRAGOSO (1869–1951). Career Army officer, one of the founders of the *Estado Novo* (q.v.) Dictatorship (1926–1974), and the longest serving President of the Republic of that regime (1926–1951). Born in Lisbon in 1869, the son of a career cavalry officer, Óscar Carmona entered the Army in 1888 and became a Lieutenant in 1894 in the same cavalry regiment in which his father had served. He rose rapidly in the Army and became a General during the turbulent First Republic, briefly served as Minister of War in 1923 and achieved public notoriety as Prosecutor for the Military in one of the famous military trials of military personnel in an abortive 1925 coup. General Carmona was one of the key supporters of the May 28, 1926 military coup which overthrew the unstable Republic and established the initially unstable Military Dictatorship (1926–1933), which was the political system that founded the *Estado Novo* (1933–1974).

Carmona took power as President upon the ousting of the May 28th coup leader, General Gomes da Costa (q.v.), and guided the military Dictatorship through political and economic uncertainty until the regime settled upon empowering Professor António de Oliveira Salazar (q.v.) with extraordinary fiscal authority as Minister of Finance (April 1928). Elected in a managed election based on limited male suffrage in 1928, President Carmona served as the Dictatorship's President of the Republic until his death in office in 1951 at age 81. In political creed, a moderate Republican not a Monarchist, General (and later Marshal) Carmona played an essential role in the Dictatorship which involved a division of labor between Dr. Salazar who, as Prime Minister since July 1932, was responsible for the daily management of the government and Carmona, who was responsible for managing civil-military relations in the system, maintaining smooth relations with Dr. Salazar and keeping the armed forces officer corps in line and out of political intervention.

Carmona's amiable personality and reputation for personal honesty, correctness and hard work combined well with a friendly relationship with the civilian Dictator Salazar. Especially in the period 1928–1944, in his more vigorous years in the position, Carmona's role was vital in both the political and ceremonial aspects of his job. Carmona's ability to balance the relationship with Salazar and the pressures and demands from a sometimes unhappy Army officer corps which, following the civilianization of the regime in the early 1930s, could threaten military intervention in politics and government, was central to the operation of the regime.

After 1944, however, Carmona was less effective in this role. His tiring ceremonial visits around Portugal, to the Atlantic Islands and to the overseas empire became less frequent, younger generations of officers grew alienated from the regime and Carmona suffered from the mental and physical ailments of old age. In the meantime, Salazar assumed the lion's share of political power and authority, all the while placing his own appointees in office. This, along with the regime's political police (PVDE or PIDE), Republican National Guard (qq.v.) and civil service as well as a circle of political institutions which monopolized public office, privilege and decision-making, made Carmona's role as mediator-intermediary between the career military and the largely civilian-managed system significantly less important. Increasingly feeble and less aware of events around him, Carmona died in office in April 1951 and was replaced by Salazar's chosen appointee, General (and later Marshal) Francisco Craveiro Lopes, who was elected President of the Republic in a regime-managed election. See SALAZAR, ANTÓNIO DE OLIVEIRA.

CARVALHO, OTELO SARAIVA DE (1934–). The Army Major who planned and managed the military operational aspects of the military coup which overthrew the Estado Novo (q.v.). A career Army officer who entered his profession in the 1950s and who held important positions in several of the colonial wars in Portugal's African territories during 1961–1974, Saraiva de Carvalho was born in Mozambique (q.v.) in 1934 and made his life's ambition to become a stage actor. In his career, he was influenced by service with Portugal's most senior Army officer,

General António de Spínola (q.v.), who served the Dictatorship both as Commissioner and Commanding General of Armed Forces in the colony of Guinea-Bissau (q.v.). Contact with African nationalist elements as well as familiarity with increasingly available Marxist-Leninist literature both in Africa and in Portugal, transformed Saraiva de Carvalho into a maverick and a revolutionary who sought to overthrow the Portuguese Dictatorship at home by means of military intervention in politics.

Known as "Otelo" (Othello) in the media and to much of the Portuguese public, Saraiva de Carvalho played a significant role in the period of April 25, 1974–November 25, 1975, when the country experienced a Leftist Revolution and a trend toward a Dictatorship of the Left. Eventually the head of COPCON, the Armed Forces Movement's special unit for enforcing "law and order" and for ensuring that the government was not overthrown by military insurrectionism, Saraiva de Carvalho became a political personality in his own right. This somberly handsome figure became the darling of the radical Left, including anarchist factions.

With the swing of the political pendulum away from the radical Left after the November 25, 1975 abortive Leftist coup, Carvalho's military career was ended and his role in politics shifted. He was dismissed from the COPCON command, arrested and held in prison for a period. After his release, he entered the political wilderness, unhappy that the revolution he envisioned for Portugal, an unorthodox Marxist-Leninist one, was not happening. Still carrying the torch for the notion of a "Socialist paradise" in which the State would play only a small role, the hero of the 25th of April (q.v.) re-entered politics and ran for President of the Republic on two occasions. In 1976, he received a respectable 16% of the vote, but in the 1981 elections his vote was negligible. Accused of involvement in several terrorist factions' conspiracies and violence, Carvalho was arrested and imprisoned. After a long and sensational trial, "Otelo" was released and acquitted. Of all the memoirs of the 1974 Revolution, *Alvorada em Abril* (Reveille in April), his contribution, was the most charming and revealing. See ARMED FORCES MOVEMENT; CAPTAINS, MOVEMENT OF THE; TWENTY-FIFTH OF APRIL.

CASTLES, PORTUGUESE. "Castles in Spain," still a common phrase in English, can conjure up romantic images of scenery in neighboring Spain. Though less well known, "Castles in Portugal" are also quite numerous and equally remarkable, romantic and scenic. Virtually all have been fully restored since the 1930s when preparations began for the 1940 Double Centenary celebrations. Major Portuguese castles are listed below and several of them have individual entries in this Dictionary; when they do this is noted with an asterisk (*). This is by no means an exhaustive list.

Lisbon region
São Jorge Castle
Palmella Castle**
Belém Tower*
Moorish Castle, Sintra
Pena Palace, Sintra*

Tagus River valley
Castle of Torres Novas/Castle
of São Filipe (Setúbal)**
Castle of Almourol

Central Portugal
Castle of Abrantes
Castle of Belver
Castle of Torres Vedras
Castle of Óbidos
Castle of Peniche
Castle of Leiria
Castle of Ourém
Castle of Tomar
Castle of Pombal
Castle of Montemor-o-Velho

Northern Portugal
Castle of Louzã
Castle of Feira
Castle of S. João da Foz
Castle of Chaves

Southern Portugal
(Alentejo province mainly)
Castle of Silves (Algarve)
Castle of Marvão
Castle of Vide
Castle of Alter do Chão
Castle of Arronches
Castles of Elvas
Castle of Estremoz**
Castle of Salir
Castle of Beja
Castle of Mértola

Castle of Guimarães
Castle of Lanhoso
Castle of Montalegre
Castle of Valença

**Indicates Castle is now a Pousada (State Inn) where visitors can stay.

Castle of Monção Castle of Bragança
Castle of Penedono Castle of Celórico da Beira
Castle of Belmonte Castle of Sabugal

CASTRO, INÊS DE (?–1355). Born in Galicia, Inês de Castro came from an important Castilian family and went to Portugal in the retinue of the Castilian Princess, Constança, who married Prince Pedro (q.v.), royal heir to the throne of King Afonso IV. Inês and Pedro fell in love, had one or two children and continued their relationship, despite the existence of the approved royal marriage of Pedro and Constança. This contributed to the premature death of Pedro's legitimate wife and introduced once again the fear of Castilian intervention in Portugal into royal court politics. Pedro's father, King Afonso IV, feared that Inês' Castilian family might meddle in succession politics and threaten the future of Pedro and Constança's legitimate son, Fernando. Taking advice from leading counsellors, King Afonso had Inês murdered in 1355. For a while, Pedro rebelled against his father's action, but later a truce was declared.

Historians debate what happened next, but in the following century, after Pedro's death, a legend or myth grew up in Spain which became the basis for the romantic story of the corpse of Inês and Pedro. The legend was adopted in various novels, operas, songs, poetry and folklore and was noteworthy in the literature of France, Portugal and other countries. It was said that Pedro tracked down and killed all who had been involved in Inês' murder, then disinterred her corpse, put it on the throne and acclaimed it as Queen of Portugal in a ceremony. *See* PEDRO I, KING.

CATHERINE OF BRAGANZA, QUEEN OF ENGLAND (1638–1706). The daughter of King John IV and Queen Luísa de Gusmão and born at Vila Viçosa. In 1659, Catherine was a prospective bride of King Louis XIV of France, the "Sun King," but the marriage negotiations failed. In 1661, marriage negotiations began in London under the auspices of Portugal's Ambassador, Dom Francisco de Melo (q.v.), and it was arranged that Catherine would marry King Charles II of England (q.v.). The marriage arrangements were confirmed in the famous Anglo-

Portuguese Treaty of June 23, 1661, one of the keystones of the ancient Anglo-Portuguese Alliance (q.v.), and Catherine's dowry was established. As a result, England received from Portugal some two million cruzados (about £350,000 in English money at the time) and the cession of Tangier, Morocco, and Bombay, India.

In May 1662, Catherine arrived in England at Portsmouth harbor and began a residence of some 30 years. While Catherine contributed a mighty dowry and introduced the custom of tea-drinking to her husband's country, she failed to adjust either to the climate or the culture and remained a melancholy exile. Her staunch Catholic faith made her suspect among the English Anglican majority and Charles II's unfaithfulness marred their relationship. Charles died in 1685, but Catherine remained in England until 1692. When she returned to Portugal, she lived in Bemposta Palace and supported the controversial Methuen Treaty (1703) (q.v.) and maintenance of the Anglo-Portuguese connection. Before her death in 1706, she was named Regent twice in 1704 and 1705.

CAVACO SILVA, ANÍBAL ANTÓNIO (1939–). Leading figure in post-1974 Portugal, Social Democrat leader, Prime Minister since 1985. Born in the Algarve in 1939, Cavaco Silva was educated in Faro and Lisbon (q.v.) and in 1964 obtained a degree in Finance at the University of Lisbon. Like many of the younger leaders of post-1974 Portugal, Cavaco Silva underwent an important part of his professional training abroad; in December 1973 he received a Doctorate in Economics from York University, Great Britain. He entered academic life as an Economics and Finance Professor in 1974 and taught until he entered politics full-time in 1980, when he was named Minister of Finance in the Sixth Constitutional Government of Social Democrat (PSD) leader and Premier, Sá Carneiro (q.v.). He was elected a PSD deputy to the Republican Assembly in October 1980. Following the general legislative elections of October 1985, Cavaco Silva was named Prime Minister of the 10th Constitutional Government. His party, the PSD, strengthened its hold on the legislature yet again in the 1987 election when, for the first time since the 1974 Revolution, Portugal was ruled by a party with a clear majority of seats in the Legislature.

Cavaco Silva, who has emphasized a strong free enterprise and de-nationalization policy in the framework of economic rejuvenation, has been Prime Minister since 1985 and in the elections of 1987 and 1991 his party won a clear majority of seats in the Assembly of the Republic (more than 50%) which encouraged stability and economic progress in post-Revolutionary Portugal. *See* POLITICAL PARTIES.

CHURCH, CATHOLIC. The Catholic Church and the Catholic religion or faith in Portugal together represent the oldest and most enduring of all institutions in the country. Since its origins as an institution go back at least to the middle of the 3rd century AD, if not earlier, the Christian and later the Catholic Church is much older than any other institution or major cultural influence such as the Monarchy (lasted 770 years) or Islam and Muslim factors (540 years). Indeed, it is older than Portugal (852 years). "The Church," despite its changing doctrine and form, is 1750 years old.

In its earlier period, the Church played an important role in the Reconquest of Portugal as well as in the colonization and settlement of various regions of the shifting Christian-Muslim frontier as it moved south. Until the rise of Absolutist Monarchy and Central Government, the Church dominated all public and private life, provided the only education available, along with the only hospitals and charity institutions. During the Middle Ages and the early stage of the overseas empire, the Church accumulated a great deal of wealth. One historian suggests that by 1700 one-third of the land in Portugal was owned by the Church. Besides land, Catholic institutions possessed a large number of chapels, churches and cathedrals, capital and other property.

Extensive periods of Portuguese history witnessed either conflict or cooperation between the Church and the increasingly intrusive State (Central Government) which was based after 1500 in Lisbon (q.v.). The Monarchy and the nobility challenged the great power and wealth of the Church especially after the acquisition of the first overseas empire (1415–1580). When King João III (q.v.) requested the Pope to allow Portugal to establish the Inquisition (q.v.) (Holy Office) in the country and the request was finally granted in 1531, royal power more than religion was the chief concern. The Inquisition acted as a judicial arm of the Catholic Church in order to root out heresies, primarily Judaism and Islam and later Protestantism. But the Inquisition also played a part in strengthening royal power and jurisdiction.

The Church's power and prestige came under direct attack for the first time in governance under the Marquis of Pombal (1750–1777) (q.v.) when the King's Chief Minister placed Regalism above the Church's interests. In 1759, the Jesuits were expelled from Portugal, though they were allowed to return after Pombal left office. Pombal also harnessed the Inquisition and put in place other anti-clerical measures. With the rise of Liberalism and secular concerns after 1820, considerable Church-State conflict occurred. The new Liberal staté weakened the power and position of the Church in various ways: in 1834 all religious orders were suppressed and their property confiscated both in Portugal and in the empire; and in the 1830s and 1840s, agrarian reform programs confiscated and sold large portions of Church lands. By the 1850s, Church-State relations had improved, various religious orders were allowed to return and the Church's influence was largely restored. By the late 19th century, Church and State were closely allied again, Church roles in all levels of education were pervasive and there was a popular Catholic revival underway.

With the rise of Republicanism and the early years of the First Republic, especially from 1910–1917, Church-State relations reached a new low. A major tenet of Republicanism was anti-clericalism and the belief that the Church was as much to blame as the Monarchy for the backwardness of Portuguese society. The Provisional Republican Government's 1911 Law of Separation decreed the secularization of public life on a scale unknown in Portugal. Among the new measures which Catholics and the Church opposed were: legalization of divorce; appropriation of all Church property by the State; abolition of religious oaths for various posts; suppression of the Theology School at Coimbra University; abolition of Saints' days as holidays; abolition of nunneries and expulsion of the Jesuits; closing of seminaries; secularization of all public education at all levels and banning of religious courses in schools.

After considerable civil strife over the religious question under the Republic, President Sidónio Pais (q.v.) restored normal relations with the Holy See and made concessions to the Portuguese Church. Encouraged by the apparitions at Fátima (q.v.) between May and October 1917, which caused a great sensation among the rural people, a strong Catholic reaction to anti-clericalism ensued. Backed by various new Catholic organizations such as the "Catholic Youth" and the Academic Center of Christian Democracy (CADC), the Catholic revival influenced government and politics under the Dictatorship. Premier Salazar (q.v.) was not only a devout Catholic and member of the CADC, but his formative years included nine years in the Viseu Catholic Seminary preparing to be a priest. Under the Dictatorship, it is true, Church-State relations greatly improved and Catholic interests were protected. On the other hand, Salazar's no-risk Statism never went so far as to restore to the Church all that had been lost in the 1911 Law of Separation. Most Church property was never returned from State ownership and, while the Church played an important role in public education to 1974, it never recovered the influence in education it had enjoyed before 1911.

Today the majority of Portuguese proclaim themselves Catholic and the enduring nature of the Church as an institution seems apparent everywhere in the country. But there is no longer a monolithic Catholic faith and there is growing diversity of religious choice in the population. There is an increasing number of Protestant Portuguese as well as a small, but growing number of Muslims. The Muslim community even erected a Mosque which is located, ironically, near the Spanish Embassy. In the 1990s, Portugal's Catholic Church as an institution appeared to be experiencing a revival of influence. While Church attendance and piety statistics were arguable, several Church institutions retained an importance in society which went beyond the walls of the thousands of churches: a popular, flourishing Catholic University, Radio Renascença, the country's most listened-to radio station, and a new private television channel owned by the Church. See FÁTIMA; INQUISITION; SALAZAR, ANTÓNIO DE OLIVEIRA.

COIMBRA, CITY OF. Located on the north bank of the Mondego River, in what was the Beira Litoral province on old maps and now the capital of Coimbra district, this city of about 60,000 people remains one of the few cities besides the capital, Lisbon (q.v.). It is also the site of one of Portugal's most important and its most ancient university. Coimbra lies on the Lisbon-Oporto highway and during much of the reconquest era (ca. 850–1250) was on the southern edge of the Christian kingdom of Portugal. Coimbra was the capital of Portugal from 1139 to 1385 and six kings were born in the city. It takes its name from nearby Conimbriga (q.v.). *See* COIMBRA, UNIVERSITY OF.

COIMBRA, UNIVERSITY OF. Portugal's oldest and most prestigious university and one of Europe's oldest, the University of Coimbra and its various roles have a historic importance which supersedes merely the educational. For centuries, the University formed and trained the principal elites and professions which dominated Portugal. For more than a century certain members of its faculty entered the Lisbon government. A few, such as Law Professor Afonso Costa (q.v.), Mathematics instructor Sidónio Pais (q.v.), Anthropology Professor Bernardino Machado and Economics Professor António de Oliveira Salazar (q.v.), became Premiers and Presidents of the Republic. In such a small country with relatively few universities until recently, Portugal counted Coimbra's University as the educational cradle of its leaders and knew its academic traditions as an intimate part of national life.

Established in 1290 by King Dinis (q.v.), the University first opened in Lisbon (q.v.) but was moved to Coimbra in 1308, and there it remained. University buildings were placed high on a hill in a position which physically dominates Portugal's third city. While sections of the medieval university buildings remain, much of what today remains of the old University of Coimbra dates from the Manueline era (1495–1521) and the 17th and 18th centuries. The main administration building along the so-called Via Latina is Baroque in the style of the 17th and 18th centuries. Most prominent among buildings adjacent to the central core structures are the Chapel of São Miguel, built in the 17th century, and the magnificent University Library, of the era of wealthy King João V (q.v.), built between 1717 and 1723. Created entirely by Portuguese artists and architects, the Library is unique among historic monuments in Portugal. Its rare book collection, a sight in itself, is complemented by exquisite gilt wood decorations and beautiful doors, windows and furniture. Among visitors and tourists, the Chapel and Library are the prime attractions to this day.

Elaborate, ancient traditions and customs inform the faculty and student body of Coimbra University. Tradition flourishes, though some customs are more popular than others. Instead of residing in common residences or dormitories as in other countries, in Coimbra until recently students lived in the city in "Republics," private houses with domestic help hired by the students. Students wore typical black academic gowns. Efforts during the 1974 Revolution and aftermath to abolish the wearing of the gowns, a powerful student image symbol, met resistance and generated controversy. In romantic Coimbra tradition, students with guitars sang characteristic songs, including Coimbra *fado* (q.v.), a more cheerful song than Lisbon *fado,* and serenaded other students at special locations. Tradition also decreed that at graduation graduates wore their gowns but burned their school (or college or subject) ribbons (*fitas*), an important ceremonial rite of passage.

The University of Coimbra, while it underwent a revival in the 1980s and 1990s, no longer has a virtual monopoly over higher education in Portugal. By 1970, for example, the country had only four public and one private university and the University of Lisbon had become more significant than ancient Coimbra. By 1990, diversity in higher education was even more pronounced: there were now five private universities and fourteen autonomous public universities not only in Lisbon and Oporto (q.v.), but at provincial locations. Still, Coimbra retained an influence as the senior university, some of whose graduates still entered national cabinets and distinguished themselves in various professions.

COMMEMORATIONS, PORTUGUESE HISTORIC. As in so many other activities of Portugal and her people, in historic commemorative work the past always seems present. For more than a century, Portugal has planned and sponsored a variety of historic commemorations related to the Discoveries era and age of glory of historic Portugal. The Columban centenary commemorations, involving Spain (q.v.) and Italy in particular, have gained greater world attention. Portugal, nevertheless, has a history of her own commemorations.

Whatever the political ideology of the governmental system involved, Portugal's historic commemorations have been continuous and well-planned and have sought to stir national pride as well as regime loyalty. Portugal's official efforts in public commemoration date at least back to 1880, when Portuguese celebrated the 300th anniversary of the death of the national epic poet, Luís de Camões (q.v.). Others followed that sought to arouse national remembrance and encourage notions of national revival and focused either on biographical or national discovery dates. The next major commemoration was in 1894, when Portugal commemorated the 400th anniversary of the birth in 1494 of Prince Henry the Navigator (q.v.) and, in 1897–1899, the 400th anniversary of Vasco da Gama's (q.v.) discovery of the sea route to India.

The 20th century has seen the most elaborate and publicized historic commemorations for Portugal. Besides its extensive propaganda program beginning in the 1930s, the *Estado Novo* (q.v.) Dictatorship put considerable effort into extensive historic commemorations with at least a dual purpose: to encourage national pride and international respect as well as regime loyalty. At least three national commemorations are worthy of note here, though there were scores of other events on a smaller scale. From June–December 1940, Portugal held the grand Double Centenary celebrations which celebrated Portugal's emergence as an independent monarchy and state in 1140 (800 years) and the restoration of independence from Spain in 1640 (300 years). More than five months of activities included expensive publications of books and tourist materials, exhibits, academic conferences, and an outstanding kind of Lisbon World's Fair known as the "Exposition of the Portuguese World," staged at Belém, in front of Jerónimos (qq.v.), and involving the unveiling for the first time of the new Monument of the Discoveries (q.v.).

Two other commemorations of the Dictatorship deserve mention: the 1947 celebration of the 800th anniversary of the Portuguese taking of Lisbon (1147) from Moorish forces and the 1960 commemoration activities marking the 500th anniversary of the death of the central figure of the Portuguese Discoveries,

Prince Henry the Navigator. The latter set of events took place during a time of political sensitivity, when the government's African policy was under strong international pressures.

Since the 1974 Revolution, Democratic Portugal has put substantial resources into commemorating various persons and events of the era of the Discoveries. In 1980, Portugal's scholars celebrated the 400th anniversary of the death of national poet Camões in many books, articles, exhibits and conferences. But this would all be overshadowed by the celebration of the 500th anniversary of the Portuguese Discoveries that would run from 1988 to 2000. This elaborate effort involved the establishment of a government agency called the "National Committee for the Commemoration of the Portuguese Discoveries," headed by one of Portugal's most eminent scholars on the subject, Dr. Vasco Graça Moura. Commemoration began in 1988 with the celebration and reenactment of the 1488 voyage of navigator Bartolomeu Dias from Lisbon to beyond the Cape of Good Hope, in South Africa. The 12-year cycle, the longest Discoveries commemorations of any century and of any Western country, put the 1992 Columban Quincentenary events somewhat in the shade. It was scheduled to end in 2000, marking the 500th anniversary of the year that Portugal's Pedro Álvares Cabral (q.v.) discovered Brazil (q.v.). *See* DISCOVERIES, MONUMENT OF.

CONIMBRIGA. South of the present city of Coimbra, Conimbriga was a Roman settlement of some importance which is currently undergoing archaeological excavations and restoration of the houses, streets and walls of this ancient community. As of the early 1990s, between one-third and one-half of the excavations were complete and were being carried out by Portuguese archaeologists, a team of French archaeologists and other international experts. A remarkable tourist site for extended visits and study tours, the nearby museum and Conimbriga offer unique insight into Roman life. For example, one can view the restored Roman plumbing, water systems and even a kind of sauna system in several elegant villas and extensive, beautiful mosaics. *See* COIMBRA.

CONSTITUTIONS. Beginning with the 1822 Constitution, which was imposed on a hesitant King João VI on his return from

Brazil, Portugal has had six different constitutions of varying longevity. Most of them have undergone one or more major revisions. The following list indicates the political system and its dates, the dates of the Constitution adopted, and the dates of major revisions. It should be noted that the 1976 Constitution of Democratic Portugal is still in the process of revision.

Constitutional Monarchy (1822–1910)
    1822 Constitution (in effect: 1822–23, 1836–38)
    1826 Constitution (*Carta* = Charter)
        (in effect: 1826–28, 1834–36; reinstituted,
        1842–1910) revised: 1852, 1885, 1895, 1896.
    1838 Constitution (in effect: 1838–42)
First Parliamentary Republic (1910–1926)
    1911 Constitution (in effect: 1911–1933)
        revised: 1919, 1920, 1921.
Estado Novo Dictatorship (1926–1974)
    1933 Constitution (in effect: 1933–1974)
        Included 1930 Colonial Act;
        revised 1945, 1951, 1959, 1971.
Democratic Republic (1974–)
    1976 Constitution (in effect: 1976–)
        revised 1982, 1989.

CORPORATIVISM. Corporativism or Corporatism, a social and economic doctrine or ideology, has been influential on several occasions in the 20th century. Based on Catholic social doctrines, Corporativism began to enjoy a certain vogue among conservative parties in the First Republic. The Dictatorship adopted the doctrine as one of its main ideologies and strategies after 1930, though it took decades for the Corporative system to be instituted in any comprehensive way. Salazar (q.v.) and his ruling group advocated the Corporative system in the 1933 Constitution and the National Labor Statute of September 1933, but it was not until after a 1956 Law that the system was put into operation.

    The *Estado Novo's* (q.v.) intention was to have greater control over the economy than the weak First Republic had managed by means of eliminating social conflict as well as the inevitable struggle between labor and management. New State doctrine declared that the regime under a Corporative system would be "neither bourgeois nor proletarian." The idea was that corporativism in Portugal would be largely self-regulating and would promote social peace and prosperity. In fact, the corporative system became simply another part of the large State bureaucracy in the 1950s, 1960s and 1970s. Under this system, management was organized in guilds (*Grémios*) and labor in official unions (*Sindicatos*). The state also organized special employer-employee institutes for rural workers (*Casas do Povo* or "Houses of the People") and for fishermen (*Casas dos Pescadores* or "Houses of Fishermen").

An elaborate bureaucratic structure administered this cumbersome system. A Chamber of Corporations, representing all professions and occupations, was the upper chamber of the national Legislature in Lisbon. One major aim or strategy of the system was to prevent labor strikes or lockouts, but after 1942's widespread strikes and later labor unrest it was clear that opposition labor groups, some organized by the Portuguese Communist Party, had engineered their own labor union system parallel to the Corporative system. After the April 25, 1974 Revolutionary coup (q.v.), the Provisional Government abolished the New State's Corporative system.

CORTES. Under the Portuguese Monarchy, an assembly or kind of proto-parliament of various classes. While historians debate its historical origins, its earliest form as an assembly which was more than a royal council was present before 1211. At first only clerical and noble groups were represented and later elements of the people. Its business was to discuss fiscal matters (taxes) and it was convened by the Portuguese Monarch. The *Cortes'* powers and functions varied but its golden age of prestige coincided with the 14th and 15th centuries. As the Monarchy acquired more independent wealth from the overseas expansion and empire, it depended less on the *Cortes* for revenue. Under King João III (q.v.), as the Monarchy garnered greater power and control, the *Cortes* was seldom consulted and the King was asked to call the *Cortes* to meet at least every ten years. While it met during the 17th century, it did not meet at all during the reigns of the Absolutist, Regalist Kings João V (q.v.) and José I, with Pombal (q.v.) as Chief minister. The last *Cortes* met in 1828 in order to acclaim Dom Miguel as an Absolutist King. Later, under the subsequent Constitutional Monarchy (1834–1910), legislative assemblies were given different names (House of Deputies, Chamber of Peers, etc.). *See* LEGISLATURES, POR-TUGUESE.

COSTA, AFONSO (1871–1937). Leading political and government figure of the first parliamentary Republic (1910–1926), Portuguese Republican Party (PRP) leader and notable lawyer. Afonso Costa, like so many Portuguese political figures in the 20th century, was trained as a lawyer and taught as a law professor at a university, in his case, Coimbra University (q.v.). A brilliant student and a radical activist in student politics in his day, Costa soon both embodied and symbolized radical Republican politics and the effort to replace the Monarchy. As Minister of Justice in the 1910–1911 Provisional Government of the turbulent First Republic, Afonso Costa was the author of radical anti-clerical laws which helped to polarize the political struggles of the fledgling representative system. The leader of the radical wing of the PRP, known in that day as "The Democrats," Afonso Costa was the youngest cabinet officer in the Provisional Government, at age 39. A small but tenacious man, he was a strong speaker and debater in the noisy sessions of the Republic's Congress. Afonso Costa was Prime Minister three times during the First Republic (1913–1914, 1915–1916 and April–December 1917). His third Premiership was abruptly ended with the Sidónio Pais (q.v.) military coup of December 8, 1917. Costa was arrested but soon went into exile in Paris. Except for a few visits to Portugal, Costa remained in Paris as an international lawyer with a lucrative practice. Though asked to "save the Republic" by taking office again, Costa refused. Following a period in which he conspired from abroad to overthrow the Dictatorship, he died in Paris in 1937.

- D -

DELGADO, GENERAL HUMBERTO (1906–1965). Pioneer Air Force advocate and flyer, senior officer who opposed the *Estado Novo* (q.v.) and oppositionist candidate in the 1958 Presidential elections. One of the young Army lieutenants who participated in the May 28, 1926 coup which established the Military Dictatorship, Delgado was a loyal regime supporter during its early phase (1926–1944) and into its middle phase (1944–1958). An important advocate of an Army Air Force, a daring pilot, and a proponent of assisting the Allies with air bases in the Azores (q.v.) in World War II, Delgado spent an important part of his career after 1943 outside of Portugal. On missions in Europe and North America for the government and armed forces, the Air Force General came to oppose the Dictatorship in the 1950s. In 1958 he stood as the oppositionist candidate in the Presidential elections and his regime candidate opponent was Admiral Américo Tomás (q.v.). Delgado received considerable popular support in the cities during the campaign during which he and the coalition of varied political movements, including the Communist Party and Movement of Democratic Unity, were harassed by the regime police, PIDE (q.v.). When the managed election results were "tallied," Delgado had won more than 25%, including heavy votes in the African colonies, an embarrassment to the regime, which promptly altered the electoral law so that universal male suffrage was replaced by a safer electoral college (1959).

When legal means of opposition were closed to him, Delgado conspired with dissatisfied military officers who promised support but soon abandoned him. The government had him stripped of his job, rank and career and, in 1959, fearing arrest by the PIDE, Delgado sought political asylum in the Embassy of Argentina. Later he fled to South America and organized opposition to the regime, including liaison and plotting with Henrique Galvão (q.v.). Delgado traveled to Europe and North Africa to rally Portuguese oppositionists in exile and, in 1961–1962, dabbled in coup plots. Delgado had a role in the abortive coup at Beja, in January 1962, when the regime crushed the attempt of one Army unit to rebel. Brave to the extent of taking risks against hopeless odds, Delgado dreamed of instigating a popular uprising on his own. With his Brazilian secretary as his companion, Delgado made an appointment with destiny on the Spanish frontier with Portugal in February 1964. Neither he nor his companion were seen alive again and later their bodies were discovered in a shallow grave and investigations since have proved that they were murdered by PIDE agents in a botched kidnapping plot. When the true story of what happened to the "Brave General" was revealed in the world press, the opposition's resolve was strengthened and the *Estado Novo's* image reached a new low. Posthumously, General Delgado was honored in numerous ways since the Revolution of April 25, 1974.

DINIS, KING (1261–1325). Medieval Portugal's most talented Monarch, known as both "The Farmer King" and "The Poet King." Grandson of Alfonso X *"El Sabio"* ("The Learned") of Castile and Leon, and son of Afonso III (q.v.) of Portugal, Dinis ruled from 1279 to 1325. Dinis' fruitful reign helped strengthen Portugal as a nation and state, in an era of dangers and uncertainty. Dinis was a patron of learning, a noted poet who is known in tradition as the *"Rei-Trouvador"* ("Troubadour-King"), founder of the Universities of Lisbon and Coimbra (q.v.) and an influence on several translations made into Portuguese and other important acts. Dinis was also the King who decreed that Portuguese would be the official language of the country in legal and judicial activities.

DISCOVERIES, MONUMENT OF THE. Located on the Tagus shore in Belém, not far from the Tower of Belém and the Jerónimos Monastery (qq.v.), the Monument of the Discoveries is a stone tribute of relatively recent origin. Built originally in 1940 as part of the Dictatorship's Double Centenary commemorative Exposition of the Portuguese World, the Monument of the Discoveries was constructed of temporary, light materials. Unlike most of the Exposition's constructions, however, the Monument was not torn down after the Exposition closed in December 1940. It remained in place and was reconstructed out of permanent stone materials in time for the 1960 Celebrations of the 500th anniversary of the death of Prince Henry (q.v.).

The Monument is the work of sculptor Leopoldo de Almeida, faces into the Tagus on Belém shore, and is complemented by an enormous mosaic windrose of points of the compass contributed by the Union of South Africa, which is set in the open square just inland from the Monument. This modern construction forms an imposing caravel in full sail, with Prince Henry the Navigator up at the prow and a group of the country's chief navigators and sailors behind him. Notably, Columbus, who sailed for Spain (q.v.) is not among them! *See* COMMEMORATIONS, PORTUGUESE HISTORIC.

DIU, BATTLE OF (February 2, 1509). One of the more decisive battles in world maritime history, ended for 100 years any real threat to Portugal's command of the Indian Ocean and helped establish the West's naval hegemony in the Indian Ocean. Portugal's first Viceroy in India, Francisco de Almeida (qq.v.), sailed his fleet into Diu harbor and engaged an Egyptian and Gujerati fleet. Almeida's fleet and soldiers effectively destroyed the Muslim fleet and forces in the course of a day's bloody fighting. After the battle, the Muslim powers were unable to challenge Portugal's maritime strength for a considerable period. Not long afterwards, Portugal added Diu to its port conquests and that enclave in India (q.v.) remained a Portuguese possession until the invasion of Nehru's Indian army in December 1961.

DOURO, RIVER. This river in the Iberian Peninsula is about 485 miles (1,000 kilometers) long and thus shorter than the Tagus (q.v.). Known as the *Rio Douro* in Portuguese and the *Rio Duero* in Spanish, it rises in north-central Spain (q.v.), first flows west to northeast Portugal, then turns south and forms a section of the Luso-Spanish frontier and ultimately flows west into the Atlantic Ocean about two miles (three kilometers) south of Oporto (q.v.). Within Portugal, the Douro passes through deep gorges and steep hills and has rapids. Along sections of the Douro River grow the vineyards of the Port wine (q.v.) industry and in Oporto, along its banks, are found the so-called wine lodges of the Port wine companies. *See* OPORTO; PORT WINE.

- E -

EANES, RAMALHO (1935-). Career Army officer who played an important part in the revolutionary Armed Forces Movement (q.v.) which organized the 1974 coup, a key figure in the defeat of a Leftist military coup in November 25, 1975 and President of the Republic during two terms. Eanes was born near Castelo Branco and entered the Army School in 1953 at age 18. After promotion to Lieutenant in 1957, he served for a period in Portuguese India (q.v.). He served several tours in Portugal's African wars including Mozambique, (1961–1964 and 1966–1968), Guinea-Bissau (1969–1971) and Angola (January 1974 until the April 25, 1974 coup) (qq.v.). He participated in the Armed Forces Movement's conspiracy to topple the Dictatorship and later held important posts when the military governed Portugal during the period 1974–1975. One key post was as head of the Portuguese Radio and Television system, an important position in the Revolution's intense war of words and debates. In the failed Leftist coup attempt on November 25, 1975, Eanes, now promoted to Lieutenant Colonel, played a pivotal role in the triumph of the moderate Military party. In December 1975, he was named Army Chief of Staff. General Ramalho Eanes was twice elected and served two full terms as President of the Republic, in 1976–1981 and 1981–1986. In the 1976 Presidential elections, Eanes received about 61% of the vote and in that of December 1980, 56.4%. *See* ARMED FORCES MOVEMENT.

ECONOMY. Portugal's economy, under the influence of the European Economic Community (EEC) (q.v.), grew rapidly as of 1985–1986, and through 1992 the average annual growth was 4–5%. It is important, however, to place this current growth, which includes some not altogether desirable developments, in historical perspective. On at least three occasions in this century, Portugal's economy has experienced severe dislocation and instability: during the turbulent First Republic (1911–1925); during the Dictatorship, when the world Depression came into play (1930–1939); and during the aftermath of the 1974 Revolution (1974–1977). At other periods, and even under the Dictatorship, there were eras of relatively steady growth and development, despite the fact that Portugal's weak economy lagged behind industrialized Western Europe's economies, perhaps more than the Salazarist group wished to admit to the public or to foreigners.

For a number of reasons, Portugal's backward economy underwent considerable growth and development following the beginning of the colonial wars in Africa in early 1961. Recent research findings suggest that, contrary to a "stagnation thesis" that the *Estado Novo* (q.v.) economy during the last fourteen years of this Corporativist (q.v.), authoritarian regime experienced little or no growth, there were important changes, policy shifts, structural evolution and impressive growth rates. In fact, the average annual Gross Domestic Product growth rate (1961–1974) was about 7%. The war in Africa was one significant factor in the post-1961 economic changes. The new costs of finance and spending on the military and police actions in the African and Asian empires in 1961 and thereafter forced changes in economic policy.

Starting in 1963–1964, the relatively closed economy was opened up to foreign investment and Lisbon began to use deficit financing and more borrowing at home and abroad. Increased foreign investment, residence and technical and military assistance also had effects on economic growth and development. Salazar's Government moved toward greater trade and integration with various international bodies by signing agreements with the European Free Trade Association and several international finance groups. New multinational corporations began to operate along with foreign-based banks in the country. Meanwhile, foreign tourism increased massively from the early 1960s on and the tourism industry experienced unprecedented expansion. By 1973–1974, Portugal received more than 8 million tourists annually for the first time.

Under the Caetano (q.v.) period of the Dictatorship (1968–1974), other important economic changes occurred. High annual economic growth rates continued until the world energy crisis inflation and a recession hit Portugal in 1973. Caetano's system through new development plans modernized aspects of the agricultural, industrial and service sectors and linked educational (q.v.) reforms with plans for social change. It also introduced cadres of forward-looking technocrats at various levels. The general motto of Caetano's version of the Dictatorship was "Evolution With Continuity," but Lisbon was unable to solve the key problems which were more political and social than economic. As the boom period went "bust" in 1973–1974, and growth slowed down greatly, it became clear that Caetano and his governing circle had no way out of the African wars and could find no easy compromise solution to the need to democratize Portugal's restive society. The economic background of the April 25, 1974 (q.v.) military *golpe* was a severe energy shortage caused by the world energy crisis and Arab oil boycott as well as high general inflation, increasing debts from the African wars and a weakening currency. While the regime prescribed greater Portuguese investment in Africa, in fact Portuguese businesses were increasingly investing outside of the *escudo* area in Western Europe and the United States (q.v.).

The 1974 Revolution and a period of political and social turmoil during two years following the surprise *golpe* dislocated a weakening economy. Production, income, reserves and annual growth fell drastically during 1974–1976. Amidst labor-management conflict, there was a burst of strikes and income and productivity plummeted. Ironically, one factor which cushioned the economic impact of the Revolution was the significant gold reserve supply which the Dictatorship had accumulated, principally during Salazar's (q.v.) years. Another factor was emigration from Portugal and her former colonies in Africa which to a degree reduced pressures for employment. The sudden infusion of more than 600,000 refugees from Africa did increase the unemployment rate which in 1975 was 10–15%. But, by 1990, the unemployment rate was down to about 5–6%.

After 1985, Portugal's economy experienced high growth rates again which averaged 4–5% through 1992. Substantial economic assistance from the EEC and individual countries such as the United States (q.v.) as well as the political stability and administrative continuity which derived from majority Social Democrat Governments starting in mid-1987, supported new growth and development in the EEC's second poorest country. With rapid infrastructural change and some unregulated development, Portugal's leaders harbored a justifiable concern that a fragile environment and ecology were under new, unacceptable pressures. Among other improvements in the standard of living since 1974 was an increase in per capita income. By 1991 the average minimum monthly wage was about 40,000 *escudos* and per capita income was about $5,000 per annum. *See* EMPIRE, PORTUGUESE OVERSEAS; EUROPEAN ECONOMIC COMMUNITY; HEALTH; INTRODUCTION, SOCIETY AND ECONOMY.

EDUCATION. Portugal's educational system has long been troubled by several disturbing trends: a relatively high level of mass illiteracy in rural areas, fewer educational opportunities for women, an overcentralized, inefficient and underfunded national educational system and a basic lack of educational reforms at various levels. Progress in reducing the illiteracy rate has been made in recent decades:

Illiteracy Rate (1970–1990)

1970	25.8%
1973	24%
1990	20%

There have been several recent eras of educational reform including 1970–1974, during the Caetano period of the *Estado Novo* (qq.v.), and since 1985 in Democratic Portugal. Among the needed reforms have been increased funds for education, improved teacher education, decentralization of the rigidly centralized educational system, benefits of the new civil freedoms of speech and the press and improvement in secondary and higher education in the rural districts. The following chart reflects changes in education since the April 25, 1974 Revolution (q.v.).

	1973–1974	1987–1988
Primary School students	1.19 million	1.18 million
Teachers	48,352	41,518
Secondary School students	369,033	596,060
Teachers	21,875	68,811
University students	58,605	100,000 (estim.)
Professors	3,676	11,014
Number of Art Schools		27
Universities	14	19
Private		8
Public (National)		11

EGAS MONIZ, DR. ANTÓNIO CAETANO (1874–1955). Pioneer physician and neurosurgeon, sometime Republican political figure and Minister during the First Republic and Portugal's only Nobel Prize winner. Trained as a doctor at Coimbra University's (q.v.) Medical School, he was named a Professor in 1902. In 1911, after having studied at several clinics in France, Egas Moniz was transferred to the Chair of Neurology at the University of Lisbon. In 1903, he began his involvement in politics when he was elected a deputy to the Monarchy's parliament. During the early and middle phases of the First Republic, Egas Moniz became one of the more important moderate Republican personalities in the Constituent Assembly, a leading member of Almeida's Evolutionist Party, a founder of the Centrist Party and a staunch supporter of Presidentialism and President Sidónio Pais (q.v.). In a sense a prophet without honor during some of the more difficult phases of the turbulent Republic, Egas Moniz was Portugal's Minister to Spain in 1917–1918 and then Portugal's Minister of Foreign Affairs. During 1919, he headed Portugal's delegation to the Versailles Peace Conference. Exhausted and disillusioned with politics and government service by mid-1919, he devoted the remainder of his active life to medical practice and neurological research and writing.

In 1927 after intensive experimentation, Egas Moniz performed the first cerebral angiography on a patient; this X-ray provided vital information on the brain, in terms of blood circulation in the brain, the most significant finding in half a century. In 1935, he pioneered a new type of brain operation. His great contributions to medicine and to neuro-surgery were finally recognized in 1949, when Egas Moniz was awarded the Nobel Prize for the discovery of the uses of leucotomy in certain psychoses. To date, he is the only Portuguese to receive such an honor. His two fascinating memoirs (*Confidências de um Investigador Científico* (1949) and *A Nossa Casa* (1950)) are among the more significant and prescient of Portuguese memorial works in modern times. A tenacious collector of plastic arts, his collection is housed in the Egas Moniz House-Museum at Avanca (near Aveiro), northern Portugal, and other memorabilia related to this outstanding scientist are located in the Egas Moniz Museum, Lisbon.

EMPIRE, PORTUGUESE OVERSEAS (1415–1975). Portugal was the first Western European state to establish an early modern overseas empire beyond the Mediterranean and perhaps the last colonial power to decolonize. A vast subject of complexity which is full of myth as well as debatable theories, the history of the Portuguese overseas empire involves the story of more than one empire, the question of imperial motives, the nature of Portuguese rule and the results and consequences of empire, including the impact on subject peoples as well as on the mother country and its society. Here, only the briefest account of a few such questions can be attempted.

As a preliminary, it would be noted that there were various empires or phases of empire since the capture of the Moroccan city of Ceuta in 1415. There were at least three Portuguese empires in history:

First empire (1415–1580)
Second empire (1580–1640 and 1640–1822)
Third empire (1822–1975)

With regard to the second empire, the so-called Phillipine period (1580–1640), when Portugal's empire was under Spanish domination, could almost be counted as a separate era. During that period, Portugal lost important parts of her Asian holdings to England (q.v.) and also sections of her colonies of Brazil (q.v.), Angola (q.v.) and West Africa to Holland's conquests. These various empires could be characterized by the geography of where Lisbon invested its greatest efforts and resources to develop territories and ward off enemies.

The first empire (1415–1580) had two phases. First came the African coastal phase (1415–1497), when the Portuguese sought a foothold in various Moroccan cities but then explored the African coast from Morocco to past the Cape of Good Hope in South Africa. While colonization and sugar farming were pursued in the Atlantic islands as well as in the islands in the Gulf of Guinea like São Tomé and Príncipe (q.v.), for the most part the Portuguese strategy was to avoid commitments to defending or peopling lands on the African continent. Rather, Lisbon sought a seaborne trade empire where the Portuguese could profit from exploiting trade and resources (such as gold) along the coasts and continue exploring southward to seek a sea route to India (q.v.). The second phase of the first empire (1498–1580) began with the discovery of the sea route to Asia, thanks to Vasco da Gama's (q.v.) first voyage in 1497–1499, and the capture of strong points, ports and trading posts in order to enforce a trade monopoly between Asia and Europe. This Asian phase produced the greatest revenues of empire Portugal had garnered, yet ended when Spain (q.v.) conquered Portugal and commanded her empire as of 1580.

Portugal's second overseas empire began with Spanish domination and ran to 1822, when Brazil won her independence from Portugal. This phase was characterized largely by Brazilian dominance of imperial commitment, wealth in minerals and other raw materials from Brazil and the loss of a significant portion of her African and Asian coastal empire to Holland and England. A sketch of Portugal's imperial losses either to native rebellions or to imperial rivals like England and Holland follows:

Morocco (North Africa) (sample only)

Arzila—taken in 1471; evacuated in 1550s; lost to Spain in 1580, which returned city to a Sultan.

Ceuta—taken in 1415; lost to Spain in 1640 (loss confirmed in 1668 treaty with Spain).

Tangiers—taken in 15th century; handed over to England in 1661 as part of Catherine of Braganza's dowry to King Charles II.

West Africa

Fort/Castle of São Jorge da Mina (now Ghana)—taken in 1480s; lost to Holland in 1630s.

Middle East

Socotra isle—conquered in 1507; Fort abandoned in 1511; used as water resupply stop for India Fleet.

Muscat—conquered in 1501; lost to Persians in 1650.

Ormuz—taken, 1505–1515 under Albuquerque; lost to England who gave it to Persia, 17th cent.

Aden (entry to Red Sea)—unsuccessfully attacked by Portugal (1513–1530); taken by Turks in 1538.

India

Ceylon (Sri Lanka)—taken by 1516; lost to Dutch after 1600.

Bombay—taken in 16th century; given to England in 1661 treaty as part of Catherine of Braganza's dowry for Charles II.

East Indies

Moluccas—taken by 1520; possession confirmed in 1529

Saragossa treaty with Spain; lost to Dutch after 1600; only East Timor remaining.

After the restoration of Portuguese independence from Spain in 1640, Portugal proceeded to revive and strengthen the Anglo-Portuguese alliance (q.v.), with international aid to fight off further Spanish threats to Portugal and drive the Dutch invaders out of Brazil and Angola. While Portugal lost her foothold in West Africa at Mina to the Dutch, dominion in Angola was consolidated. The most vital part of the imperial economy was a triangular trade: slaves from West Africa and from the coasts of Congo and Angola were shipped to plantations in Brazil; raw materials (sugar, tobacco, gold, diamonds, dyes) were sent to Lisbon; Lisbon shipped Brazil colonists and hardware. Part of Portugal's War of Restoration against Spain (1640–1668) and its reclaiming of Brazil and Angola from Dutch intrusions was financed by the New Christians (Jews converted to Christianity after the 1496 Manueline order of expulsion of Jews) who lived in Portugal, Holland and other low countries, France, and Brazil. If the first empire was mainly an African coastal and Asian empire, the second empire was primarily a Brazilian empire.

Portugal's third overseas empire began upon the traumatic independence of Brazil, the keystone of the Lusitanian enterprise, in 1822. The loss of Brazil greatly weakened Portugal both as a European power and as an imperial state, for the scattered remainder of largely coastal, poor, and uncolonized territories which stretched from the bulge of West Africa to East Timor (q.v.) in the East Indies and Macau (q.v.) in south China, were more of a financial liability than an asset. Only two small territories balanced their budgets occasionally or made profits: the cocoa islands of São Tomé and Príncipe in the Gulf of Guinea and tiny Macau, which lost much of its advantage as an entrepot between the West and the East when the British annexed neighboring Hong Kong in 1842. The others were largely burdens on the treasury. The African colonies were strapped by a chronic economic problem: at a time when the slave trade and then slavery were being abolished under pressures from Britain and other western powers, the economies of Guinea (q.v.), São Tomé/Príncipe, Angola and Mozambique (q.v.) were totally dependent on revenues from the slave trade and slavery. During the course of the 19th century, Lisbon began a program to reform colonial administration in a newly rejuvenated African empire, where most of the imperial efforts were expended, by means of replacing the slave trade and slavery with legitimate economic activities.

Portugal participated in its own early version of the "scramble" for Africa's interior during 1850–1869, but discovered that the costs of imperial expansion were too high to allow effective occupation of the hinterlands. After 1875, Portugal participated in the international "Scramble for Africa" and consolidated its holdings in west and southern Africa, despite the failure of the *contra-costa* (to the opposite coast) plan which sought to link up the interiors of Angola and Mozambique with a corridor in central Africa. Portugal's expansion into what is now Malawi, Zambia and Zimbabwe (eastern section) in 1885–1890 was thwarted by its oldest ally Britain, under pressure from interest groups in South Africa, Scotland and England. All things considered, Portugal's colonizing resources and energies were overwhelmed by the African empire which she possessed after the frontier-marking treaties of 1891–1906. Lisbon could barely administer the massive area of five African colonies whose total area comprised about 8% of the area of the colossal continent. The African territories alone were many times the size of tiny Portugal and as of 1914 Portugal was the third colonial power in terms of size of area possessed in the world.

The politics of Portugal's empire were deceptive. Lisbon remained obsessed with the fear that rival colonial powers, especially Germany and Britain, would undermine and then dismantle her African empire. This fear endured well into World War II. In developing and keeping her potentially rich African territories (especially mineral-rich Angola and strategically-located Mozambique), however, the race against time was with herself and her subject peoples. Two major problems, both chronic, prevented Portugal from effective colonization (i.e. settling) and development of her African empire: the economic weakness and underdevelopment of the mother country and the fact that the bulk of Portuguese emigration after 1822 went to Brazil, Venezuela, the United States and France, not to the colonies. These factors made it difficult to consolidate imperial control until it was too late, that is, until local African nationalist movements had organized and taken the field in insurgency wars which began in three of the colonies during the years 1961–1964.

Portugal's belated effort to revitalize control and to develop in the truest sense of the word Angola and Mozambique after 1961 had to be set against contemporary events in Europe, Africa and Asia. While Portugal held on to a backward empire, other European countries like Britain, France and Belgium were rapidly decolonizing their empires. Portugal's failure or unwillingness to divert the large streams of emigrants to her empire after 1850 remained a constant factor in this question. Prophetic were the words of the 19th century economist Joaquim Oliveira Martins who wrote in 1880 that Brazil was a better colony then for Portugal than Africa and that the best colony of all would have been Portugal itself. As of the day of the military coup in Lisbon (April 25, 1974), which sparked the final process of decolonization of the remainder of Portugal's third overseas empire, the results of the colonization program could be seen to be modest compared to the numbers of Portuguese emigrants outside the empire. Moreover, within a year, of some 600,000 Portuguese residing permanently in Angola and Mozambique, all but a few thousand had fled to South Africa or returned to Portugal.

In 1974 and 1975, most of the Portuguese empire was decolonized or, in the case of East Timor, invaded and annexed by a foreign power before it could consolidate its independence. Only historic Macau, scheduled for transfer to the People's Republic of China in 1999, remained nominally under Portuguese control as a kind of footnote to imperial history. If Portugal now lacked a conventional overseas empire and was occupied with the challenges of integration in the European Community (q.v.), Lisbon retained another sort of informal dependency which was a new kind of empire: the empire of her scattered overseas Portuguese communities from North America to South America. Their numbers were at least six times greater than that of the last settlers of the third empire. See ANGOLA; BRAZIL; GUINEA; LUSO-TROPICALISM, THEORY OF; MOZAMBIQUE; ROSE-COLORED MAP; SÃO TOMÉ; TIMOR, EAST; ULTIMATUM, ENGLISH.

ENGLAND (GREAT BRITAIN AFTER 1707). Next to Spain (q.v.), the country with which Portugal has had the closest diplomatic, political and economic relations into contemporary times and during much of her history as a nation. Today the two countries retain the formal bonds of the world's oldest diplomatic alliance. Whatever the diplomatic ups and downs of the Alliance, England and Portugal increasingly linked their economies starting with the Methuen treaties (q.v.) in the early 18th century. "English woolens for Portuguese wines" was the essence of this trade arrangement, but many other products were traded between two peoples with quite different religious and cultural features. Among economic links, now traditional, are those in banking and finance, manufacturing, agriculture and trade. Portugal joined Britain in several international economic organizations well before it entered the European Community (q.v.) in 1986: European Free Trade Association (1959), International Monetary Fund, World Bank and General Agreement on Tariffs and Trade. Tourism, too, has long been a key connection. Ever since the 1700s, English travelers have enjoyed the sun and citrus fruits of Portugal and Madeira (q.v.) for their health, early privileged tourists. Another significant link is one of the largest foreign communities in Portugal. Both have increased considerably since the early 1960s when cheap air fares began. Among European Community members, Britain remains one of Portugal's largest foreign investors. *See* ANGLO-PORTUGUESE ALLIANCE; CATHER-INE OF BRAGANZA; METHUEN, TREATY OF; PORT WINE; WINDSOR, TREATY OF.

ESTADO NOVO. The name the Dictatorship (1926–1974) called itself. *"Estado Novo"* or "New State" was a name which may have been influenced by an earlier regime's name for itself, *"Republica Nova"* or "New Republic," led by President Sidónio Pais (1917–1918) (q.v.) in the First Republic (1910–1926). The name *"Estado Novo"* appears for the first time in 1930, during the Military Dictator-ship phase; it caught on with supporters of the regime and became official. *See* SALAZAR, ANTÓNIO DE OLIVEIRA; SALA-ZARISM; TWENTY-EIGHTH OF MAY.

ESTORIL. Composed of the towns of São Pedro, São João, Monte Estoril and Estoril, and located about 15 miles (32 kilometers) west of Lisbon (q.v.) along the coast, Estoril forms the heart of a tourist region. Once described in tourist literature as the Sun Coast (*Costa do Sol*), this coast—in order not to be confused with a region with a similar name in neighboring Spain (*Costa del Sol*)—has been renamed the "Lisbon Coast." Its origins go back to several developments in the late 19th century which encouraged the building of a resort area which would take advantage of the coast's fine climate and beaches from Carcavelos to Cascais such as the fact that sporty King Carlos (1889–1908) and his court liked summering in Cascais (apparently the first tennis in Portugal was played here), then only a simple fishing village, the medicinal spring waters in Estoril and the inauguration (1889) of a new train line from Lisbon to Cascais, a convenient way of bringing visitors before the age of automobiles and superhighways.

As a high-class resort town, Estoril was developed beginning in the 1920s and 1930s due in part to the efforts of the entrepreneur Fausto de Figueiredo, whose memorial statue graces the now famous Casino Gardens. Soon Estoril possessed a gambling Casino, restaurants and several fine hotels, including the elegant Hotel Palácio-Estoril, which opened in 1932.

Estoril's beginnings as a small but popular international resort and watering spot were slow and difficult, however, and what Estoril became was determined in part by the international economy and politics. The resort's backers and builders modeled Estoril to a degree on Nice, a much larger, older and better known resort in the French Riviera. The name "Estoril," in fact, which was not found on Portuguese maps before the 20th century, was a Portuguese corruption of the French word for a mountain range near Nice. Estoril hotel designs, such as that for what reputedly became the most luxurious hotel outside Lisbon, the Hotel Palácio-Estoril, looked to earlier hotel designs on the French Riviera.

It was remarkable, too, that Estoril's debut as a resort area with full services (hotels, casino, beach, spa) and sports (golf, tennis, swimming) happened to coincide with the depth of the world Depression (1929–1934) which seemed to threaten its future. Less expensive, with a more reliably mild year-round climate and closer to England and North America than the older French Riviera, the "Sun Coast" which featured Estoril had many attractions. The resort's prosperity was guaranteed when large numbers of middle class and wealthy Spaniards migrated to the area after 1931, during the turbulent Spanish Republic and subsequent bloody Civil War (1936–1939). World War II (when Portugal was neutral) and the early stages of the Cold War only enhanced the Sun Coast's resort reputation. After 1939, numbers of displaced and de-throned ex-royalty from Europe came to Portugal to live in a sunny, largely tax-free climate. In the early 1950s, Estoril's Casino became known to millions of readers and arm-chair travelers when it was featured in one of the early James Bond books by Ian Fleming, the novel *Casino Royale* (1953).

ESTRELA MOUNTAINS. The Estrela mountain range (*Serra da Estrela*), about 75 miles (160 kilometers) long in the Beira Alta district of north-central Portugal, boasts the highest peaks in the country. The highest point is about 6,532 feet (2,000 meters). Frequently seen from neighboring areas with snow-capped peaks, the Estrela ("star" in Portuguese) mountains feature Portugal's only downhill (winter) skiing facilities. This is an area of Beira Alta district (or "province" in previous administrative divisions) where wolves still survive and are common in local oral tradition.

EUROPEAN ECONOMIC COMMUNITY (EEC). In 1978, Portugal began negotiations with the EEC to become a member and, in January 1986, along with Spain (q.v.), Portugal joined that organization. Since joining the EEC, Portugal's economy has received many benefits: loans, grants, technical assistance and other economic, social and educational advantages which are worth billions of dollars. Most of Portugal's trade is with EEC members and Portugal's economy is tied now to EEC plans and planning, standards and rules and philosophy. Starting in January 1993, by previous agreement, all EEC tariff barriers for many goods (excluding agricultural goods until 1995–1996 in Portugal's case) were removed and there is concern in Portugal that many small and medium-sized businesses (which are the norm) will not survive the new competition from richer member states. Next to Greece, Portugal remains the poorest, least developed EEC country and there is anxiety in Lisbon that following new pressures for the EEC to give massive assistance to former Soviet bloc countries in Eastern Europe and to allow them in time to join the EEC Portugal will be at a disadvantage. *See* ECONOMY.

ÉVORA, CITY OF. Located about 68 miles (140 kilometers) southeast of Lisbon, the city of Évora is the capital of Évora district, and formerly the capital of old Alentejo province. Its current population is over 35,000. In Roman Lusitania (q.v.) its name was *"Liberalitas Julia."* Conquered by various invaders thereafter, including the Muslims, the city was reconquered by the Christian Portuguese in 1165. For a time during the 15th and 16th centuries, Évora was the site of the royal court's residence. It has a unique architectural heritage and its center includes a Roman temple (Temple of Diana) as well as many medieval and renaissance buildings in Gothic, Manueline (q.v.) and the later Baroque styles. Like Tomar, Santarém, Braga, Coimbra (qq.v.) and Óbidos, Évora can be classified as a Museum-City. Recognizing this, on November 25, 1986, UNESCO declared Évora's city center to be protected and registered as a "World Treasure" as well as the "Patrimony of Humanity," the first time such honors were granted to a Portuguese city. Besides the Corinthian-styled Roman Temple of Diana, Évora has the oldest standing aqueduct in Portugal (ca. mid-16th century). In the 1980s, the University of Évora was revived. There is also a reconstructed Roman aqueduct in Évora as well as a 13th century Gothic Cathedral. *See* PROVINCES, PORTUGAL'S (HISTORIC).

- F -

FADO. Traditional urban song and music sung to the accompaniment of two stringed instruments by a woman or man. The Portuguese word, *fado,* derives from the Latin word for fate (*fatum*) and the *fado* is sung by *fadistas* whose usage does not distinguish the sex of the singer. Traditionally, wherever the *fado* is performed, the singer—who is often but not always a woman wearing a shawl around her shoulders—is accompanied by the Portuguese *guitarra,* a twelve-stringed mandolin-like instrument or lute, and the *viola,* a Spanish guitar. There are at least two contemporary variations of the *fado*: the Lisbon *fado* and the Coimbra or University student *fado*. While some authorities describe the song as typical of the urban working classes, its popularity and roots are wider than only this group and it appears that, while the song's historic origins are urban and working class, its current popularity is more universal. The historic origins of the *fado* are not only obscure but hotly debated among scholars and would-be experts. Some suggest that its origins are Brazilian and African, while others counter and say that there is a Muslim, North African element mixed with the Hispanic.

After the 1974 Revolution, there was talk that the *fado*'s days were numbered as a popular song that seemed to be identified as an obsolete, regime-encouraged entertainment that like a drug or soporific encouraged passivity. In the new Portugal, however, the *fado* has not lost its general popularity among various classes as well as among an increasingly large number of visitors and tourists. The *fado* is performed in restaurants, cafes and special *fado* houses, not only in Portugal and other Lusophone countries like Brazil, but wherever Portuguese communities gather abroad. While there do not appear to be schools of *fado, fadistas* learn their trade by apprenticeship to senior performers, both men and women. Portugal's most celebrated *fadista* remains Amália Rodrigues who, now in her 70s, still performs in public. She made her main American debut in New York's Carnegie Hall in the 1950s and about the same time Americans were charmed by a popular song of the day, "April in Portugal," an American version of a traditional Portuguese *fado* called *"Fado de Coimbra,"* about Coimbra University's (q.v.) romantic traditions. The predominant tone of the Lisbon variation of the *fado,* sung often in the districts of Alfama, Mouraria, Bairro Alto and Alcântara, is that of nostalgia, *saudade,* sadness and regret. Traditionally, the Coimbra version has a lighter, less somber tone. *See* SAUDADES.

FÁTIMA. Village in central Portugal, site of a Catholic shrine and pilgrimage center and place associated with cult of "Our Lady of Fátima." Near this small village in the so-called "Cove of the Lions," the Virgin Mary reportedly appeared before three peasant children, shepherds, on the 13th of each month from May to October 1917. The children were told that they were being addressed by "Our Lady of the Rosary" and that a chapel should be built there in her honor. Fátima soon became, in effect, the Portuguese Lourdes, one of the great Catholic shrines and pilgrimage centers. In 1932, the Catholic Church (q.v.) authorized devotion to Our Lady of Fátima and a large shrine and basilica were constructed near the site of the incidents. In 1967, Pope Paul VI visited Fátima. Fátima has become a center of devotion for millions of persons in the last decades as well as the topic of a continuing controversy between believers and skeptics and critics. Debates about the significance of what happened at Fátima in 1917 and the aftermath will continue, but it is a fact that the development of Fátima as a Catholic shrine and pilgrimage center occurred amidst a Catholic revival in Portugal during the first third of the 20th century. *See* CHURCH, CATHOLIC.

FIDALGO. Refers to a noble or person of noble lineage. The word derives from the expression *"filho de algo"* (son of something) which came into common usage during the 13th century in Portugal, with an equivalent in neighboring Spain (q.v.). Eventually, the word became synonymous with "noble" and implied possession of "wealth." Entry into the class of *fidalgos* was highly desirable and service in the overseas empire after 1415 could provide the impetus for such social mobility.

FIFTH OF OCTOBER. An important national holiday called "Republic Day" in Portugal. It commemorates what happened on October 5, 1910, when Republican forces overthrew the Monarchy and established the first Portuguese Republic (1910–1926). During the Dictatorship (1926–1974), Republicans and other opponents of the authoritarian regime would mark that day in pilgrimages and political meetings at Lisbon cemeteries where the honored dead from the First Republic lie in tombs and graves. Since April 25, 1974, the Fifth of October has reassumed greater importance as a *national* holiday.

FILIPE I, KING (1527–1598). Known to history usually as Fillipe II of Spain (q.v.), this Spanish monarch was the first King of the

Phillipine dynasty in Portugal, or Filipe I. He ruled Portugal and its empire from 1580 to 1598. The son of Carlos V (Charles V) of Spain and the Hapsburg empire and of Queen Isabel of Portugal, Filipe had a strong claim on the throne of Portugal. On the death of Portugal's King Sebastião (q.v.) in battle in Morocco in 1578, Filipe presented his claim and candidacy for the Portuguese throne. In the Cortes (q.v.) of Almeirim (1579), Filipe was officially recognized as King of Portugal by that assembly which was dominated by the clerical and noble estates. This act, however, did not take into account the national feeling of the Portuguese people. A portion of the people supported a Portuguese claimant, the Prior of Crato, and they began to organize armed resistance to the Spanish intrusion. In 1580, Filipe sent a Spanish army across the Portuguese frontier under the Duke of Alba. Both on land and at sea Spanish forces defeated the Portuguese. At the Cortes of Tomar (1581), Filipe was proclaimed King of Portugal. Before returning to Spain in 1583, Filipe resided in Portugal.

There were grave consequences for Portugal and her scattered imperial holdings of the Spanish overthrow of Portugal's hard-won independence. Just how bitter these consequences were is reflected in how Portuguese history and literature traditionally termed the Spanish takeover: "The Babylonian Captivity." Portugal suffered from the growing decline, decadence and weaknesses of her Spanish master. Beginning with the destruction of the Spanish Armada (1588), which used Lisbon as its supply and staging point, Spanish rule over Portugal was disastrous. Not only did Spain's brave enemies—especially England, France (qq.v.) and Holland—attack continental Portugal as if it were Spain, they also attacked and conquered portions of Portugal's vulnerable, far-flung empire. *See* INTRODUCTION, PORTUGAL UNDER SPANISH RULE.

FIRST OF MAY. An important holiday for organized labor and a Labor Day for many countries in Europe, among them Portugal. Traditionally, beginning in the last decades of the Monarchy, this was a day when labor groups, including unions of laborers, would demonstrate and commemorate European Labor Day in Portugal. When unions were given legal status during the First Republic, the First of May was a day during which labor openly organized demonstrations of solidarity and strength. During the Dictatorship, when traditional unions did not enjoy legal status but had to be part of official labor syndicates in the Corporatist (q.v.) system, May First was a day when labor challenged the regime's labor policies and the control of the streets. An important test of democratic Portugal occurred on May 1, 1974, following the military coup of April 25th (q.v.). Freedom to celebrate that labor holiday was now present, but some observers feared violence, disorder and confusion as long repressed forces of labor emerged in the streets. That May First celebration, however, went smoothly and there were media estimates that one million Portuguese marched in the capital's streets peacefully that day.

FIRST OF DECEMBER. For centuries and until recently an official Portuguese national holiday each year. On December 1, 1640, in Lisbon a Portuguese Revolution overthrew Spanish rule and restored national independence. The First of December was long celebrated as a holiday which was to impart feelings of national loyalty and patriotism in the people and mark the end of the 60-year period of Portugal's subjugation to Phillipine Spain. *See* FILIPE I, KING; WAR OF RESTORATION.

FLAG, PORTUGUESE NATIONAL. Portugal's current national flag was adopted under the First Republic on June 19, 1911. In the center of two fields of bright green and red, which symbolize Portugal's land and the blood shed for the good of the nation, are two shields which are superimposed on an armillary sphere in yellow. Most significant is the use of the symbol of the armillary sphere which suggests Portugal's historic role in exploration of the globe and the spirit of scientific discovery. All regimes since the First Republic have adopted this flag unchanged. The armillary sphere was an ancient astronomical device comprised of a globe surrounded by rings which represented celestial movements and their measurement.

FRANCE. The continental European country with which Portugal has had the closest and most friendly relations since the Middle Ages and whose culture since early modern times has been the most important model for Portugal's culture. Beginning in the Reconquest, French groups assisted Portuguese in fighting the

Muslims and Portugal's first royal dynasty was Burgundian. Various French religious orders settled in Portugal and brought new skills and ideas. Franco-Portuguese relations in diplomacy went through various phases after a virtual break between the two countries during the Hundred Years' War and Castile's campaigns to conquer Portugal up to the battle of Aljubarrota (1385) (q.v.), when France was the main ally of Castile. France gave Portugal vital assistance in the 16th and 17th centuries against Spanish aggression. French aid was given to Dom António, Prior of Crato, who opposed Phillip II's domination of Portugal, and to Restoration Portugal during the War of Restoration (1640–1668) (q.v.). With the important exception of the disastrous Napoleonic invasions and war (1807–1811), Franco-Portuguese relations in diplomacy commerce and culture were exceptionally good since the first quarter of the 19th century.

In part as a response to unpopular Castilianization during Spain's (q.v.) domination, Portuguese found French culture a comforting, novel foil and prestigious alternative. Despite England's (q.v.) dominance in matters commercial, diplomatic and political under the oldest Alliance, French culture and politics came to enjoy primary importance in Portugal. Even in commerce, France was Portugal's third or fourth best customer during the 19th century. Especially between 1820 and 1960, French influence provided a major model for the Portuguese educated classes. A brief list of some key political, literary, philosophical and artistic ideas Portugal eagerly embraced is suggestive. Dom Pedro IV's (q.v.) 1826 Charter (*A Carta*) was directly modeled on an early French constitution. French models of Liberalism and Socialism prevailed in politics, Impressionism in art, Romanticism and Realism, Parnassianism and Symbolism in literature, Positivism and Bergsonianism in philosophy, etc. During the 18th and 19th centuries, the Portuguese language, including vocabulary and orthography (spelling), experienced extensive Frenchification. French became Portugal's second language and provided access to knowledge and information vital for the education and development of isolated Portugal.

French cultural influences became pervasive and entered the country by various means: through the French invasions before 1811, trade and commerce, improved international communication and transportation, Portuguese emigration to France, which became a mass movement after 1950, and close diplomatic and intellectual relations. An example of the importance of French culture until recently, when British and American cultural influences have become more significant, was that works in French dominated foreign book sections in Portuguese bookstores. If Portugal retained the oldest diplomatic link in world history with England, its chief cultural model until recently was France. Until after the 1974 Revolution, the largest portion of Portugal's educated elite studying abroad resided in France and took French higher degrees. The pattern of Portuguese students in higher education abroad has diversified in the years since and now a significant portion are studying in other European continental states as well as in Britain and the United States (q.v.). Diplomatic posts in France rank high in the pecking order of Portugal's small Foreign Service.

FRANCO, GENERALÍSSIMO FRANCISCO (1892–1975). Spain's (q.v.) soldier-dictator whose Nationalists won the Spanish Civil War (1936–1939) and who ruled Spain from 1939 to 1975, when he died. General Franco's personal and diplomatic relations with Portugal's dictator, António de Oliveira Salazar (q.v.), ever since the late 1930s were a significant element in the *Estado Novo's* (q.v.) foreign policy in World War II and the Cold War. Salazar played a key role in helping convince Franco and his ruling group during the menacing years of 1939–1941 not to join the Axis powers in World War II. For his part, Franco supported Salazar's concept of an Iberian bloc of states in various diplomatic and political initiatives beginning with the Luso-Spanish agreements signed in 1939 and 1940. During the Cold War, Franco's Spain pursued a policy which gave support to Salazar's *Estado Novo. See* SPAIN.

FREYRE, GILBERTO (1900–1987). World famous Brazilian sociologist and scholar whose writings (1933–1960) formed the basis for the so-called theory of "Luso-Tropicalism" (q.v.). Born in Recife but receiving his higher degrees in the United States under American scholars, Freyre wrote a pioneering volume on the history of the colonization of Brazil (q.v.), under the influences of the Portuguese, Amerindians and black Africans. This first major work on Brazil, with the English title of *The Masters and the Slaves,* generated controversy over the precise role of Portugal in expansion and colonization in the world. The 1933 book and later writings up to the 1960 Commemoration of the 500th anniversary of Prince Henry the Navigator's death formed the foundation for certain interpretations which the Dictatorship later used to support its policy of continuing Portuguese colonial rule in Africa and Asia.

- G -

GALVÃO, HENRIQUE (1895–1970). Army officer and oppositionist of the *Estado Novo* (q.v.) Dictatorship. A career Army officer with considerable service in the African colonies, especially as an administrator in Angola (q.v.) in the 1930s, Galvão was an enthusiastic supporter of the Dictatorship in its early phase (1926–1944). As a young officer he supported the "28th of May" coup (q.v.) against the Republic and soon held middle level posts in the Dictatorship. An early booster of the cultural and political potential of the radio and public spectacles, Galvão did little soldiering but more administration in radio and was appointed to manage the June-December 1940 Exposition of the Portuguese World in Lisbon. After a tour of the African colonies as Inspector-General, he presented a confidential report (1947) to the regime's National Assembly in Lisbon. His findings revealed widespread abuse of authority and forced labor and semi-slavery in Angola and other colonies.

The regime's suppression of this report and the negative response precipitated Galvão's break with Salazar's (q.v.) government. Galvão was harassed by the political police (PIDE) (q.v.) and arrested and tried for treason in 1952. Imprisoned, he escaped disguised as a woman from Santa Maria hospital in 1959 and fled to South America, where he organized opposition groups to the Dictatorship. In early 1961, Galvão got world media coverage when he led a group of about a dozen Iberian dissidents who participated in an early act of political terrorism: the hijacking at sea of the Portuguese ocean liner, *Santa Maria,* drawing the attention of the world's journalists and public to the flaws in the *Estado Novo* and attempting to arouse a revolution against the Lisbon authorities by sailing the liner to Portuguese Africa (São Tomé or Angola). This bold enterprise failed, the liner and the hijackers were interned in Brazil, and Galvão continued in the political wilderness as an adventurer-oppositionist. He died in South America in 1970, the same year as his *bête noire*, Dr. Salazar.

GAMA, VASCO DA (1468?–1524). Navigator, conqueror and Fleet Commander of the Portuguese ships which discovered the sea route to India, 1497–1498. Born in Sines and trained in navigation, Vasco da Gama was named commander of four, by today's standards, very small vessels, which left the Tagus (q.v.) from Belém on July 8, 1497. The fleet sailed via the Cape Verde Islands down the African coast and passed the Cape of Good Hope, South Africa, on November 18, 1497. After cruising up the coast of East Africa, Vasco da Gama's ships reached Mombasa and then Melinde, where a friendly Sultan permitted a famous Indian Ocean pilot, Ahmed ben Majid, to assist Vasco da Gama in the voyage east to the west coast of India (q.v.). The Portuguese reached Calicut, India, on May 18, 1498. Vasco da Gama's missions were to discover the route to India, tap into the spice markets of Asia and contact and make treaties with Christian rulers there. Perhaps the greatest of Portugal's discoverers and sea explorers, Vasco da Gama accomplished these missions, though liaison with Christian princes proved illusory, and Portugal broke the spice monopoly of the Venetian-Asian system and began the process of prying open Asia to Western trade, conquest and empire.

The first of Da Gama's ships returned to Lisbon in July 1499 and Da Gama himself returned later in the summer. In the age of exploration, in a different league even than Columbus' first voyage to the West Indies, Vasco Da Gama's feat stands unequaled: the distance from Portugal to India by the most direct route around the Cape of Good Hope was 10,000 miles (22,000 kilometers) by sea under severe conditions typical of the age of sail. The entire round trip took two years and out of about 170 crew members only 55 returned to Lisbon. King Manuel of Portugal showered the navigator-commander with honors. Da Gama made another voyage to Calicut (1502–1504) and died in government service in India in 1524. Along with other famous navigator-conquerors of the Age of Discoveries as well as the national epic poet Camões (q.v.), Vasco da Gama is buried in the Jerónimos Monastery, Belém (qq.v.).

GENERATION OF 1895. Refers to a historic group of Portuguese colonial soldiers and war heroes who fought in Portuguese African colonial wars and, more specifically, to those Portuguese soldiers who participated as combatants in the 1895 campaign in southern Mozambique (q.v.) against the African Gaza kingdom of King Gungunyane. Among the soldiers who were part of this victorious but bloody campaign in Portuguese East Africa were Joaquim Mousinho de Albuquerque (q.v.), Eduardo Costa, Aires de Ornelas, Paiva Couceiro and Gomes da Costa (q.v.), some of whom later played roles in domestic politics in Portugal. *See* ALBUQUERQUE, JOAQUIM MOUSHINHO DE; GOMES DA COSTA, MANUEL.

GOLPISMO. Portuguese word for tendency or practice of military intervention in public affairs or politics, or the fact of military coups overthrowing governments. This expression derives from the word *"golpe"* ("blow" or "coup"). It came into use in the 19th century, when the word *"pronunciamento"* (q.v.) also became part of the common vocabulary. *See* PRONUNCIAMENTO.

GOMES DA COSTA, MANUEL DE OLIVEIRA (1863–1929). Marshal of the Portuguese Army, Commander of Portugal's forces in Flanders in World War I and leader of the military coup which overthrew the First Republic in May 1926. Trained at the Military College, Gomes da Costa rose from the rank of private to General during the period 1883 to 1917. His career began with important colonial service in India and Mozambique (qq.v.) in suppressing insurgencies in the 1890s. He served with Mousinho de Albuquerque (q.v.) in the Gaza campaigns (1896–1897), Mozambique and later in Angola and São Tomé (qq.v.). His most notable service was in Portugal's intervention in World War I as he helped organize the first Brigade and commanded the first Division of Portugal's Expeditionary Corps (CEP) which entered combat on the Western front in May 1917. For his role in the battle of Lys, in April 1918, when German forces badly mauled the Portuguese sector, Gomes da Costa was decorated by Portugal with the Tower and Sword medal. During the latter part of the First Republic, he was dispatched to the colonies on missions to divert him from domestic politics since he had joined the Reformist Party (PR).

As the most senior and best known career Army officer, Gomes da Costa was invited by former CEP comrades to join in military conspiracies to overthrow the Democrat-dominated First Republic. On May 28, 1926, in Braga, he launched the military coup with the pronouncement "To Arms, Portugal!" The General's famous name and forceful personality gave the military movement necessary prestige and won public opinion's confidence for the political moment. Gomes da Costa, however, was not suited to political maneuvering and administrative efficiency and, on July 9, 1926, he was dismissed as Minister of War by other Generals including future President Óscar Carmona (q.v.) and then exiled to the Azores (q.v.). For political effect and as a consolation prize to the leader whose individual daring had helped create the *abertura* (opening) which allowed the coup to succeed, the Military Dictatorship honored Gomes da Costa, even in exile, with promotion to Marshal of the Army. In ill health on his return from the isolated Azores in late 1927, he died less than two years later in Lisbon. There is a statue of Gomes da Costa in a square in Braga, designed by Barata Feyo, which honors the General of the "28th of May" (q.v.) coup d'etat.

GRAMIDO, CONVENTION OF (1847). Agreement signed by representatives of the parties in conflict in the Patuleia (q.v.) civil war (1846–1847), involving the siege of Oporto (q.v.). At Gramido, near Oporto, the following parties negotiated and signed a convention or agreement in order to stop the armed conflict: the Oporto Junta led by José Passos; the Lisbon government of Queen Maria II's (q.v.) Constitutional Monarchy; and the emissaries of the intervening foreign powers England, France and Spain (qq.v.). While the force of the intervening foreign armies and fleets convinced the Oporto rebels to negotiate and to capitulate, the provisions of the Convention of Gramido were not recognized, ratified or fulfilled by the triumphant Portuguese government in Lisbon nor by the foreign powers that had dispatched armed forces to Portugal. *See* PATULEIA.

GUADIANA, RIVER. The Guadiana River is about 515 miles (1200 kilometers) long in Spain (q.v.) and Portugal, one of the Peninsula's longest rivers with the Tagus and Douro (qq.v.). It rises in south-central Spain, flows west to Portugal's border, turns south and forms two sections of the frontier between Spain and Portugal. It then empties into the bay of Cadiz. Sections of the Guadiana form the border between the Algarve district and Spain.

GUARDA NACIONAL REPUBLICANA (GNR). The "Republican National Guard" is Portugal's national highway and traffic police and rural and urban constabulary. Established in 1911, under the first parliamentary Republic, in order to protect the novice Government in the capital and in main cities, the GNR became a kind of second army. While it was recruited from the career Army officer corps and noncommissioned ranks, the GNR was based on a historic precedent (the Monarchy had a Municipal Guard with similar functions) and a political necessity (the need to be a deterrent and bulwark against threatening Army insurrections) during a time of political instability. With increasingly heavy weaponry, a much enlarged GNR became a source of controversy as the Republic ended and the Military Dictatorship was established (1926–1933) and grew into the "New State" system. The Dictatorship eventually reduced its strength, but maintained it as a reserve force which might confront a potentially unreliable Army in the capital and main cities and towns. In post-1974 Portugal, GNR personnel can be seen in their distinctive uniforms and dealing with highway safety, traffic, the drug problem, and serious crimes. While the main headquarters is at Carmo barracks (Carmo Square), Lisbon, where Premier Caetano surrendered to the Armed Forces Movement (qq.v.) on April 25, 1974, GNR detachments are found all over the country.

GUIMARÃES. This city in Braga District, which is known as the cradle of Portuguese nationality, has origins which precede both the Monarchy and the nation. Portugal's first King Afonso Henriques (q.v.) was born in Guimarães and it was here that the first *Cortes* (q.v.) was held where it was decided in 1093 to give the government of the County of Portugal to the Burgundian Count Henry, the father of Afonso Henriques, later King of Portugal. In 1853 Guimarães was declared a city by Queen Maria II (q.v.). Long a symbol of the founding of Portugal, Guimarães' classic granite castle has many historic associations. It was here that the official opening of the 1940 Double Centenary celebrations occurred. For a small population, Guimarães has a large number of medieval monuments, including churches, palaces and chapels.

GUINEA. Former West African colony of Portugal until its independence in September 1974, Guinea-Bissau (not to be confused with Guinea-Conakry, its neighbor to the east and south) was the scene of Portuguese activity at least on the coast since the mid-15th century. Its area is about 14,000 square miles (36,120 square kilometers). Portugal established a few forts and trading posts on the coast of what became Guinea-Bissau and slave trade became the major economic activity until the mid-19th century. Portugal's coastal presence was not expanded to the tropical interior until the 19th century when Lisbon supported various so-called "pacification" campaigns. African rebellions continued, however, to 1936.

With the formation of the African Party for the Independence of Guinea and Cape Verde (PAICG), the principal nationalist movement, in 1956, African resistance increased. Between 1963 and 1974, a war of insurgency against Portuguese colonial rule was fought in the country. Unlike Portugal's territories in southern Africa—Angola and Mozambique (qq.v.)—Guinea-Bissau did not have Portuguese settlement of any consequence and the major private company which dominated the territory's economy (Companhia União Fabril) withdrew most of its assets by 1972. An important part of the alienation and radicalization of the Armed Forces Movement's (q.v.) officers took place in the grueling bush war in Guinea-Bissau. After the revolution in Lisbon, Portugal granted independence to this country. *See* ARMED FORCES MOVEMENT.

GULBENKIAN, CALOUSTE SARKIS (1869–1955). Armenian oil tycoon, philanthropist and art connoisseur-collector who settled in Portugal in World War II and whose donated wealth forms the basis for the Gulbenkian Foundation, Lisbon (qq.v.). Born in Scutari, Turkey, when it was part of the Ottoman Empire, Calouste Gulbenkian made a huge fortune and became one of Europe's wealthiest individuals through investment in Iraqi petroleum. While the oil business and investments were his work, the appreciation and collection of rare art represented his passion. During the 1920s and 1930s, he purchased a rich collection of Western and Oriental art. Some of it was loaned to great museums in London and Washington and some of it was displayed in his mansion in Paris on Avenue d'Iena.

Gulbenkian's life and the fate of his possessions were changed by the fortunes of World War II and by residence in Portugal. In April 1942, Gulbenkian fled Vichy France and settled in Portugal. Between his arrival and his death in July 1955, he made dispositions of his possessions and wealth which have had an almost incalculable impact on Portugal's arts, culture, science and education. After declining to build a museum for his unmatched art collection either in London or Washington, D.C., Gulbenkian decided to build such a home for his precious collection in Portugal and to endow an international Foundation in Lisbon. Since his death in 1955 and inauguration of the Foundation headquarters in the late 1960s, a Museum and a Contemporary Arts Museum have opened and Portuguese and other Lusophone arts and science circles have greatly benefited. *See* GULBENKIAN FOUNDATION.

GULBENKIAN FOUNDATION AND ASSOCIATED MUSEUMS AND INSTITUTES. In 1956, a year after the death of the Armenian philanthropist and art collector in Lisbon, the Gulbenkian Foundation was established in Portugal, Gulbenkian's adopted country of retirement. The work of this Foundation has had both an internal impact on Portugal's arts, sciences, health and education and an international impact in the advancement of Portuguese Studies in the world. The modern building housing the Foundation's staff and library was completed in the late 1960s and Gulbenkian's art collection was moved from Paris and other cities to a Museum adjacent to the Foundation offices. In the early 1980s, a Museum of Contemporary Arts was completed nearby. The income from the Gulbenkian endowment of the Foundation supports not only philanthropic social projects, but a wide variety of the arts, including organizations which offer performance seasons such as a ballet group and orchestras. Besides the Headquarters, the Museum and Contemporary Arts Museum at Avenida de Berna, Lisbon, the Foundation supports institutions in other districts of the Lisbon region, and has a program of scholarly grants for Portuguese as well as international scholars and students in various disciplines. The Foundation, in terms of annual giving, is one of the largest such institutions in Western Europe. *See* GULBENKIAN, CALOUSTE SARKIS.

- H -

HEALTH. While public health has improved considerably in the past two decades and there has been a greater rate of improvement in this area since the 1974 Revolution, severe public health problems continue to plague the country. The death rate has decreased and life expectancy has increased (in 1989–1990, life expectancy was about 71 for males and 78 for females), but public health problems in Portugal continued to be severe and statistics especially in rural Portugal were typical of many poor countries. Recent improvements in the health picture include an improved medical educational system, better medical technology and an increased number of doctors and medical personnel. There has also been some increase in the number of hospitals (in 1975, there were 229 hospitals and, in 1990, there were 239) and in the number of beds available for patients. Basic health knowledge in the general population, however, remains low, especially in rural areas. Medical resources were best, an old story in Portugal, in the major cities of Lisbon, Oporto and Coimbra (qq.v.). An important sign was that as more women entered the professional fields there were more women doctors. Observers noted that public health and medical improvements were closely linked to reforms in education (q.v.) and better living conditions in both urban and rural area where substandard housing, sanitation facilities, hygiene and clean water supplies remained persistent problems. *See* ECONOMY; EDUCATION.

HENRIQUES, KING AFONSO (1105?–1185). The first King of Portugal, known as "The Founder" in Portuguese history and tradition, the former Burgundian Count who established Portugal as an independent kingdom from Castile and Leon. The independence of Portugal was established on the field of battle by 1139 or 1140. Afonso Henriques had his main capital at Coimbra (q.v.) and devoted most of his reign to 1185 to two main enterprises: ensuring the continued separation of Portugal from the kingdoms of Castile and Leon and the reconquest from the Muslims of the western parts of the Iberian Peninsula which became part of Portugal. In 1147, with the assistance of English and Flemish crusaders on the way to the Holy Land, Afonso Henriques' forces conquered the city of Lisbon (q.v.) from the Muslims following an extended siege. Beginning in 1143, Afonso Henriques had received formal recognition of the independence of Portugal and of his legitimacy as King of Portugal from the Pope in Rome, but it was only in 1179 that the Papal communications first began to employ the royal title Afonso Henriques had created and established as "The Founder" of the country of Portugal. Afonso Henriques died in 1185 at the unusual age of nearly 80 years and is known in Portuguese history as Afonso I.

HENRY OF AVIZ, PRINCE (1394–1460). Known to the Portuguese as "O Infante Dom Henrique," as an heir to his father's throne, Prince Henry the Navigator was born in Oporto (q.v.). His Father was King João I (1357–1433) and his Mother was Philippa of Lancaster (qq.v.), daughter of John of Gaunt. As a young Prince, Henry won his knighthood as a member of the Portuguese expedition which captured the Moroccan city of Ceuta in 1415, the beginning of Portugal's overseas expansion and the onset of the European age of exploration and discovery.

The life and work of Prince Henry are steeped in centuries of myth and legend. Reliable historical research suggests that the Prince played a key role in the early phases of the Portuguese discoveries due to his patronage of expeditions, sailors and navigators and his use of the important funds of the knightly Order of Christ of which he was in control. Prince Henry, nevertheless, was not solely responsible for more than one third of the exploration ventures during his time, possessed strongly medieval ways, did not create the so-called "School of Sagres" for navigators and certainly was ignorant of much Renaissance science. While he did participate nobly in the Ceuta adventure, as far as the voyages down the coast of Africa and into the Atlantic until his death in 1460 are concerned, Prince Henry was a stay-at-home, an armchair geographer who did not visit Africa beyond Morocco.

HERCULANO, ALEXANDRE (1810–1877). One of Portugal's greatest historians and one of its giants in 19th century writing and literature. Born in Lisbon (q.v.) to a middle class family, Herculano studied commerce and diplomacy. At age 21, he enlisted in Dom Pedro's Liberal armed forces but was forced to flee to exile in England and then France (qq.v.). Later he was part of the victorious Liberal expeditionary force which landed near Oporto (q.v.). He began his serious studies in Oporto, but soon re-located to Lisbon where he worked as a journalist. In 1839, he was named to the post of Director of the Royal Library at Ajuda Palace and at Necessidades Palace (qq.v.) and thus began to prepare to write his classic work, *História de Portugal,* a major study which when completed took the history of the country only up to the end of the 13th century. The first volume of the work with which his fame as a historian is most closely associated, *História de Portugal,* was published in 1846. But Herculano was a versatile writer who wrote novels, essays and poetry as well as history.

In addition to being a man of words, he was a man of action who was active in exchanges with other *literati* and who did government service. Herculano, for example, was on the Commission which revised the Civil Code of Portugal. His historical writings influenced future generations of writers because of his literary style and above all because of his objective, scientific approach to research and conclusions, and because he broke through the legend and myth which had surrounded ancient and medieval Portuguese history. Dissatisfied with politics and public life, Herculano retired to a farm in the country (at Vale de Lobos) in 1859 and worked as a farmer as of 1866.

- I -

IBERIANISM. The belief or creed that a unified Iberian Peninsula in which Spain (q.v.) and Portugal would be incorporated in the same political unit would enhance those countries' place in Europe, lay a basis for revival of the Iberian states from a position of decline and lead to needed social improvements. Iberianism became popular in certain Leftist groups, including Socialists, in both countries in the 19th century, although it was a more popular idea in Spain than it was in Portugal. Sometimes Iberianism was expressed in the form of advocating an Iberian federal union or Federation. *See* SPAIN.

INDIA, PORTUGUESE. Formerly a Portuguese colony and all that remained of Portugal's Indian holdings of the 16th and 17th centuries, Goa, Damão and Diu are located on the western coast of the Indian sub-continent. These three enclaves, comprising an area of about 1,537 square miles (3,400 square kilometers), were acquired by Portugal during the 16th century after the initial voyage of Vasco da Gama (1497–1499) (q.v.) which discovered the sea route to the Indies from Portugal. Beginning in 1510, Goa was the capital of the Portuguese State of India which had jurisdiction over Portugal's holdings in eastern Africa as well as in Asia. Goa became not only an administrative capital but a center for religion and education. Various Catholic religious orders, such as the Franciscans, Dominicans and Jesuits, used Goa as a base for missionary efforts in Asia. Most notable among them was St. Francis Xavier (q.v.). Goa enjoyed a kind of colonial golden age in the 16th and 17th century when various churches, seminaries and colleges flourished there. Eventually Goa was bypassed as the capital of Portuguese India was transferred first to Mormugão and later to Pangim.

For religious and political reasons, not economic, Portugal held on to Portuguese India, when confronted after World War II with Indian nationalism. Pressures to leave Goa, Damão and Diu mounted throughout the 1950s, following the independence of India in 1947. In December 1961, after numerous alarms and efforts by Indian and Goan nationalists to employ passive resistance to oust Portuguese control, India's Nehru ordered the Indian Army to invade, conquer and annex Goa,

Damão and Diu and incorporate them as part of the Indian Union. With most of her armed forces in the African territories at the time and with Britain refusing to allow the use of British bases to reinforce Portugal's small garrison in Portuguese India, Portuguese armed forces had no chance and resisted only briefly. Premier Salazar's (q.v.) Government dealt harshly with the forces which surrendered in India and were made prisoners of war. Lisbon negotiated their release without enthusiasm. Resentment against the Dictatorship's treatment of the army in India was one of the stated reasons later for the conspiracy and 1974 coup of the Armed Forces Movement (q.v.). *See* ARMED FORCES MOVEMENT; EMPIRE, PORTUGUESE; XAVIER, ST. FRANCIS.

INQUISITION, PORTUGUESE. Known also as the Holy Office of the Inquisition, Portugal's Inquisition was established in 1536 under King João III (q.v.) and was finally abolished only in 1821. The initial motives for establishing this Church (q.v.) institution were more political than religious; King João III saw it as an instrument to increase central power and royal control in Portugal. Permission for its foundation was granted by the Papacy in Rome, but the Inquisition's judges and officers were appointed by the Portuguese King not by the Papacy. Seven years after its establishment, the Inquisition's first victims were burned at the stake in Évora. Eventually, the Holy Office of the Inquisition became a kind of state within a state with its own bureaucracy, censors who acted as a "thought police" over the faithful as well as over heretics or dissidents, and police who maintained their own prisons. The period of this infamous institution's greatest power to persecute, prosecute and execute heretics was during the 16th and 17th centuries. During Pombal's (q.v.) administration (1750–1777),the Inquisition's power was curtailed. By 1821, when it was abolished by reformist governments, the Inquisition no longer had much significance.

For centuries, however, the Inquisition generated fear and was able to control considerable wealth, the goods and property confiscated from victims. In the history of Portuguese politics and culture, the Inquisition has symbolized cruel oppression, the spirit of discrimination and religious persecution of heretics and minorities, including Jews who were often forcibly converted. It created an era of censorship of intellectual activity, injustice, bigotry, racism and anti-Semitism and raised questions about the role and power of the Catholic Church in society and the relationship between the Church and State. Some opponents of the *Estado Novo* (q.v.) Dictatorship quite justifiably compared the Inquisition's control of free thought and action with that of the *Estado Novo* in their day. *See* CHURCH, CATHOLIC; JOÃO III, KING; NEW CHRISTIANS.

INTEGRALISM. A conservative political doctrine which had some influence on the designers and managers of the *Estado Novo* (q.v.) Dictatorship after 1926. Strongly influenced by the French writer Charles Maurras and his *Action Française,* Portuguese Integralists formed a group called "Integralismo Lusitano" and in 1914 began publishing a periodical in Coimbra (q.v.) called *Nação Portuguesa.* This advocated restoration of the Monarchy in Portugal, but a monarchy which was described as "organic, traditionalist and anti-parliamentary," where Portugal would be ruled by a very strong executive or State. The Integralists made numerous attacks on the First Republic and, undoubtedly, Salazar (q.v.) and his circle were influenced by this set of ideas. Its main doctrine of a return to Monarchy, however, doomed it to failure and the death of its main ideologue and writer, António Sardinha in 1925, deprived it of its greatest thinker. *See* SALAZARISM.

ISABEL, SANTA (SAINT ELIZABETH OF PORTUGAL) (1269–1336). Known to the Portuguese as the "Holy Queen" Isabel, she was born in Spain (q.v.), the daughter of Pedro III of Aragon. At the tender age of 12, she was married to Portugal's King Dinis (q.v.), who was a better monarch than he was a husband. Isabel became widely known and famous for her peacemaking among her warring family and between Portugal and Castile, her piety and devotion and her good works in supporting and building convents, chapels, hospitals, refuges for the homeless and wayward, orphanages and shelters for abused women. Widowed in 1325, she moved near the Santa Clara Convent in Coimbra (q.v.) and continued her pious deeds. She died on July 4, 1336, the day now celebrated as her feast day, and was buried in Coimbra. She was beatified in 1516 and was canonized in 1625 by Pope Urban VIII. See DINIS, KING.

- J -

JERÓNIMOS, MONASTERY OF (MOSTEIRO DO JERÓNIMOS).
Located at Belém, west of Lisbon (qq.v.), the Monastery and Cathedral of Jerónimos is the most magnificent of the Age of Discoveries monuments. Ordered built as a gift to the monastic Order of Hieronymites by King Manuel I (q.v.), following the return of Vasco da Gama's (q.v.) ships from the discovery of India in 1499, Jerónimos was constructed between 1502 and 1525. The purpose of this massive building was to commemorate the Portuguese discovery of the sea route to India. Its location, at the time of its building very close to the water, was near the Restelo beach, the departure point for Da Gama's voyage.

One of Portugal's premier tourist attractions, Jerónimos consists of a Church and Claustrum and a portion of the convent, partially destroyed in the 1755 Lisbon earthquake. The architectural style was an innovation, later named after the King who helped finance constructions from the new imperial wealth from Africa and Asia, the Manueline style (q.v.); more recently, students employ the term, "Atlantic Baroque." For example, columns, pillars and door frames are decorated elaborately with stone sculpted in the form of maritime objects: ship ropes, coral, sea life, sailors, and plant life and sea weeds.

Jerónimos is located inland from the Monument of the Discoveries (q.v.), along the Avenida Marginal west of Lisbon, in an open square once the main site of the 1940 Double Centenary Exposition of the Portuguese World, a kind of Lisbon World's Fair. See DISCOVERIES, MONUMENT OF THE; MANUELINE ARCHITECTURAL STYLE.

JOÃO I, KING (1383–1433). An illegitimate son of King Pedro I (reign: 1357–1367) (q.v.), João I was the founder of the Aviz dynasty of Portuguese Kings and Master of the Order of Aviz. João's reign was essential in furthering the cause of Portugal's independence from a threatening Castile (Spain) and João's armies with English assistance defeated the Castilian pretenders in 1385 at the great battle of Aljubarrota (qq.v.). In order to show gratitude to God, João ordered the beginning of the construction of the great Abbey at Batalha (q.v.). João's marriage to the English princess, Philippa of Lancaster (q.v.), daughter of John of Gaunt, was another vital element in the strengthening of the country and in the prelude to overseas empire. Philippa gave João six children, among them the scholarly Prince Dom Pedro and his brother, the Infante Dom Henrique or Henry of Aviz (q.v.), known to history outside Portugal as "Prince Henry the Navigator."

JOÃO III, KING (1502–1557). Portugal's most talented and accomplished monarch of the late Renaissance Period, known as "The Perfect Prince" in literature and tradition. João III was the fifteenth King of Portugal, the son of King Manuel I (q.v.). Well-educated by brilliant tutors, including the Humanist Luís Teixeira, João at age 12 was introduced to the study of royal governance by his father. During his reign, Portugal reached the apogee of its world imperial power at least in terms of coastal area and number of different continents over which the scattered territories were spread. Portugal had a tenuous hold on various Moroccan cities and during João's reign she was forced to abandon most of the North African fortresses, due to Muslim military pressures. It was to the colonization and exploitation of giant Brazil, though, that João turned imperial attention. In diplomacy, no other monarch during the Aviz dynasty was as active; negotiations proceeded with Spain, France (qq.v.) and the Holy See. In domestic affairs, João III reinforced Absolutist tendencies and built up royal power. It was João, too, who introduced the Holy Office (Inquisition) (q.v.) in Portugal in 1536, after lengthy negotiations. The King encouraged a flowering of Humanist culture as well and among favored intellectuals were the great writers Gil Vicente (q.v.) and Damião de Góis.

João III's reign was a vital turning point in the history of Portugal's first overseas empire (1415–1580). He found the empire at its zenith, yet when he died it was showing grave signs of weakness not only in Morocco, but in Asia, where rival European powers and the Turks were on the move. Portugal's very independence from Spain and even the royal succession were under a cloud when João III died in 1557 without a son to succeed him. Following tragic deaths of his children, João's only indirect heir was Sebastião (q.v.), a grandson, who succeeded to rule a menaced Portugal. *See* SEBASTIÃO I, KING.

JOÃO IV, KING (1604–1656). The Duke of Braganza who headed the Revolution of 1640 in order to restore Portugal's independence from Spain (q.v.) and who became King João IV, the first of the Braganza dynasty to rule. Under the so-called "Babylonian Captivity," Portugal was ruled by the Phillipine dynasty of Spain during 1580–1640. The rebellion of Catalonia against Spain in mid-1640 and restiveness in Portugal provided an opportunity and the occasion for the small country to organize a Revolution and overthrow Spanish rule. João, Duke of Braganza, was an heir of the Aviz dynasty and Portugal's most formidable noble and largest landowner. His power base was in the Alentejo province, his Palace at Vila Viçosa. The revolution of December 1, 1640 (q.v.), a day which remains a national holiday in Portugal, was successful. Portugal recovered its independence, and João was proclaimed João IV of Portugal.

With slim national resources to repel reassertions of Spanish control, King João IV built an effective administration and fought a series of wars with Spain. He was aided in the effort by Portugal's oldest ally, England (q.v.), and was able to repel subsequent Spanish invasions. An important Anglo-Portuguese treaty which renewed the alliance was signed in 1654, but the King died only two years later and did not live to see the signing of the decisive 1668 Luso-Spanish treaty which formally ended Spain's efforts to take back Portugal. In Portuguese history, João retains the title of "The Restorer" and is a central figure in "The Restoration" era.

JOÃO V, KING (1689–1750). The son of King Pedro II (q.v.) and Maria Sofia Neubourg, João was acclaimed King in 1707. By any measure, his long reign (43 years) had a significant impact on Portuguese government, arts and culture. The early period was consumed with anxiety over continental European affairs, especially the menacing War of Spanish succession which ended in 1714. João then shifted his emphasis to the commercial and political interests of the Atlantic empire, to the Church (q.v.) and religious affairs and to reinforcing the Anglo-Portuguese Alliance (q.v.). Under João, there was intensive development of colonization and exploitation in Portuguese America, namely Brazil (q.v.).

In spite of the State's usual fiscal woes, the Monarchy and the nobility garnered considerable wealth from Brazilian diamonds, gold and other materials. Large amounts of revenue were expended on royal palaces, houses, churches, chapels and convents, and, despite the Lisbon earthquake's impact in 1755, a considerable portion of this conspicuous consumption survives in historic monuments. Most outstanding is the Baroque monstrosity, one of the largest buildings in Europe, the great Mafra Convent, which was constructed during João's reign. Through his acts of piety and bribery, João was declared "Most Faithful" Majesty by the Pope. Under royal largesse, Portuguese arts and culture were well-served and Italian Opera was introduced in Lisbon. *See* MAFRA, CONVENT OF.

- L -

LATIFUNDIA. Large farms and landed estates, generally south of the Tagus River (q.v.). Located mainly but not exclusively in the Alentejo district, southeast of Lisbon, these large, landed estates originated in Roman and then Muslim times and by the 19th century were characterized by absentee landowners, vast estates of thousands of acres which were farmed by landless peasants who provided much of the labor. Concentrated in the wheat-growing Alentejo district, the *latifundia* represented a chronic, severe social and economic problem which many successive governments failed to address or to solve. Agrarian reform attempts in the late Monarchy, the First Republic and the Dictatorship failed to deal decisively with the *latifundia* problem.

Just scores of well-off families, sometimes resident in the towns or in Lisbon, owned most of the land while most of the work on this land, a crucial food-producing area of Portugal, was performed by poor peasants with little or no access to land ownership. Sporadic forcible occupation of land on a small scale by farm workers occurred during the first Republic, but the authorities soon repressed it. During the Portuguese Revolution of 1975 about 2.5 million acres of *latifundia* were forcibly occupied by farm workers and political supporters and there was a program of land ownership re-distribution and sharing. Agrarian reform efforts regarding both *minifundia* and *latifundia* have continued. *See* MINIFUNDIA.

LEGISLATURES. Legislative assemblies during Portugal's long history have had various names, roles and functions. Under the pre-Constitutional Monarchy, various *Cortes* (q.v.) were convoked by the monarch. From 1834 on, the Constitutional Monarchy usually featured a two-chamber legislature: a House or Chamber of Deputies and a House or Chamber of Peers (Lords). During the first parliamentary Republic (1910–1926), after the 1911 constitution was drafted and ratified by the Constituent Assembly, the two-chamber legislature was composed of a Chamber of Deputies (or "Congress") and a Senate. The legislature of President Sidónio Pais' (q.v.) "New Republic," which met for only a few weeks, was described as a "Congress." The Dictatorship's two-chamber legislature, more consultative than law-making, met from January 1935 to April 1974 and was composed of a National Assembly and a Corporative chamber. Post-1974 Democratic Portugal, which began its constitutional life in 1976, has a one-chamber legislature called the Assembly of the Republic. *See* CONSTITUTIONS; CORTES; ESTADO NOVO.

LISBON. The capital of Portugal and capital of the Lisbon district. City population, about one million; greater Lisbon area, at least 2.5 million. Located on the north bank of one of the greatest harbors in Europe, formed from the estuary of the Tagus River (q.v.) which flows into the Atlantic, Lisbon has a long and illustrious history. A site of Phoenician and Greek trading communities, Lisbon became an important Roman city. Its name, *Lisboa,* in Portuguese and Spanish, is a corruption of its Roman name, *"Felicitas Julia."* The city experienced various waves of invaders. Muslims conquered it from the Visigoths in the 8th century and after a long siege Muslim Lisbon fell to the Portuguese Christian forces of King Afonso Henriques (q.v.) in 1147.

Lisbon, built on a number of hills, saw most of its major palaces and churches constructed between the 14th and 18th centuries. In the 16th century, the city became the Aviz dynasty's main capital and seat and a royal palace was built in the lower city along the harbor where ships brought the empire's riches from Africa, Asia and Brazil. On November 1, 1755, a devastating earthquake wrecked a large part of the main city and destroyed the major buildings, killed or displaced scores of thousands of people and destroyed important historical records and artifacts. The Dictator Pombal (q.v.) ordered the city rebuilt along new lines and the main lower city center, the *baixa* ("down below"), today remains Pombaline in style with a square grid of streets, spacious squares and broad avenues. Due to the earthquake's destruction, few buildings with the exceptions of the larger cathedrals and a few palaces pre-date 1755.

Lisbon is more than the political capital of Portugal, the site of the central government's offices, the legislative and executive buildings. Lisbon is the economic, social and cultural capital of the country as well as the major educational center which contains almost half the country's universities and secondary schools.

The continuing importance of Lisbon as the country's political heart and mind, despite the justifiable resentment of its northern rival, Oporto, and the university town of Coimbra (qq.v.), was again illustrated in the 1974 Revolution which began with a military coup by an armed forces organization on April 25th. The *Estado Novo* (q.v.) dictatorship was overthrown in a largely bloodless coup organized by career junior military officers whose main strategy was directed toward the conquest and control of the capital. Once the Armed Forces Movement (q.v.) had the city of Lisbon and environs under its control by the afternoon of April 25, 1974, its mastery of the remainder of the country was assured.

Along with its dominance of the country's economy, politics and government, Lisbon's cultural offerings remain impressive. The city is a treasure house which contains hundreds of historic houses and squares, churches and cathedrals, ancient palaces and castles, some reconstructed to appear as they were before the Lisbon earthquake of 1755. There are scores of museums and libraries. Among the more outstanding museums open to the public are the Museu de Arte Antiga, the Gulbenkian Museum (q.v.), the Contemporary Art Museum and many others. *See* LISBON EARTHQUAKE.

LISBON EARTHQUAKE. On November 1, 1755, All Saints' Day, Lisbon experienced the worst earthquake known during its recorded history. The earthquake destroyed large sections of the city, including the central downtown and the great Royal Palace square, now in a different form known as "Commerce Square," but still referred to by the old name, "Square of the Palace" (*"Terreiro do Paço"*). Thousands of buildings, including more than 100 churches and 300 palaces fell down, and tens of thousands of people died. The shocks were followed by a giant tidal wave from down the Tagus River (q.v.), which drowned many, and then devastating fires which fed on the candles' conflagration of interior furnishings.

The King's Chief Minister Pombal (q.v.) was decisive in his rehabilitation and reconstruction efforts. Much of the Lisbon downtown, the *baixa* ("below"), was rebuilt and a massive grid pattern of streets grew up. Except for sections of the old Arab quarter, the *Alfama,* most of Lisbon was destroyed or rebuilt along Pombaline lines. The Lisbon earthquake became a great issue and discussion point in mid-18th century Europe and England (q.v.) and the British Parliament voted 100,000 pounds in humanitarian aid and relief to Portugal and the earthquake victims, one of the first cases of massive humanitarian aid for an international disaster from a foreign nation, albeit Portugal's oldest ally. *See* LISBON.

LUÍS I, KING (1838–1889). King Luís I was the second son of Queen Maria II (q.v.) and Dom Fernando. When his older brother, King Pedro V (q.v.), died suddenly in October 1861, he ascended the throne. Well-educated with the temperament of a writer and artist, Luís probably preferred the literary life to politics and public affairs. In the history of Portugal's literature, Luís is noted for his translations into Portuguese of several of Shakespeare's plays. During his 28-year reign, Portugal experienced a phase of the Regeneration (q.v.) and, for part of the period after 1870, relatively stable politics and a lack of military intervention in public life. During his reign, too, there was material progress and great literary accomplishment with the famous novels of Eça de Queirós and the poetry of Antero de Quental. While Republicanism became a greater force after 1871, and the first Republican deputy was elected to the Chamber of Deputies in 1878, this party and its ideology were not a threat to the Monarchy until after the reign of Dom Luís. When King Luís died in 1889, he was succeeded by his oldest son, Dom Carlos, whose stormy reign witnessed the rise of Republicanism and serious degeneration of the Monarchist cause. *See* REGENERATION.

LUSIADS, THE. Portugal's national epic poem of the Discoveries era, written by the nation's most celebrated poet, Luís de Camões (q.v.). Published in 1572, toward the end of the adventurous life of Camões, *The Lusiads* is the most famous and most often-quoted piece of literature in Portugal. Modeled in part on the style and format of Virgil's *Aeneid, Os Lusíadas* is the story of Portugal's long history and features an evocation of the Portuguese navigator Vasco da Gama's (q.v.) epic discovery of the sea route from Portugal to Asia. Part of the epic poem was composed when Camões was in royal service in Portugal's Asian empire, including in Goa and Macau (q.v.). While the dramatic framework is dominated by various deities from classical literature, much of what is described in Portugal, Africa and Asia is real and accurately rendered by the classically-educated (at Coimbra) poet Camões who witnessed both the apogee and the beginning of decline of Portugal's seaborne empire and world power.

While the poet praises imperial power and greatness, Camões has a prescient nay-sayer. "The Old Man of Restelo," on the beach where Vasco da Gama is about to embark for Indian adventures, criticizes Portuguese expansion beyond Africa to Asia. Camões was questioning if the high price of Asian empire was worth it for the nation and gave voice to those anti-Imperialists and "Doubting Thomases" in the country who opposed more overseas expansion beyond Africa. It is interesting to note that in the Portuguese language usage and tradition since the establishment of *The Lusiads* as a national poem, "The Old Man of Restelo" ("*O Velho do Restelo*") came to symbolize not a wise Cassandra with timely warnings that Portugal would be fatally weakened by empire and might fall prey to neighboring Spain (q.v.), but merely a Doubting Thomas in popular sentiment. *The Lusiads* soon became universally celebrated and accepted and has been translated into many languages. In the history of criticism in Portugal, more has been written about Camões and *The Lusiads* than about any other author or work in Portuguese literature, now more than a thousand years in the making. *See* CAMÕES, LUÍS DE.

LUSITANIA (AND LUSITANIANS). Pre-Roman ancient Iberians who inhabited what became known to the Romans as the province of Lusitania. Little is known of the Lusitanians, considered to be the ancestral "race" of native Portuguese and scholars debate the extent to which Lusitanians had Celtic roots and traits. The Greek scholar Strabo's account of the Lusitanians' customs is the only detailed picture of a people who had a warlike reputation and who may have practiced human sacrifice. The Lusitanians fiercely resisted Roman conquest and a chief figure of resistance over many years was the hunter-shepherd Viriatus (q.v.). Eventually the Lusitanians were subdued by the Romans. In mythology, Lusitania and Lusitanians owed their origins to a founding father, known in legend as *"Lusus."* Thus, the prefix signifying Portuguese language and culture is *"Luso,"* as in "Luso-Brazilian," etc. *See* LUSO; VIRIATUS.

LUSO. Portuguese prefix meaning "Portuguese." Derives from the ancient Roman term for the province of Lusitania and from the name of the native inhabitants, Lusitanians. In myth, the ancestor of all Lusitanians was one "Lusus." Today Luso is also the name of a town in central Portugal which has famous mineral waters.

LUSO-TROPICALISM, THEORY OF. An anthropological and sociological theory or complex of ideas allegedly showing a process of civilization relating to the significance of Portuguese activity in the tropics of Africa, Asia and the Americas since 1415. As a theory and method of social science analysis, Luso-Tropicalism is a 20th century phenomenon which has both academic and political (foreign and colonial policy) relevance. While the theory was based in part on French concepts of the "science of tropicology" in anthropology, it was Gilberto Freyre (q.v.), an eminent Brazilian sociologist-anthropologist, who developed Luso-Tropicalism as an academic theory of the unique qualities of the Portuguese style of imperial activity in the tropics. In lectures, articles and books during the period 1930–1960, Freyre coined the term "Luso-Tropicalism" to describe Portuguese civilization in the tropics and to claim that the Portuguese, more than the other European colonizing people, successfully adapted their civilization to the tropics.

From 1960 on, the academic theory was co-opted to lend credence to Portugal's colonial policy and determination to continue colonial rule in her large, remaining African empire. Freyre's "Luso-Tropicalism" theme was featured in the elaborate Fifth Centenary of the Death of Prince Henry the Navigator celebrations held in Lisbon in 1960 and in a massive series of publications produced in the 1960s to defend Portugal's policies in her empire, the first to be established and the last to decolonize in the Third World. Freyre's academic theory and his international prestige as a scholar who had put the sociology of Brazil (q.v.) on the world map were eagerly adopted and adapted by the Lisbon government. A major thesis of this interesting but somewhat disorganized mass of material was that the Portuguese were less racist and prejudiced toward the tropical peoples they interacted with.

As African wars of insurgency began in Portugal's empire during 1961–1964, and as the United Nations put pressures on Portugal, Luso-Tropicalism was tested and challenged not only in academia and the press, but in international politics and diplomacy. Following the decolonization of Portugal's empire during 1974 and 1975 (though Macau remained the last colony to the late 1990s), debate over the notion of Luso-Tropicalism died down. With the onset of the 500-year anniversary celebrations of the Portuguese Age of Discoveries and Exploration, beginning in 1988, however, a whiff of the essence of Luso-Tropicalism reappeared in selected aspects of the commemorative literature. *See* COMMEMORATIONS, PORTUGUESE HISTORIC; FREYRE, GILBERTO.

- M -

MACAU. Portuguese colonial territory in south China. Portugal's last colony, in effect, and by agreement scheduled to be turned over to the People's Republic of China in 1999. Since Portuguese traders first settled in Macau in 1557, this tiny territory of 7 square miles (15.7 square kilometers) has been a Portuguese colony headed by a Portuguese administration. Long a dependency of the Viceroyalty of Goa, Portuguese India (q.v.), Macau's prosperity depended on the vicissitudes of diplomatic and trade relations between China and the West. For nearly three centuries (ca. 1557–1842), Macau was the only Western entrepot-outpost-enclave-colony on the China coast. Even after Japan expelled Western traders in the 17th century, Macau had a key role as the link between China and the West. This role changed after Britain seized neighboring Hong Kong (1842) as a colony. Thereafter, Macau fell into the shadow of a booming Hong Kong.

While it was a remote dependency of Portugal in the Far East, Macau has long played a multiplicity of roles: China's window on the West, preempted in the 1840s by Hong Kong; sanctuary and refuge for various waves of refugees from China or Hong Kong; because of its peculiar international status and location, a center of vice (gambling, smuggling, prostitution and drug traffic); and a meeting place and exchange point for the Chinese and Portuguese civilizations.

Following the 1974 Revolution, Lisbon offered to return Macau to mainland China, but the offer was refused and negotiations between China and Portugal ensued. While China controls Macau's economy, a small Portuguese administration, with only nominal authority, will remain in Macau until 1999, when China resumes its sovereignty.

MADEIRA ISLANDS, ARCHIPELAGO OF. An autonomous region of Portugal in the Atlantic Ocean which consists of the islands of Madeira and Porto Santo and several smaller isles. The capital of the archipelago is Funchal on Madeira Island and the islands have a total area of 308 square miles (794 square kilometers) and are located about 700 miles (1500 kilometers) southwest of Lisbon. Discovered uninhabited by Portuguese navigators between 1419 and 1425, but probably seen earlier by Italian navigators, the Madeiras were named *"Madeira"* (wood or timber) because of the extensive forests found on the islands' volcanic hills and mountains. Prince Henry the Navigator (q.v.) was first responsible for the settlement and early colonization of these islands.

The Madeiran economy was soon dominated by sugar plantations which were begun when the Portuguese transplanted sugar plants from the Mediterranean. In the 15th, 16th and 17th centuries, Madeira was worked largely by black African slaves brought from West Africa and the Islands produced sugar, cereals and wine. Eventually the Islands' fortunes were governed by a new kind of wine called "Madeira," developed in the 17th century. Madeira was produced using a heating process and became famous as a sweet, fortified dessert wine popular both in England (q.v.) and in British North America. It was a favorite drink of America's Thomas Jefferson. The Madeira wine business was developed largely under English influence, management and capital, though the labor was supplied by African slaves and Portuguese settlers. Two other main staples of these islands' economic fortunes were initially developed due to the initiatives of English residents as well. In the 18th century, Madeira became an early tourist and invalid spot for England and the islands' tourist facilities began to be developed. It was an English woman resident in the 19th century who introduced the idea of the Madeiran embroidered lace industry, an industry which ships its fine products not only to Portugal but all over the world.

Since the 1950s, with new international airline connections with England and Portugal, the Madeiras have become a popular tourist destination and, along with Madeira wine, tourism became a major foreign exchange earner. Among European and British visitors especially, Madeira Island has attracted visitors who like flower and garden tours, challenging mountain walks and water sports. Over the last century, there has been a significant amount of Madeiran emigration, principally to the United States (California and Hawaii being the favored residential states), the Caribbean and, more recently, South Africa. Since 1976, the Madeiras have been, like the Azores Islands (q.v.), an Autonomous Region of Portugal.

MAFRA, PALACE AND CONVENT OF. One of the Iberian Peninsula's largest structures, Mafra Palace and Convent remains Portugal's most colossal historic monument-building. About 30 miles (70 kilometers) north-northwest of Lisbon (q.v.), the complex is located in the town of Mafra, one of Portugal's most ancient settlements. First ordered built by the extravagant King João V (q.v.) in 1711, the massive Mafra Palace was not completed until decades later by poorly-paid labor. With perhaps the larger building of Phillip II of Spain's Escorial Palace and Convent in mind, King João V dedicated the rival enterprise to celebrating the birth of a child to his Austrian Queen; this child, who was a girl, became Queen of Spain. A veritable army of workers—at one time 45,000—constructed the massive building which some thought would never be completed. In fact, after it was finally begun in 1717, the building was finished in 1735.

The most extravagant project of João's expansive reign, Mafra Palace and Convent's style and spirit are heavy, but this is offset by the magnificent baroque library and the music which comes from the 50-bell carillon that is still in use. The wonders of Mafra can be imagined from just a few of the building figures; there are, for example, 5,200 doorways and 2,500 windows. Some of the wealth in royal coffers that paid for Mafra came from "the King's Fifth" out of the diamonds and gold in Portugal's richest colony, Brazil (q.v.). The manner in which this historic monument is not only a tourist site, but actually utilized for a variety of purposes is a fascinating case of Portugal as a "museum-state." Mafra today provides space for two museums, offices of the Mafra City Hall (*Câmara Municipal*), an elementary school and an Army regiment. It is also used as a church. *See* JOÃO V, KING.

MANUEL I, KING (1469–1521). King Manuel I, named "The Fortunate" in Portuguese tradition, ruled from 1495–1521, the zenith of Portugal's world power and imperial strength. Manuel was the 14th King of Portugal and the ninth son of Infante Dom Fernando and Dona Brites as well as the adopted son of King João II (reigned: 1481–1495) (q.v.). Manuel ascended the throne when the royal heir, Dom Afonso, the victim of a riding accident, suddenly died. Manuel's three marriages provide a map of the royal and international history of the era. His first marriage (1497) was to the widow of Dom Afonso, late heir to the throne. The second (1500) was to the Infanta Dona Maria of Castile and the third marriage (1518) was to Dona Leonor, sister of King Carlos V (Hapsburg Emperor and King of Spain).

Manuel's reign featured several important developments in government, such as the centralization of State power and royal Absolutism, overseas expansion, namely the decision in 1495 to continue on from Africa to Asia and the building of an Asian maritime trade empire, and innovation and creativity in culture, with the emergence of Manueline (q.v.) architecture and the writings of Gil Vicente (q.v.) and others. There was also an impact on population and demography with the expulsion or forcible conversion of the Jews. In 1496, King Manuel I approved a decree that forced all Jews who would not become baptized as Christians to leave the country within 10 months. The Jews had been expelled from Spain in 1492. The economic impact on Portugal in coming decades or even centuries is debatable, but it is clear that a significant number of Jews converted and remained in Portugal and became part of the Portuguese establishment.

King Manuel's decision in 1495, backed by a Royal Council and by the *Cortes* (q.v.) called that year, to continue the quest for Asia by means of seeking an all-water route from Portugal around Africa to India was momentous. Sponsorship of Vasco da Gama's (q.v.) first great voyage (1497–1499) to India was the beginning of an era of unprecedented imperial wealth, power and excitement. It became the official goal to create a maritime monopoly of the Asian spice trade and keep it in Portugal's hands. When Pedro Álvares Cabral's (q.v.) voyage from Lisbon was dispatched in 1500 to India, its route was deliberately planned to swing southwest into the Atlantic, thus sighting "The Land of the Holy Cross," or Brazil (q.v.), which soon became a Portuguese colony. Under King Manuel, the foundations were laid for Portugal's Brazilian and Asian empire, from Calicut to the Moluccas. Described by France's King Francis I as the "Grocer King," with his command of the mighty spice trade, King Manuel approved of a fitting monument to the new empire: the building of the magnificent Jerónimos Monastery and Church (q.v.) where, after his death in 1521, both Manuel and Vasco da Gama were laid to rest. *See* GAMA, VASCO DA; JERÓNIMOS.

MANUEL II, KING (1890–1932). The last reigning King of Portugal and the last of the Braganza dynasty to rule. Born in 1890, the son of King Carlos I and Queen Amélia, young Manuel witnessed the murder of his father and his elder brother, the heir apparent, Dom Luís, by anarchists in the streets of Lisbon, on February 1, 1908. In the same carriage as his mortally wounded father and brother, and himself wounded, Manuel survived to ascend the throne. His brief reign was troubled by political instability, factionalism and rising Republicanism. As the Republican revolution succeeded, Manuel and his family, including the Queen Mother Amélia, fled from the bombarded Necessidades Palace in Lisbon to the Mafra Palace (qq.v.). Rather than abdicate or remain as a prisoner of the Republic, Manuel fled by ship to exile in England (q.v.), where he remained for the rest of his life. Occupying himself with his hobby of collecting rare Portuguese books, Manuel died prematurely at age 42, in 1932, at his estate south of London.

MANUELINE ARCHITECTURAL STYLE. An innovative, unique architectural and art style named after King Manuel I (reigned: 1495–1521) (q.v.). In the middle of the 19th century, Portuguese Romantic writers, including the great Almeida Garrett, began to describe the unusual architectural style developed during Manuel's reign as "Manueline." In recent years, some scholars have termed the style "Atlantic Baroque" instead, because it combines themes of maritime life and a grotesque, even wild look. The style continued some years after Manuel's death in 1521. Both civil and religious architecture were affected by the style. It appears in private houses as well as in historical monuments such as Jerónimos Monastery (q.v.) and the famous "Tomar Window" of the Order of Christ Chapel in Tomar. Typical of Manueline decorations are the sea life and maritime themes of coral, ropes, buoys, cork, ship rigging, sea weeds and other sea plant life, tropical fruits and vegetables and figures of mariners, all rendered in stone. *See* JERÓNIMOS; MANUEL I, KING.

MARIA I, QUEEN (1734–1816). Daughter of King José I (1750–1777), she married her uncle Pedro III, her father's brother.

Upon assuming her reign and becoming Queen in 1777, with the death of her father, Maria I dismissed the Marquis of Pombal (q.v.), the King's Chief Minister. Known in Portuguese history by the nickname of "The Pious," Maria was extremely religious and in her brief reign attempted to reverse dictator Pombal's statist, anti-clerical policies . . . but to little avail. Her life and reign were transformed by family tragedies and by personal reactions to the news of the cataclysmic events in France. Maria's mental weakness was exacerbated progressively with the death of her consort Pedro (1786) and her eldest son João (1788) and gravely affected by news of the French Revolution and its excesses (1789–1792). In 1792, she became insane and ceased to reign while her son João took her place and, in 1799, became Prince Regent. When, in 1807, the royal family fled on a British fleet to Brazil (q.v.) as France (q.v.) occupied Portugal, mad Maria, restrained, it was said, in an iron cage, was taken along. In 1816, while the royal court remained in Brazil, she died in Rio de Janeiro. *See* JOÃO VI, KING.

MARIA II, QUEEN (1811–1853). Born Maria da Gloria, daughter of Pedro IV (q.v.) of Portugal (Pedro I of Brazil) and his first wife Archduchess Leopoldina of Austria, in Rio de Janeiro, the future Queen was named Regent at age 7, on the death of King João VI (1826). By an agreement, her father Pedro abdicated the throne of Portugal on her behalf with the understanding that she would marry her uncle Dom Miguel (q.v.), who in turn was pledged to accept a Constitutional Charter written by Pedro himself. Backed by the Absolutist party, including his reactionary mother Queen Carlota Joaquina (q.v.), Dom Miguel returned from his Austrian exile in 1828 and proceeded to scrap the 1826 Charter of Pedro and rule as Absolutist King of Portugal, placing the nine-year old Maria da Gloria in the political wilderness. Emperor Pedro I of Brazil (who had been Pedro IV of Portugal before he abdicated in Maria's favor) responded by deciding to fight for his daughter's cause and for the restoration of the 1826 Charter. Maria's Constitutional Monarchy, throne and cause were at the center of the "War of the Brothers" (q.v.) a tragic civil war from 1831–1834. With foreign assistance from England (q.v.), Pedro's army and fleet prevailed over the Miguelite forces by 1834. By the Convention of Évora-Monte, signed by Generals of Miguel and Pedro, Miguel surrendered unconditionally, peace was assured and Miguel went into exile.

At age 15, Maria da Gloria was proclaimed Queen of Portugal, but her personal life was tragic and her reign a stormy one. Within months of the victory of her Constitutionalist cause, her chief advocate and counsellor, her father Pedro, died of tuberculosis. Her all too brief reign was consumed in childbirth (she died in childbirth, bearing her eleventh child in 1853 at age 34) and in ruling Portugal during one of the modern era's most disturbed phases. During her time on the throne, there were frequent military insurrections and interventions in politics, various revolutions, the siege of Oporto, the Patuleia revolt, the Maria da Fonte revolt (qq.v.), rebellion of leading military commanders (Marshals) and economic troubles to boot. Maria was a talented monarch and helped raise and educate her oldest son Pedro, who succeeded her as King Pedro V (q.v.), one of Portugal's most remarkable rulers of recent centuries. Late in her reign, the Constitutional Monarchy system settled down, enjoyed greater stability and began the so-called "Regeneration" (q.v.) era of economic development and progress. *See* MARIA DA FONTE; PATULEIA; PEDRO V, KING; REGENERATION.

MARIA DA FONTE. A 19th century rural rebellion of peasants against the Central Government as well as the legendary name of a peasant woman rebel. Beginning in northern Portugal in a village called Vieira do Minho, women led supposedly by one called "Maria of the Fountain" were provoked to rebellion by new laws regarding health regulations (burial customs) and tax assessments. Mobs raided the village administrative center, burned records and attacked officials. The insurrection spread throughout Minho province into Tras-os-Montes in 1846. The Costa Cabral Government was in office in Lisbon (q.v.) and failed to get the legislative chambers to support suppression of the rural uprising. The Maria da Fonte affair led to pressures to dismiss the Costa Cabral Government in order to mollify the rural rebels. Queen Maria II (q.v.) consented to the resignation of the Government and the appointment of a successor. The Costa Cabral brothers then fled to exile in Spain (q.v.). The name and concept of "Maria da Fonte" in folklore, songs and tradition came to symbolize the idea of justified rural discontent and direct action against arbitrary action by the Central Government embodied by Lisbon. Following the end of the Maria da Fonte risings in northern Portugal, a great deal of mythology attached to the original events. See MARIA II, QUEEN.

MELO, FRANCISCO MANUEL DE (1608–1666). One of Portugal's two greatest prose writers of the 17th century, along with Father António Vieira (q.v.), and one of the greatest in both Spain (q.v.) and Portugal in early modern times. Noted as a prose writer for his clarity, wit, satire and realism, Melo lived through the supreme dramas of his time: the final struggle between the Inquisition and the New Christians (qq.v.), the loss and also recovery of parts of Portugal's overseas empire as well as the independence of Portugal from Spain in 1640, following 60 years of Castilian rule. Melo was born in Lisbon to a noble family of Spanish descent. His profession was soldiering and, later, diplomacy. After he participated in the restoration of Portugal's independence and in the triumph of the Braganza dynasty as the ruling royal family of Portugal, Melo was imprisoned and exiled to Brazil (q.v.). He ended his life as a diplomat on important missions in London, Rome and Paris.

Educated by the Jesuits in a Lisbon school, Melo led the life of a man of action rather than that of a sedentary scribbler. His greatest works, some written in Castilian, some in Portuguese, gave him fame outside Portugal and well after his relatively brief life span. His *Historia de los Movimientos y Separación de Cataluña* (1645) is a classic, eye-witness account of the 1640 Catalan revolt against Castile. Among other works which mark the author's enduring accomplishment are his *Cartas Familiares* (1664), *Apólogos Dialogaes,* his short histories, *Epanáforas* (1649–1659), and his internationally popular *Carta de Guia de Casados* ("Guide Map for Married Persons"), which was translated into English first in 1697 by Captain Stevens as *The Government of a Wife* and was a minor bestseller of the early modern age.

MENDES, ARISTIDES DE SOUSA (1885–1954). Career Portuguese diplomat whose extraordinary assistance to Jewish and other refugees in 1940 France (q.v.) led to his career's ruin, but posthumous fame and recognition. A conventional member of Portugal's governing elite, and devoutly Catholic, Aristides de Sousa Mendes was educated like his twin brother, who was also a diplomat, at Coimbra University (q.v.). He entered Portugal's Foreign Service, Consular track, in 1910 and served in a variety of posts in Europe, Africa, Latin America and the United States. Less successful as a diplomat than his brother César, who briefly served as Foreign Minister and attained the rank of ambassador, Aristides de Sousa Mendes was assigned to be Portuguese Consul in Bordeaux, France, in 1938. When thousands of desperate refugees fleeing the German armies poured in to Sousa Mendes' Consulate in June 1940, Lisbon ordered him to cease signing visas to enter Portugal.

Defying his superiors' orders, Sousa Mendes signed perhaps as many as 20–30,000 visas, after deciding not to charge fees to applicants. Because of his action in Bordeaux and at the Franco-Spanish frontier, where he also assisted refugees to escape the Nazi terror, Sousa Mendes was dismissed from his post and recalled to Lisbon. Following his suspension from service and the granting of a minuscule pension, the former diplomat and his family fell into poverty and obscurity. Through the efforts of his family and helpful foreign diplomats, Israel in 1967 declared Sousa Mendes a Hero of Conscience of World War II and a Righteous Gentile. In the 1980s, Portugal's government officially rehabilitated and recognized posthumously this obscure but heroic figure and his deeds were celebrated in books, journals, newspaper articles and TV films.

METHUEN TREATY (1703). Named for the British envoy to Lisbon, John Methuen, the commercial treaty which came to be known by his name was signed on December 27, 1703. This treaty followed the May 1703 treaties of alliance between Portugal, England (q.v.) and the Low Countries and the Hapsburg Empire which were related to the War of Spanish Succession. The Methuen Treaty stipulated that thenceforth Portuguese wines would be favored as exports to England in the same way that English woolen imports to Portugal would have advantages. Since England was not importing French wines due to a war with France (q.v.) and since English merchant-shippers in Portugal would benefit from the agreement, the Methuen Treaty was viewed as advantageous to all parties involved. With only three articles, the Treaty agreed that both Portuguese wines and English woolens would be exempt from custom duties and that each nation had to ratify the Treaty within two months. The Methuen Treaty became the keystone of Anglo-Portuguese commercial relations for at least the next century, but several historians have suggested that it favored England more than Portugal. *See* ANGLO-PORTUGUESE ALLIANCE; PORT WINE.

MIGUEL I, KING (1802–1866). The third son of Dom João VI and of Dona Carlota Joaquina (q.v.), Miguel was barely five years of age when he went to Brazil (q.v.) with the fleeing royal family. In 1821, with his mother and father, he returned to Portugal. Whatever the explanation for his actions, Miguel always took Carlota Joaquina's part in the subsequent political struggles and soon became the supreme hope of the reactionary, clerical, Absolutist party against the Constitutionalists and opposed any compromise with liberal Constitutionalism or its adherents. He became not only the symbol but the essence of a kind of reactionary Messianism in Portugal during more than two decades, as his personal fortunes of power and privilege rose and fell. With his personality imbued with traits of wildness, adventurism and violence, Miguel enjoyed a life largely consumed in horseback riding, love affairs and bullfighting.

After the independence of Brazil (1822), Miguel became the principal candidate for power of the Traditionalist Party which was determined to restore Absolutist royal power, destroy the Constitution and rule without opposition. Involved in many political conspiracies and armed movements beginning in 1822, including the coups known to history as the "Vila Francada" (1823) and the "Abrilada" (1824), which were directed against his father King João VI, in order to restore Absolutist royal power. These coup conspiracies failed due to foreign intervention, and the King ordered Dom Miguel dismissed from his posts and sent into exile. He remained in exile for four years. The death of King João VI in 1826 presented new opportunities in the Absolutist party, however, and the dashing Dom Miguel remained their great hope for power.

His older brother Dom Pedro IV (q.v.), then Emperor of Brazil, inherited the throne and wrote his own constitution, the

Charter of 1826, which was to become the law of the land in Portugal. However, his daughter Maria, only seven, was too young to rule, so Pedro, who abdicated, put together an unusual deal. Until Maria reached her majority age, a Regency headed by Princess Isabel Maria would rule Portugal. Dom Miguel would return from his Austrian exile and, when Maria reached her majority, Maria would marry her uncle Miguel and they would reign under the 1826 Charter. Miguel returned to Portugal in 1828, but immediately broke the bargain. He proclaimed himself an Absolutist King, acclaimed by the usual (and last) 1828 Cortes (q.v.), dispensed with Pedro's Charter and ruled as an Absolutist. Pedro's response was to abdicate the Emperorship of Brazil, return to Portugal, defeat Miguel and place his young daughter on the throne. In the civil war called "The War of the Brothers" (1831–1834) (q.v.), after a seesaw campaign at sea and on land, Miguel's forces were defeated and he went into exile, never to return to Portugal. *See* JOÃO VI, KING.

MINIFUNDIA. Small land-holdings or farms, mainly north of the Tagus River (q.v.). Owned by individual farmers, these small farms are typical of north and central Portugal and in area usually range between one and three acres only. One political base for the center and right-wing parties in this century has been the farmers of the *minifundia*. *See* LATIFUNDIA.

MONDEGO, RIVER. The only major river in Portugal with its sources entirely inside Portugal. The Mondego River rises in the Estrela mountain range, flows through Coimbra and into the Atlantic Ocean north of the Tagus River (qq.v.). Associated with the romantic songs (including *fado*) and poetry of Coimbra University (q.v.) students in tradition, the Mondego is a picturesque sight as it flows to the sea through Beira Alta and Beira Baixa districts. The Mondego is about 130 miles (280 kilometers) long. *See* COIMBRA, CITY OF; COIMBRA, UNIVERSITY OF.

MOZAMBIQUE. Presently an independent African state and formerly Portugal's main colonial territory in East Africa. After Angola (q.v.), Portugal's largest colony in Africa with some

297,000 square miles (784,090 square kilometers). Lisbon controlled sections of what is now Mozambique from the early 16th century to 1975. In its long history as a Portuguese colony and outpost, Mozambique was influenced by its geography and its position in the Portuguese empire. Mozambique's location adjacent to industrializing South Africa was an important factor in its economic life. The colony's location on the sea route to Portugal's empire in India, mainly Goa, and its administrative subordination to Portuguese India (q.v.) during centuries were also important historical factors.

Until the 20th century, except for sections of the disease-ridden Zambezi valley, what little Portuguese colonization there was remained coastal. After 1910, Portuguese colonization in the interior burgeoned and plantations of sugar, cotton and other crops were developed. As in Angola and other African colonies of Portugal, long after slavery was abolished in the 19th century, forced labor of Africans continued into the 1960s in Mozambique. In 1964, a colonial war in Mozambique began, a conflict between Portuguese armed forces and nationalist forces of the Front for the Liberation of Mozambique (FRELIMO). This conflict ceased following the 1974 Revolution in Portugal. Mozambique obtained its independence in July 1975. *See* PORTUGUESE EMPIRE.

- N -

NATIONAL UNION. See UNIÃO NACIONAL.

NECESSIDADES, PALACE OF. Necessidades Palace is a sprawling, massive 18th century Palace in western Lisbon. As in the cases of Mafra and Belém Palaces (qq.v.), "The Palace of the Necessities" was ordered built by King João V (q.v.) on the site of an old chapel dedicated to "Our Lady of Necessities." The original 18th century building consists of a chapel, palace and convent and contains a considerable amount of historic artifacts and art. As the current headquarters of Portugal's Foreign Service and Ministry of Foreign Affairs, Necessidades is a working "museum-palace" with many different sections. Various monarchs resided in the rose-colored building. During the course of the October 5, 1910 Republican Revolution in Lisbon, Necessidades Palace was where the last reigning King, Manuel II (q.v.), spent his last night as sovereign before escaping to Mafra Palace en route to exile in England (q.v.). Damage from Republican naval shelling to the Palace has since been repaired. One section of the Palace houses the Ministry of Foreign Affairs' official library and archives, where several centuries of records of external relations are deposited. *See* JOÃO V, KING.

NEW CHRISTIANS. Term applied to Portuguese of Jewish descent who had been converted to Christianity after the 1496 expulsion of Jews law of King Manuel I (q.v.). Jews had settled in Portugal since the early years of the Monarchy and by the late 15th century a significant minority of Jews was dominant in agriculture, medicine, crafts, finance and government. Part of King Manuel's marriage contract with a Spanish princess decreed the expulsion of Jews in Portugal, following what had occurred in Spain (q.v.) in 1492. Those persons who had converted to Christianity after the 1496 expulsion law in order to avoid having to leave Portugal were termed "New Christians" ("*Cristãos-Novos*") to distinguish them from "Old Christians," the remainder of the Christian population. For centuries thereafter, New Christians suffered persecution and discrimination in Portugal both at the hands of the Inquisition (after 1536) (q.v.) and of other sectors of society. It was not until the laws passed by the Pombal (q.v.) regime in the 1770s that official discrimination in holding public office in Portugal was ended in the case of the New Christians. *See* INQUISITION, PORTUGUESE; MANUEL I, KING.

NEW REPUBLIC (1917–1918). Known in Portuguese as the "*República Nova*" regime, the New Republic was an authoritarian and presidentialist phase of the disturbed First Republic (1910–1926), when Major Sidónio Pais (q.v.) organized a military coup, overthrew the Democrats' system and established a brief, fragile New Republic which he hoped would reconcile Monarchists and Republicans, Conservatives and Liberals, anti-clericals and clericals. The New Republic abruptly collapsed following the December 1918 assassination of Sidónio Pais, who

had been elected President of the Republic in the spring of
1918. *See* PAIS, SIDÓNIO.

NEW STATE. See ESTADO NOVO.

NORTON DE MATOS, JOSÉ (1867–1955). One of Portugal's most
important and influential colonial administrators of the 20th
century African empire, a central figure in the management of
Portugal's dispatch of an army to Flanders in World War I and
oppositionist candidate in the 1949 Presidential elections.
Trained as an Army engineer, he attended Coimbra University
(q.v.) and became a stalwart Republican. During much of the
1890s, he served in Portuguese India (q.v.) where he came under
the influence of the style and policies of the British *Raj*. During
the First Republic, he held a number of important posts in the
empire and in Portugal: Governor-General of Angola (1912–
1915) (q.v.), Colonial Minister (1915) and Minister of War
(1915–1917), during which service he was instrumental in
organizing the mobilization and dispatch of Portugal's Expeditionary Force (CEP) to the Western front in 1917. Later, he
served as High Commissioner and Governor-General of Angola
(1921–1924) and was named Portugal's Minister to Britain
(1924–1926).

Dismissed from his London post by the Military Dictatorship
in 1926, Norton de Matos never held an official post again and,
as he opposed both the Military Dictatorship and the *Estado
Novo* (q.v.), he found it difficult to practice his engineering
profession, in retirement from the Army. However, he remains
important in post-1926 colonial policies and concepts and
attempted to put them into practice after 1945. In 1949,
General Norton de Matos was the oppositionist candidate in the
Presidential elections and opposed the regime incumbent,
Marshal Óscar Carmona (q.v.). Using the law, police harass-
ment and other means, the Dictatorship persecuted Norton de
Matos' followers and disrupted his campaign. Just before the
rigged election was to be held, the aged General withdrew his
candidacy, rightfully claiming fraud and intimidation. A tough
if liberal reformist in colonial affairs, the senior colonial
authority wrote his final book *A Nação Una* in 1953 and called
for the regime to implement his basic reform ideas and to

improve treatment of Africans in labor and race relations. Norton de Matos' prescient warnings about African policies were largely ignored, while Lisbon followed his key strategic and development concepts. *See* CARMONA, ANTÓNIO ÓSCAR.

- O -

OPORTO, CITY OF. Known as *Porto* in Portuguese, it is the second largest city after Lisbon (q.v.) and a major commercial-industrial center of northern Portugal as well as the outlet of the Port wine (q.v.) industry. Capital of Oporto district, it is also "capital of the north," in effect. The current population of the city is approximately 400,000 and that of Greater Oporto, over 800,000. Oporto lies on the right (north) bank of the Douro River (q.v.), about two miles (three kilometers) from its mouth. Its harbor is Leixões. Several bridges connect the city to the other bank, including the famous Eiffel Bridge, built in the 19th century by the builder of the Eiffel Tower of Paris. Among the notable historic buildings are many churches, a Gothic medieval Cathedral, Bishop's palace and the Tower of the Clérigos. There are also interesting museums and libraries. Oporto's economy has been dominated for three centuries by the Port wine shippers and industry; the wine, in fact, is named after the city itself. In recent decades, however, the local economy has become diversified and industry and manufacturing have begun to surpass Port wine in importance.

The city of Oporto, proud of its hard-working reputation and its preeminence and anticipation in supporting liberal political causes, has an ancient rivalry with the capital Lisbon. Since 1820, when the first liberal, constitutional movement burst forth in Oporto, the city has often anticipated Lisbon in supporting liberal political causes. Other cases occurred in the 19th century, including the January 1891 Republican revolt at Oporto, and in the 20th century, including Oporto's fervent support of the Presidential candidacy of the ill-fated General Humberto Delgado (q.v.) in 1958. It is noteworthy, too, that one of the most enduring critics of the Dictatorship in its middle and late years (1940s–1960s) was a Bishop of Oporto, who was exiled and penalized by the regime.

Whether it is in soccer (*futebol*), liberal causes, hard work or politics, Oporto and its inhabitants nurse a fierce local pride that they are better than Lisbon. In Portuguese tradition, Oporto residents are known as "tripe-eaters" (*tripeiros*), as opposed to Lisbon residents, known as "lettuce-eaters" (*alfacinhas*). Despite Lisbon's dominance of the print media, the city of Oporto has supported some of the country's more important daily newspapers, starting in the 19th century. *See* LISBON; PORT WINE.

OURIQUE, BATTLE OF (July 25, 1139). The battle between the forces of the newly proclaimed King of Portugal, Afonso Henriques (q.v.), "The Founder," and Muslim forces where the Christian forces triumphed. The probable site of this battle whose history is clothed in legend is near the present city of Santarém. It is possible that the Muslims near that city then resumed payment of tribute to Afonso Henriques and that the triumph prepared the Portuguese forces for the coming assault on Lisbon (q.v.), held by the Muslims, which was successful eight years later. Among the legends about the battle of Ourique is one that the Christians won due to the divine intervention of the Lord. Firm historical evidence about this battle, however, remains slight. *See* HENRIQUES, KING AFONSO.

- P -

PACHECO, DUARTE (1900–1943). One of Portugal's outstanding civil engineers and the most energetic and accomplished Cabinet Minister in the early phase of the *Estado Novo* (q.v.), Duarte Pacheco was born in 1900 in Loulé, Algarve province. As Director and instructor in the Higher Technical Institute, Lisbon, Pacheco trained several generations of urban planners and engineers and served in several key posts in the Dictatorship: Minister of Education, President of the Lisbon *Câmara Municipal* (City Hall), and on two occasions between 1932 and 1943 the premier Minister of Public Works and Communications in the history of the regime. As a relatively liberal Republican in a regime of conservatives, Monarchists and crypto-Monarchists and Integralists, Duarte Pacheco was a political maverick but a highly respected, if controversial, man of action. His Public Works Ministry helped to transform the look of the capital, Lisbon, improve urban planning and housing, create the remarkable Double Centenary Exposition of the Portuguese World at Belém (q.v.) in 1940, and construct a number of key edifices for various institutions. In November 1943, he was killed in a tragic automobile accident. His influential memory still lives in the oral tradition of the new Portugal's Ministry of Public Works and sets a high standard of excellence.

PAIS, SIDÓNIO (1872–1918). Leading political figure during the First Republic, Minister to Berlin for the Republic and ill-fated President of the Republic (1917–1918) as well as founder of the "New Republic" (q.v.) system. Born in the Minho district to a family of modest means, Sidónio Pais was one of the most brilliant students in mathematics of his generation at Coimbra University (q.v.), the pre-1926 crucible for so many of Portugal's future political leaders. Following his doctorate in mathematics at Coimbra, he became a faculty member at that institution and entered Republican politics. He joined Brito Camacho's (q.v.) moderate Republican Party, the Unionists, and served as Portugal's Minister to Berlin, 1912–1916.

A reserve Army major, Pais was ambitious as well as idealistic and sought to reform the Republic's turbulent, inefficient system. He headed the military coup and insurrection of December 5–8, 1917, which overthrew the Afonso Costa (q.v.) government and ousted the Portuguese Republican Party from power. Sidónio Pais engineered a novel regime called "The New Republic" during 1917–1918 and was elected President of the Republic in the spring of 1918. This new government sought to reconcile Monarchists and Republicans and to stabilize politics. Described by admirers as "half prince, half condottiere," Sidónio Pais' experiment was short-lived and soon collapsed in chaos. Pais was assassinated by a fanatic Republican at Rossio railroad station on December 14, 1918. *See* NEW REPUBLIC.

PATULEIA, REVOLT AND CIVIL WAR OF (1846–1847). An important 19th century civil war which featured political forces centered at Oporto pitted against the Lisbon government of Queen Maria II's (qq.v.) Constitutional Monarchy. It began with a military insurrection in Oporto on October 6, 1846. A Provisional Junta, led by the Septembrist José da Silva Passos (1800–1863), proclaimed goals included the ousting of the Lisbon government of the day and the restoration of the 1822 Constitution. Foreign intervention was sparked when the Oporto Septembrist Junta was joined by Miguelist rebels. On the pretext of preventing a restoration of a Miguelist Absolutist Government, England, France and Spain (qq.v.) intervened and dispatched armies and fleets to Portugal. Queen Maria II requested foreign assistance, too, and worked to safeguard her throne and political system. While an English fleet blocked Portugal's coast, Spain dispatched armies which crossed the Portuguese frontier in both south-central and northern Portugal. A siege of Junta forces which lasted almost eight months followed. On June 12, 1847, the foreign powers presented an ultimatum to the Oporto Junta which, though it tried to continue resistance, decided to negotiate and then to capitulate to the foreign forces and the Lisbon government. With the signing of the controversial Convention of Gramido (1847), the Patuleia civil war ended. *See* GRAMIDO, CONVENTION OF.

PEACE TREATY OF 1668, LUSO-SPANISH. Spain (q.v.) and Portugal signed the Peace Treaty of February 13, 1668, that ended the War of Restoration (q.v.) which had continued since 1641. The negotiations were mediated by England (q.v.) who guaranteed that the peace would be kept. By this important document, both states promised to return their respective conquests during that war, with the exception of the city of Ceuta in Morocco which declared for Spanish sovereignty and which was not returned to Portugal. Spain's signing of the Treaty also signified that Portuguese independence was definitively recognized. *See* WAR OF RESTORATION.

PEDRO I, KING (1320–1367). The eighth King of Portugal and fourth son of King Afonso IV and Beatriz of Castile. His second marriage as Prince and heir was to a daughter of a Castilian *hidalgo* (in Portuguese, *fidalgo* [q.v.]), Constança Manuel. In Constança's retinue from Spain came the alluring Lady-in-waiting, Dona Inês de Castro, a Gallician of Castilian stock. The notorious love affair between Inês and Pedro soon sparked a bitter conflict between Pedro and his father King Afonso and led to the premature death of Pedro's wife Beatriz. Fearing the menace of Castilian intervention in Portuguese affairs using Inês' connection with Pedro, Afonso ordered the murder of Inês in 1355. Reacting to this tragedy, Pedro rebelled and went to war against his father, though a truce was called after a short period and Afonso died in 1357. Pedro became noted in his brief reign of a decade for avoiding war and for a record of even-handed justice. The legend that Pedro disinterred the corpse of Inês de Castro and proclaimed it Queen grew up after Pedro's death in 1367 and became a popular theme in European literature centuries later. *See* CASTRO, INÊS DE.

PEDRO II, KING (1648–1706). The 23rd King of Portugal who ascended the throne in 1668. This followed the 1667 coup d'etat which deposed Pedro's handicapped brother King Afonso VI, who was later held under house arrest in the Azores and then in the National Palace of Sintra (qq.v.) for the remainder of his life. Pedro then married his sister-in-law. During his reign, Pedro signed the great peace treaty of 1668 with Spain, thus ending the War of Restoration (qq.v.). With increased revenues from mineral exploitation in Brazil (q.v.), Portugal's national finances under Pedro were strengthened. With his chief minister, the Count of Ericeira, Pedro promoted the establishment of early basic industries.

PEDRO IV, KING (also EMPEROR PEDRO I OF BRAZIL) (1798–1834). The first Emperor of Brazil (q.v.) and restorer of the liberal, Constitutional Monarchy as well as the throne of his daughter Queen Maria II (q.v.). Born in Queluz Palace, the second son of the Regent João VI and Carlota Joaquina (q.v.), Pedro at age 9 accompanied his parents and the remainder of the Braganza royal family as they fled the French invasion to Brazil in late 1807. Raised and educated in Brazil, following the return of his father King João VI to Portugal, Pedro declared the independence of Brazil from Portugal in the famous "cry of Ipiranga," on September 7, 1822. As Emperor Pedro I of Brazil, he ruled that fledgling nation-state-empire from 1822 to 1831, when he abdicated in favor of his son Pedro, and then went to Portugal and the Azores (q.v.).

Pedro's Absolutist brother, Miguel (q.v.), following the death of their father João VI in 1826, had broken his word on defending Portugal's Constitution and had carried out an Absolutist Counter-Revolution which was supported by his reactionary mother Carlota Joaquina. Pedro's daughter Queen Maria II of Portugal, who was too young to assume the duties of monarch of Portugal, had lost her throne to King Miguel, in effect, and Pedro spent the remainder of his life restoring the Constitutional Monarchy and his young daughter to the throne of Portugal. In the 1832–1834 "War of the Brothers" (q.v.), Pedro IV's armed forces triumphed over those of Dom Miguel and the latter fled to exile in Austria. Exhausted from the effort, Pedro died on September 24, 1834, and was buried in Lisbon. In 1972, his remains were moved to Ipiranga, Brazil. *See* MARIA II, QUEEN; WAR OF THE BROTHERS.

PEDRO V, KING (1837–1861). Of all Portuguese Kings in the 18th and 19th centuries, the best educated and most intellectually talented. Pedro was the first-born son of Queen Maria II (q.v.) and Prince Ferdinand of Saxe-Coburg-Gotha. Exceptionally well-educated, Prince Pedro traveled extensively abroad, which was unusual for a Portuguese royal heir in that day, and was educated under his mother's watchful eye. He was blessed with a brilliant memory, a fine imagination, shrewd political judgement and a fund of learning. Pedro demonstrated a keen interest not only in common political affairs such as fell within a Constitutional monarch's concerns, but with a variety of subjects including science, emigration, diplomacy and the African colonies. He carried on a lively correspondence with royal relatives abroad including Queen Victoria of England to whom he was related through his father. When his mother Queen Maria II died tragically at age 34 in childbirth, 16-year-old Pedro became Regent. He ascended the throne at age 18 and was a model monarch. He ruled formally from 1855 to 1861, when he died of typhus. His brief but significant appearance as an enlightened ruler was a sad case of unfulfilled promise. *See* MARIA II, QUEEN.

PENA, NATIONAL PALACE OF. High above the National Palace of Sintra (q.v.), on the top of the Sintra mountain range, lies Pena Palace, a product of 19th century imagination and work. Constructed during the 1840s and 1850s, following the acquisition of a ruined ancient convent on the site, the Palace was ordered constructed by the consort of Queen Maria II (q.v.), the German prince Ferdinand. It was destined to become the favorite summer residence of the royal family, a cooler spot than even the National Palace in the square below and with a view unmatched in Portugal. From the top of Pena Palace, on a clear day, one can see the Atlantic ocean to the west and north and Lisbon (q.v.) to the east and south.

The Palace's romantic situation overlooking Sintra and beyond, a place made famous in 19th century English literature by the writings of Lord Byron and William Beckford and a host of lesser known travelers, is fully supported in the bizarre architecture of the building itself. Designed by a German military architect, Baron Von Eschweg, whose statue stands nearby on another mountain peak so that his spirit may contemplate his famous handiwork, the Palace's styles combine ancient, medieval and modern forms. To visitors who know Disney World castles, Pena may appear to be a Magic Kingdom building. Besides the Gothic and Manueline (q.v.) styles, the Moorish touch is present in towers and a minaret. The interior rooms are rich in *azulejos* (q.v.) and historic furniture of the Victorian era.

PEREIRA, PEDRO TEOTÓNIO (1902–1972). Teotónio Pereira was one of the most important political figures in the higher ranks of the Dictatorship, present at the creation of the *Estado Novo* (q.v.) and, for more than a decade, a potential successor of Premier Salazar (q.v.). Born in Lisbon and trained as a mathematician and insurance actuarian, Pereira was one of the few *Estado Novo* high officials to have studied abroad (in Switzerland). At age 31 he was named the first Under Secretary of State for Corporations and played an important role in constructing a Corporative (q.v.) system. He was Minister of Commerce and Industry (1936–1937) and, in 1938, was sent to represent Portugal in General Franco's Spain (qq.v.), the first of a number of top diplomatic posts he served in for the Dictatorship. At various times until he served as Minister of the Presidency (1958–1961), succeeding his rival Marcello Caetano (q.v.) in the post, Teotónio Pereira was Portugal's Ambassador to Britain, Brazil, NATO and the United States. One of the most influential personalities of the regime, Teotónio Pereira remained loyal to the aging Salazar throughout the middle and late periods of the *Estado Novo* (1944–1958; 1958–1968) and was on the short list of potential successors to Salazar in September 1968. Ill health, age and the candidacy of Caetano, however, conspired against him. He died in Lisbon in November 1972.

PEREIRA DE MELO, ANTÓNIO MARIA FONTES (1819–1887). Major 19th century political leader, engineer and mastermind of the Regeneration (q.v.) era (1851–1880). Trained in the armed forces as an engineer, Fontes Pereira de Melo participated in the suppression of the Maria da Fonte (q.v.) revolt by Saldanha's forces and, in 1851, was called to Lisbon to assume various key posts in several Ministries (Navy and Overseas; Treasury; Public Works; Commerce and Industry). In 1858, he assumed leadership of the Regenerador Party and was instrumental in directing and guiding the economic and industrial process known as the Regeneration (q.v.) after 1851. He became Prime Minister, too, on several occasions and received many honors and much recognition.

Fontes Pereira de Melo realized how far behind Portugal was in economic development and industrialization and initiated a program of building the necessary transportation infrastructure. During this era, Portugal acquired a basic network of railroads and roads and the beginnings of industrialization and participation in various export markets with Portuguese products and resources. Fontes Pereira de Melo's economic development programs marked the onset of modern economic development in Portugal and represented the apogee of political stability and financial accomplishment during the Constitutional Monarchy. *See* REGENERATION.

PESSOA, FERNANDO (1888–1935). Portugal's most celebrated and talented modern poet and one of Europe's greatest 20th century poets, now translated into many languages. Pessoa was born in Portugal but was raised and educated in South Africa and for a period English became almost his first language. He returned to Portugal at age 12 and he wrote poetry from an early age. He wrote poetry and essays both in English and in Portuguese and wrote under various names. Beyond that unusual practice, Pessoa created different personalities with names such as Alberto Caeiro, Ricardo Reis, Álvaro de Campos and Bernardo Soares, his heteronyms. He became one of Europe's greatest Modernist poets, though he did not publish much of his poetry in book form during his lifetime. His book, *Mensagem* ("Message"), published in 1934 in Lisbon and receiving a government prize, appeared only a year before his premature death at age 47. Though he had published poems in scattered, ephemeral periodicals in Portugal, much of his writings remained unpublished and stored in a family trunk.

PHILIPPA OF LANCASTER, QUEEN (1360–1415). Wife of King João I (q.v.) of Portugal and daughter of John of Gaunt, son of King Edward III. Born in England (q.v.), she was educated at home within the bosom of the royal family and little is known of her life until she was 26 and sailed to Castile with her father. The marriage of King João I and Philippa was celebrated in Oporto (q.v.) in 1387 and during the next fifteen years the Queen's life at least half of the time was expended in pregnancy and childbearing. From age 27 to 42, a remarkable physical feat for that era or any other, Philippa bore the so-called "illustrious generation" of children which included Prince Henry the Navigator (q.v.), Prince Pedro, and King Duarte (reigned: 1433–1438). Her six sons alone dominated politics for generations and though what precise role she had in their education is unclear her influence was present in continuing the Anglo-Portuguese Alliance (q.v.) and in encouraging the expansion of Portugal into North Africa. She maintained a long correspondence with her family in England, was very religious and introduced a new liturgy into the Portuguese church services. Philippa, who was a strong influence in encouraging the crusade to attack Muslim North Africa, died of the Black Plague on the eve of the epoch-making Ceuta expedition in 1415. Though she died at Odivelas, eventually her remains were transferred to the great Abbey at Batalha (1416) (q.v.), where on her fine tomb is the only faithful likeness in the form of a prostrate marble figure. *See* BATALHA, MONASTERY OF.

PIDE (POLITICAL POLICE OF DICTATORSHIP). Commonly known as the "PIDE," the *Estado Novo*'s political police was established in a definite form in 1932. The acronym of PIDE stood for *Polícia Internacional e de Defesa do Estado* or "International and Defense of the State Police," the name it was known by from 1945 to 1969. From 1932 to 1945, it was known by a different acronym: PVDE or *Polícia da Vigilância e de Defesa do Estado*. After Premier Salazar was replaced in office by Marcello Caetano (qq.v.), the political police was renamed DGS or *"Direcção Geral da Seguridade"* or "General Directorate of Security."

This force was the most infamous means of repression and a major source of fear among the opposition during the long history of the Dictatorship. While it was described as "secret police," nearly everyone knew of its existence, though its methods—in theory—were "secret." The PVDE/PIDE/DGS had functions much broader than purely repression of any opposition to the regime. It combined the functions of a border police, customs inspectorate, immigration force, political police and regime vetting administration of credentials for government or even private sector jobs. Furthermore, this police had powers of arrest, pursued non-political criminals and administered its own prison system. From the 1950s on, the PIDE extended its operations to the empire and began to suppress oppositionists directly in various colonies in Africa and Asia.

While this police became more notorious and known to the public after 1958–1961, before that new outburst of anti-regime activity it was perhaps more effective in neutralizing or destroying oppositionist groups. It was especially effective in damaging the Communist Party of Portugal (q.v.) in the 1930s and early 1940s. Yet, beginning with the unprecedented strikes and political activities of 1943–1945, the real heyday had passed. During World War II, its top echelons were in the pay of both the Allies and Axis powers, though in later propaganda from the Left, the PIDE's pro-Axis reputation was carefully groomed into a myth. As for its actual strength and resources, it seems clear that it employed several thousand officers and also had scores of thousands of informants in the general population. In new laws of 1945 this police force received further powers of 90-day detention without charge or trial and such a detention could easily be renewed. A Who's Who of the political opposition emerges from those who spent years in PIDE prisons or who were frequently arrested without charge. This political police remained numerous and well-funded into 1974 when the military coup overthrew the regime and abolished it. A major question remains: if this police knew much about the Armed Forces Movement (q.v.) coup conspiracy, why was it so ineffective in arresting known leaders and squashing the plot?

PINTO, FERNÃO MENDES (ca. 1510–1583). Soldier and adventurer in Asia and one of Portugal's greatest prose writers of the 16th century. The author of a classic, largely true adventure story and history of Portugal in Asia, the *Peregrinação*, which in popularity among 17th century readers in Iberia and Europe rivaled Cervantes' *Don Quijote*. Even less is known about Mendes Pinto's life than that of Camões (q.v.). He left as a soldier on a fleet for India in 1537 and lived in Asia for about 17 years. Besides Portuguese India (q.v.), he saw many places in Southeast Asia, China and Japan. His service for Portugal involved great personal suffering including wounds in battle, captivities and near-starvation. In later years he retired as a lay brother of the Jesuit Order in Goa and went to Japan in 1556. In 1558 he retired to Portugal where he wrote his great work, the *Peregrinação*, which can be translated as "travels." The work was not published in his lifetime, but only in 1614, and it was long considered a work mainly of fiction, an apocryphal composition. It was apparently more popular in Spain, France and England than in his homeland. Later critics and translators have concluded that much of the work is a partly true description of the Portuguese in Asia and of Asian events, coupled with a wry but honest look at the foibles of the Catholic Church (q.v.) of his day.

POLITICAL PARTIES. Portugal's political party system began only in the 19th century and the first published, distinct political party program appeared about 1843. Under the Constitutional

Monarchy (1834–1910), a number of political groupings or factions took the name of a political figure or soldier or, more commonly until the second half of the century, the name of the particular Constitution they supported. For example, some were called "Septembrists," after the group which supported the 1836 (September) Revolution and the 1822 Constitution. Others described themselves as "Chartists" after Dom Pedro IV's 1826 Charter (*"Carta"*). From the Regeneration (q.v.) to the fall of the Monarchy in 1910, the leading political parties were the Regenerators and the Progressists (or Historicals). During the first parliamentary Republic (1910–1926), the leading political parties were the Portuguese Republican Party or "The Democrats," the Evolutionists, the Unionists, various Monarchist factions, the Liberals and the Nationalists. Small Leftist parties were also established or re-established after the collapse of President Sidónio Pais' New Republic (1917–1918) (qq.v.): the Socialist Party and the Portuguese Communist Party (1921).

Under the *Estado Novo* (q.v.) Dictatorship (1926–1974) all political parties and civic associations (such as the Masons) were banned in 1935 and the only legitimate political movement allowed was the regime's creature, the União Nacional (1930–1974) (q.v.). Various oppositionist parties and factions began to participate in the rigged electoral system of the Dictatorship beginning with the municipal elections of 1942 and continuing with general elections for President of the Republic or the National Assembly (Legislature) in 1945, 1949, 1951, 1958, 1961, 1969, 1972, etc. Among these parties were elements of the Communist Party, remnants of the old Portuguese Republican Party elite, of the old Socialist Party (originally founded in 1875), various workers' groups and special electoral committees allowed by the regime to campaign during brief pre-electoral exercises.

The fall of the Dictatorship in 1974 swept away the regime's institutions and ushered in a flood of new political groups. During 1974 and 1975, about 60 new political parties and factions sprung up, but the Portuguese Communist Party remained the senior, experienced political party. During the period of fallout and adjustment to the new pluralist, multi-party system of democracy (1974–1985), four main political parties became the principal ones and garnered the largest percentage of votes in the many general and municipal elections held between the first free election of April 25, 1975 and the general election of 1985. These parties were the Portuguese Communist Party, the Socialist Party, the Social Democrat party and the Social Democratic Center Party or "Christian Democrats." Until 1985–1987, the Socialists were ahead in votes, but the Social Democrats were victorious with clear majorities in 1987 and 1991.

POMBAL, THE MARQUIS OF (SEBASTIÃO JOSÉ DE CARVALHO E MELO) (1699–1782). 18th century Dictator of Portugal and dictatorial Chief Minister of King José I (1750–1777). Born of rural nobility, the leader—who became known as the Marquis of Pombal after the title he received only in 1770—represented Portugal abroad as a diplomat in England (1740–1744) (q.v.) and Vienna (1745–1750). When the rather lazy José I became King in 1750, Pombal assumed the top cabinet post and soon acquired great authority and power. For twenty-seven years, Pombal managed the affairs of Portugal through various crises (the Lisbon earthquake of 1755) and several wars. Major goals in his political agenda included strengthening Portugal's home economy and empire, which featured resource-rich Brazil (q.v.), economic independence from the oldest ally Britain, which tended to treat Portugal like an economic and political colony, and greater power status in a Europe which considered Portugal a third or fourth rate power. Dictator Pombal's domestic agenda was imposed by repressing the power of the nobility, strengthening royal power in all spheres and suppressing the influence and position of the Jesuits (Pombal expelled the Jesuit Order from Portugal in 1759). The extent to which Pombal was successful in these endeavors remains controversial among biographers and historians, but his pivotal role in 18th century public affairs remains secure. An impressive statue of the Dictator holding a lion at his side today dominates Pombal Square, Lisbon; it was completed in 1934. *See* LISBON EARTHQUAKE; PORT WINE.

PORT WINE. Portugal's famous Port wine, a leading export, takes its name from the city of Oporto (q.v.) or *"Porto"* which means "port" or harbor in Portuguese. Sometimes described as "The

Englishman's wine," Port is only one of the many wines produced in continental Portugal and the Atlantic islands. Another noted dessert wine is Madeira wine which is produced on the island of Madeira (q.v.). Port wine's history is about as long as that of Madeira wine, but the wine's development is recent compared to that of older table wines and the wines Greeks and Romans enjoyed in ancient Lusitania (q.v.). During the Roman occupation of the land (ca. 210 BC–300 AD), wine was being made from vines cultivated in the Upper Douro River (q.v.) valleys. Favorable climate and soils (schist with granite outcropping) and convenient transportation (on ships down the Douro River to Oporto) were factors which combined with increased wine production in the late 17th century to assist in the birth of Port wine as a new product. Earlier names for Port wine (*"Vinho do Porto"*) were descriptive of location ("Wine of the Douro Bank") and how it was transported ("Wine of [Ship] Embarcation").

Port wine, a sweet, fortified, (with brandy) aperitif or dessert wine which was designed as a valuable export product for the English market, was developed first in the 1670s by a unique combination of circumstances and the action of interested parties. Several substantial English merchants who visited Oporto "discovered" that a local Douro wine was much improved when brandy (*"aguardente"*) was added. Fortification prevented the wine from spoiling in a variety of temperatures and on the arduous sea voyages from Oporto to England (q.v.). Soon Port wine became a major industry of the Douro region; it involved an uneasy alliance between the English merchant-shippers at Oporto and Vila Nova de Gaia, across the river from Oporto, where the wine was stored and aged, and the Portuguese wine growers. In the 18th century, Port wine became a significant element of England's foreign imports and of the country's establishment tastes in beverages. Port wine drinking became a hallowed tradition in England's elite Oxford and Cambridge Universities' Colleges which all kept Port wine cellars. For Portugal, the Port wine market in England, and later in France and Belgium and other continental countries, became a vital element in the national economy. Trade in Port wine and English woolens became the key elements in the 1703 Methuen Treaty (q.v.) between England and Portugal.

In order to lessen Portugal's growing economic dependence on England, to regulate the production and export of the precious sweet wine and to protect the public from poor quality, Dictator Pombal (q.v.) instituted various measures for the industry. In 1756, Pombal established the "General Company of Viticulture of the Upper Douro" to carry out these measures. The same year Pombal ordered the creation of the first demarcated wine-producing region in the world, the port-wine producing Douro region. Other wine-producing countries later followed this Portuguese initiative and created demarcated wine regions in order to protect the quality of wine produced and to ensure national economic interests.

The upper Douro valley region (from Barca d'Alva in Portugal to Barqueiros on the Spanish frontier) produces a variety of wines; only 40% of its wines are Port wine while 60% are table wines. Port wine's alcohol content varies usually between 19 and 22% and, depending on the type, the wine is aged in wooden casks from two to six years and then bottled. Related to Port wine's history is the history of Portuguese cork. Beginning in the 17th century, Portuguese cork, which comes from cork trees, began to be used to seal wine bottled to prevent wine from spoiling. This innovation in Portugal helped lead to the development of the cork industry. By the early 20th century, Portugal was the world's largest exporter of cork. *See* ANGLO-PORTUGUESE ALLIANCE; POMBAL, MARQUIS OF.

PORTUGAL. The name *Portugal* comes from the name for a pre-Roman or Roman settlement named *"Portus Cale,"* near the mouth of the Douro River (q.v.). The southern part of the Roman province of Gallaecia (now Galicia, Spain) was occupied by the Suevi (Germanic tribe) in the period of 411 AD and the town near or in what is now Oporto (q.v.) was held by the Suevi and called later *"Portucale."*

PORTUGUESA, A. The official Portuguese national anthem since 1911. *"A Portuguesa,"* which means "The Portuguese Woman," refers to the historical symbolic female figure or "Lady Republic," a Portuguese woman who wears republican garb, including a Republican banner or flag and a Phyrigian bonnet. The concept and name were modeled on the similar figure from the

French Revolution of 1789 and the name of the French national anthem, "The Woman from Marseilles," and Republican symbols from France's Third Republic. Under the constitutional Monarchy, the national anthem was called "The Hymn of the Charter," referring to the 1826 Charter or Constitution drafted by Emperor Pedro I of Brazil or Pedro IV (q.v.) of Portugal to replace the controversial 1822 Constitution.

"A Portuguesa" was composed during the popular frenzy and outcry generated by the English Ultimatum (q.v.) crisis of January 1890. Portugal capitulated to an English Ultimatum presented to Lisbon by London during an Anglo-Portuguese conflict over possession of territory in central-east Africa. Intense feelings of patriotism, xenophobia and nationalism were generated in the wake of the Lisbon government's capitulation and its subsequent resignation from office. Inspired by the popular reaction to this incident, Alfredo Keil, a Portuguese musician and opera composer of German descent, wrote the music for "A Portuguesa," whose melody bears a slight resemblance to that of the stirring "Internationale." The sentimental, bellicose lyrics were written by Keil's friend, Lopes de Mendonça.

During the remaining years of the waning Monarchy, "A Portuguesa" was sung as a rallying cry by Republican partisans who wished to abolish the Monarchy. The song's spirit is not only nationalistic, but is imbued with an imperative of Portuguese national revival in order to remind the people of their greatness of centuries ago. After the first Republic replaced the Monarchy, the Republic's Constituent Assembly adopted "A Portuguesa" as the country's national anthem in June 1911 and it has remained so ever since. The first verse with chorus imparts the spirit of the entire patriotic message of the anthem:

"A Portuguesa"

"Heroes of the sea, noble race
valiant and immortal nation,
now is the hour to raise up on high once more
Portugal's splendor.
From out of the mists of memory,
of Homeland, we hear the voices
of your great forefathers
that shall lead you on to victory!

Chorus
To arms, to arms
on land and sea!
To arms, to arms
to fight for our Homeland!
To march against the enemy guns!"

See ULTIMATUM, ENGLISH.

PORTUGUESE (LANGUAGE). In the 1990s, the Portuguese language was spoken by more than 200 million people in the world. Seven countries have Portuguese as the official language: Portugal, Brazil, Cape Verde Islands, Guinea-Bissau, S. Tomé and Príncipe Islands, Angola, and Mozambique (qq.v.). Overseas Portuguese, who number nearly four million, reside in another two dozen countries and continue to speak Portuguese. There are distinct differences between Brazilian and Continental (Portugal) Portuguese in spelling, pronunciation, syntax and grammar, but both versions comprise the same language. Next to Romanian, Portuguese is the closest of the Romance languages to old Latin. Like Gallician, to which it is intimately linked as a kind of co-language, Portuguese is an outgrowth of Latin as spoken in ancient Hispania. It began to appear as a distinct language separate from Latin and Castilian in the 9th century and historic Portuguese made its full appearance during the 12th and 13th centuries. Major changes in the language came under the influence of Castilian in the 15th and 16th centuries and there was a Castilianization of Portuguese culture during the 1580–1640 era of Spanish rule of Portugal and her empire.

The cultural aspects of Portugal reasserting her sovereignty and restoring national independence was a reaction against Castile and Castilianization. In language, this meant that Portugal opened itself to foreign but non-Hispanic influences. In the 17th, 18th and 19th centuries, French culture and French language became major influences and enriched the Portuguese languages. In international politics, there continued the impact of the Anglo-Portuguese Alliance (q.v.), a connection which has been less cultural than political and economic. For all the centuries of English influence in Portugal since the late 14th century, it is interesting how little cultural impact occurred and how relatively few words from English have entered the language. Instead, there are many more loan words from Arabic, French and Italian.

PORTUGUESE COMMUNIST PARTY (PCP). Founded in 1921, during the First Republic, the PCP remains the oldest political party in Portugal. Its rank-and-file and leadership were composed for the most part of a curious mixture of workers, intellectuals and the middle class. During the long period of the Dictatorship (1926–1974), the PCP was the premier target of the regime's political police and its members were frequently arrested, jailed and sometimes tortured. A few were murdered. Its historical reputation during this repression was of the best organized, most active and audacious of the elements of the opposition. By the time of the 1974 coup, which it did not organize, the Central Committee of the PCP among them had suffered more than 100 years in PVDE/PIDE/DGS (q.v.) prisons.

Since 1962, the PCP's Secretary-General has been the lawyer, Álvaro Cunhal, a graduate of Coimbra University (q.v.). During the Provisional Governments after April 25, 1974, Cunhal was a member of several cabinets. For many decades, the PCP's ideology and political style was Stalinist. In the general elections of 1975–1991, the PCP and its smaller allies consistently got 10–18% of the vote, but in the late 1980s its popular support began to wane. Traditionally, the PCP's following was concentrated in industrialized, urban areas as well as in the Alentejo, a land of landless peasants. In any election, then, its main vote derived from the Lisbon (q.v.) region and the Alentejo.

PRONUNCIAMENTO. Portuguese word for military coup d'état, uprising, insurrection, derived from the verb "to declare, to announce solemnly and publicly." The Spanish word is similar (*pronunciamiento*). Praetorianism or military insurrectionism became a chronic problem as well as a political tradition first in Spain (q.v.) after the Army's coup of 1812, followed by an Army insurrection in the cause of Constitutional Monarchy in 1820 in Oporto, Portugal. Both civilian and military conspiracies to use the military to intervene in public affairs, overthrow the current government and establish a "new" system became common from this time on in Iberian affairs and such activity also became common in 19th century Latin America, where Spain and Portugal had former colonies. The Portuguese word for the tendency to have *pronunciamentos* or *golpes* is referred to as *golpismo*. See ARMED FORCES MOVEMENT; FIFTH OF OCTOBER; GOLPISMO; TWENTY-EIGHTH OF MAY; TWENTY-FIFTH OF APRIL.

PROVINCES, PORTUGAL'S HISTORIC. Today continental Portugal is divided administratively into eighteen districts, each with its district capital (see map). Traditionally, Portugal is divided into historic provinces whose names reflect the multiple cultural influences of various invaders of ancient Lusitania (q.v.) from the Romans to the Muslims (Arabs and Berbers). More than a few of these names derive from the Arabic, including *"Algarve,"* a corruption of *"Al-gharb"* or *"The West"* province. The twelve historic provinces, whose names continue to be used in everyday life despite the new district system, are: in the north, Minho, Trás-os-Montes, Douro, Douro Litoral and Beira Alta; in the center, Beira Baixa, Beira Litoral, Estremadura, and Ribatejo; and in the south, Alto Alentejo, Baixo Alentejo and Algarve.

PVDE. See PIDE.

- Q -

QUEIRÓS, JOSÉ MARIA EÇA DE (1845–1900). 19th century Portugal's greatest novelist and essayist, the author of modern classics in the form of satirical novels which are still popular and considered to be relevant to contemporary concerns in Portugal. Next to Camões and Pessoa (qq.v.), the most studied, discussed and written about Portuguese writer in modern times. Eça de Queirós was a student at Coimbra University (q.v.) and a distinguished member of the so-called "Generation of 1870" which challenged both the academic establishment and the governing elite of its day. This brilliant, prolific novelist and essayist spent much of his post-university life abroad in

Portugal's foreign and consular service. his largely Realist novels portrayed Portuguese society of 1870–1900 with wit, satire, humor and wisdom. He died in Paris in 1900, but he left behind a large body of novels and essays, published and unpublished.

QUELUZ, NATIONAL PALACE OF. Considered Portugal's most beautiful former royal residence among a host of palaces, Queluz Palace was built in the 18th century. It is rightly regarded as the Portuguese mini-Versailles for several reasons. In some respects a miniature version of France's (q.v.) colossal palace and garden, Queluz with its unusual gardens and park located west of Lisbon near Sintra bears the touch of French architects and decorators, has French furniture and decor and even boasts its own small Hall of Mirrors *à la Versailles,* The Throne Room. Queluz was a favorite dwelling place of the Regent Dom João (later King João VI) and family and symbolizes Portugal's efforts to be counted as worthy of the greatest European powers' tastes and standards of the day.

Queluz' history began with a mid-17th century country house of a noble, altered to accommodate the royal princes for a summer residence away from the noise and heat of Lisbon (q.v.). Palace construction began in 1747 and lasted at least until 1786. Portuguese Baroque and neo-classical styles dominate the charming Palace's interior and exterior. The main architects were Portuguese and Italian as well as the French decorator-artist Robillon. For materials, rare woods were imported from Brazil and marble from Italy. Especially striking in the garden-park, with its own small canal and walking bridges, are the *azulejos* (q.v.) or glazed tiles along the canal. In 1908, King Manuel II transferred ownership of Queluz to the State and extensive restorations began in 1933.

- R -

REGENERATION, THE (1851–1880). An era of relative economic progress and political stability during the third quarter of the 19th century. The Regeneration followed a period of intense political instability and uncertainty (1807–1851), with inva-

COLLEGE OF THE SEQUOIAS
LIBRARY

sions, wars and civil wars, and represented the inception of modern economic and industrial development in Portugal. In terms of administrative continuity and governmental stability and accomplishment, the Regeneration was the most hopeful era of the Constitutional Monarchy (1834–1910). It began in 1851 with a military revolt led by Marshal Saldanha, one of the conquerors and victors of the Patuleia (q.v.) revolt and civil war (1846–1847) and was supported by various groups and factions which desired civic peace, order and economic improvement. Of the Regeneration leaders, Fontes Pereira de Melo (q.v.) became the major personality and mastermind of this era which witnessed the beginnings of Portugal's main railroad and road system as well as the initiation of modern industrial and commercial activities. The Regeneration affected the economies of the Lisbon and Oporto (qq.v.) regions more than the provinces, but the rural areas also benefited from the changes which came from the new economic activities. *See* PATULEIA; PEREIRA DE MELO, FONTES.

REVOLUTION OF APRIL 25, 1974. See REVOLUTION OF CARNATIONS; TWENTY-FIFTH OF APRIL.

REVOLUTION OF CARNATIONS. Refers to the Revolution of 1974–1975 which began with the military coup of the Armed Forces Movement (MFA) against the *Estado Novo* (qq.v.) Dictatorship. Carnations of many colors, but principally red carnations because of the symbolism of red for Leftist (including Socialist and Communist) views and action, were common in Lisbon flower shops during the rainy day of April 25, 1974 (q.v.) and days thereafter. The carnation appeared to embody the peaceful, bloodless, almost romantic nature of the military coup which met little or no resistance from the Dictatorship's last defenders. The only blood shed on the April 25th was spilled when the Lisbon headquarters of the political police (DGS) fired into a surging crowd of pro-coup enthusiasts who rushed the front of the building; five persons died and several people were injured. When people began to give the Armed Forces Movement troops carnations to stick in their rifles, guns and uniforms and on their helmets and caps, the idea of using the carnations as a symbol of the peaceful intentions of the MFA spread. Soon

COLLEGE OF THE SEQUOIAS
LIBRARY

various parties and even the government adopted the symbol of red carnations and this icon of change began to appear in graffiti on walls. *See* ARMED FORCES MOVEMENT; TWENTY-FIFTH OF APRIL.

ROCA, CAPE OF. Cape on the southwest central coast of Portugal (long. 9° 30/W). Today it has a lighthouse and tourist center and is famous as the westernmost point of continental Europe. It is located on the road between Ericeira-Sintra and Cascais.

ROSE-COLORED MAP. The famous map presented to the Chamber of Deputies in 1887 which indicated that Lisbon intended to occupy, claim and annex a disputed corridor of central African territory. The pink or rose-colored area on the map was that area which linked up the Portuguese colonies of Angola (q.v.) in West Africa and Mozambique (q.v.) in East Africa. Portugal's territorial interests in tropical Africa shifted from the coasts after the settlement at the 1884–1885 Berlin West Africa Conference to the interior. Thereafter, Portugal concentrated on participating in the European race for central Africa, part of the larger movement, the "Scramble for Africa."

By means of dispatching expeditions of explorers and soldiers to the hinterlands of both Angola and Mozambique, Portugal sought to fulfill the Berlin Conference's "rule" about "effective occupation." In Portugal, the old colonialists' dream of linking up the interiors of Angola and Mozambique, a notion which dated at least to the mid-18th century, was known as the "*contra-costa*" ("opposite coast") project. Much of the rose-colored section of the map comprises what is now Zambia, Malawi and Zimbabwe. The plan failed when Britain opposed Portuguese expansion into this disputed area in 1890 and sent Lisbon a threatening Ultimatum which obliged Portugal to back down. *See* ULTIMATUM, ENGLISH.

- S -

SÁ CARNEIRO, FRANCISCO LUMBRALLES (1934–1980). Important political leader in the early years of post-1974 Portugal, founder and chief of the Social Democrat party and Prime

Minister. Trained and educated as a lawyer at the University of Lisbon Law School, he was an up-and-coming young lawyer and liberal Catholic activist in the 1960s. A practicing lawyer in Oporto (q.v.), Sá Carneiro was selected to be one of a number of younger deputies in the National Assembly during the brief "opening" phase of Marcello Caetano's (q.v.) period of the *Estado Novo* (q.v.). He became a deputy upon consenting to adhere to two conditions for his selection, namely maintaining Portugal's colonial policy in Africa and advocating "social peace" through reforms. But he refused to join the regime's official movement, the *União Nacional* (q.v.). Soon discouraged by the continued intransigence of the conservative forces still controlling regime policy, despite the efforts of Caetano during 1968–1970, Sá Carneiro and several others of the recently appointed deputies resigned their posts and went into opposition.

Following the April 25, 1974 coup and revolution, Sá Carneiro and colleagues founded the Social Democrat Party. The highly respected lawyer and spokesman for centrist views became fully involved in the unstable politics of the early Third Republic. Named Prime Minister in January 1980, Sá Carneiro became the political man of the hour in Portugal. He dominated the Social Democrat Party (PPD, later renamed PSD), which formed the core of the coalition named the Democratic Alliance (AD) which was composed of the PSD, CDS and PPM. October 1980 legislative elections reaffirmed the AD's strength as a coalition which had first emerged in the December 1979 interim elections. Anxious to consolidate political power with a President who favored AD policies and eager to have the AD candidate, General Soares Carneiro, defeat the incumbent, President Eanes, Sá Carneiro undertook a vigorous campaign in the Presidential elections set for December 7, 1980. On December 4, bound for Oporto campaign stops, Sá Carneiro's plane mysteriously crashed and burned only a short distance from the Lisbon airport. Numerous controversial investigations of the causes of this tragedy have produced only greater mystery. *See* POLITICAL PARTIES.

SAGRES. A promontory near Cape Saint Vincent (q.v.), Sagres is the site where Prince Henry (q.v.) the Navigator pursued some of his exploration-related activities before his death in 1460.

Henry resided for a period on Cape Saint Vincent and the promontory which juts out into the Atlantic, but it is a myth that he established a "school" for navigators there. A lighthouse is now on the site of the ruins and the scene is dominated by the barren cliffs and the lonely, stark look of the place, a fitting spot for Prince Henry to brood about what lay south in the Atlantic. *See* HENRY OF AVIZ, PRINCE; SAINT VINCENT, CAPE OF.

SAINT VINCENT, CAPE OF (CABO SÃO VICENTE). Considered by ancient geographers as the westernmost point of Europe, Cape Saint Vincent was known as the "Sacred Promontory" on ancient maps (*Promontorium Sacrum*). It is the southwesternmost point of Portugal, some 118 miles (250 kilometers) south of Lisbon. On this bleak, barren cape or nearby at the site of Sagres (q.v.), Prince Henry (q.v.) the Navigator was active in promoting the exploration of the Atlantic and the African coast south of Morocco. It is an important tourist attraction, despite its location. *see* HENRY OF AVIZ, PRINCE; SAGRES.

SALAZAR, ANTÓNIO DE OLIVEIRA (1889–1970). The Coimbra University (q.v.) Professor of Finance and Economics and one of the founders of the Estado Novo (q.v.) Dictatorship, who came to dominate Western Europe's longest surviving authoritarian system. Salazar was born on April 28, 1889, in Vimieiro, Beira Alta province, the son of a peasant estate manager and a shopkeeper. Most of his first 39 years were spent as a student and later as a teacher in a secondary school and a professor at Coimbra University's Law School. Nine formative years were spent at Viseu's Catholic Seminary (1900–1909), preparing for the Catholic priesthood, but the serious, studious Salazar decided to enter Coimbra University instead in 1910, the year the Braganza Monarchy was overthrown by the First Republic. Salazar received among the highest marks of his generation of students and in 1918 was awarded a doctoral degree in finance and economics. Pleading inexperience, Salazar rejected an invitation in August 1918 to become Finance Minister in the "New Republic" government of President Sidónio Pais (q.v.).

As a celebrated academic who was deeply involved in Coimbra University politics, publishing works on the troubled finances of the besieged First Republic, and a leader of Catholic organizations, Salazar was not as modest, reclusive or unknown as later official propaganda led the public to believe. In 1921, as a Catholic deputy, he briefly served in the First Republic's turbulent parliament (Congress) but resigned shortly after witnessing only one session. Salazar taught at Coimbra University as of 1916 and continued teaching until April 1928. When the military overthrew the First Republic in May 1926, Salazar was offered the Ministry of Finance and held office for several days. The ascetic academic, however, resigned his post when he discovered the degree of disorder in Lisbon's government and when his demands for budget authority were rejected. As the Military Dictatorship failed to reform finances in the following years, Salazar was re-invited to become Minister of Finances in April 1928. Since his conditions for acceptance—authority over all budget expenditures, among other powers—were accepted, Salazar entered the government. Using the Ministry of Finance as a power base, following several years of successful financial reforms, Salazar was named interim Minister of Colonies (1930) and soon garnered sufficient prestige and authority to become a kind of civilian Dictator. Salazar became one of the founders of the Dictatorship known as the *Estado Novo* ("New State"), which grew out of the initial Military Dictatorship. In July 1932, Salazar was named Prime Minister, the first civilian to hold that post since the 1926 military coup.

Salazar gathered around him a team of largely academic experts in the cabinet and during the period 1930–1933 constructed a system which featured several key policies: Portuguese nationalism, colonialism (rebuilding an empire in shambles), Catholicism and conservative fiscal management. As the *Estado Novo* went through three basic phases during Salazar's long tenure in office, Salazar's role underwent changes as well. In the early years (1928–1944), Salazar and the regime enjoyed greater vigor and popularity than later. During the middle years (1944–1958), the regime's popularity waned, methods of repression increased and hardened and Salazar grew more dogmatic in his policies and ways. During the late years (1958–1968), the regime experienced its most serious colonial problems, ruling circles—including Salazar—aged and increasingly failed and opposition burgeoned and grew bolder.

Salazar's plans for stabilizing the economy and strengthening social and financial programs were shaken with the impact of the Civil War (1936–1939) in neighboring Spain (q.v.). Salazar strongly supported General Franco's (q.v.) Nationalist rebels, the eventual victors in the war. But, as the Civil War ended and World War II began in September 1939, Salazar's domestic plans had to be adjusted. As Salazar came to monopolize Lisbon's power and authority, indeed to embody the Dictatorship itself, during crises which threatened the future of the regime, he assumed ever more key cabinet posts. At various times between 1936 and 1944, he took over the Ministries of Foreign Affairs and of War (Defense), until the crises passed. At the end of the exhausting period of World War II, there were rumors that the former Professor would resign from government and return to Coimbra University, but Salazar continued as the increasingly isolated, dominating, "recluse of São Bento," that part of the parliament's buildings with the Prime Minister's offices and residence.

Salazar dominated the Dictatorship's Government in several ways: in day-to-day governance, although this diminished as the Dictator delegated wider powers to others after 1944, and in long-range policy decisions as well as in the spirit and image of the system. A lifelong bachelor who had once stated that he could not leave for Lisbon and not continue to care for his aged mother, Salazar never married, but lived with a beloved housekeeper from his Coimbra years and adopted two daughters. During his 36-year tenure as Premier, Salazar engineered the important cabinet reshuffles which reflect the history of the Dictatorship and of Portugal.

A number of times, in connection with significant events, the Dictator decided on important cabinet officer changes: April 11, 1933 (the adoption of the *Estado Novo*'s new 1933 Constitution); January 18, 1936 (the approach of civil war in Spain and the growing threat of international intervention in Iberian affairs during the unstable Second Spanish Republic of 1931–1936); September 4, 1944 (the Allied invasion of Europe at Normandy and the increasing likelihood of a Fascist defeat by the Allies, which included the Soviet Union); August 14, 1958 (increased domestic dissent and opposition following the May-June 1958 Presidential elections in which oppositionist and former regime stalwart-loyalist General Humberto Delgado garnered at least 25% of the national vote, but lost to regime candidate, Admiral Tomás); April 13, 1961 (following the shock of anti-colonial African insurgency in Portugal's colony of Angola in January–February 1961, the oppositionist hijacking of a Portuguese ocean liner off South America and an abortive military coup which failed to oust Salazar from office); August 19, 1968 (the aging of key leaders in the government, including now gravely ill Salazar, and the defection of key younger followers).

In response to the 1961 crisis in Africa and to threats to Portuguese India from the Indian Union, Salazar assumed the post of Minister of Defense (April 1961–December 1962). The failing leader, whose true state of health was kept from the public for as long as possible, appointed a group of younger cabinet officers in the 1960s, but no likely successors were groomed to take the Premier's place. Two of the older generation, Teotónio Pereira, who was in bad health, and Marcello Caetano (qq.v.), who preferred to remain at University of Lisbon or in private law practice, remained in the political wilderness.

As the colonial wars in three African territories grew more costly, Salazar became more isolated from reality. On August 3, 1968, while resting at his summer residence, the Fortress of São João do Estoril outside Lisbon, a deck chair collapsed beneath the Dictator and his head struck the hard floor. Some weeks later, as a result, Salazar was incapacitated by a stroke and cerebral hemorrhage, was hospitalized and became an invalid. While hesitating to fill the power vacuum that had unexpectedly appeared, President Americo Tomás (q.v.) finally replaced Salazar as Premier on September 27, 1968, with his former protégé and colleague, Marcello Caetano. Salazar was not informed that he no longer headed the Government, but he never recovered his health. On July 27, 1970, Salazar died in Lisbon and was buried at Santa Comba Dão, Vimieiro, his village and place of birth. See CHURCH, CATHOLIC; CORPORATIVISM; ESTADO NOVO; INTEGRALISM; SALAZARISM.

SALAZARISM. Supposedly the ideology or ideologies characteristic of the authoritarian system developed and directed by Premier

António de Oliveira Salazar (1889–1970) (q.v.), who governed Portugal as Premier from 1932 to 1968, and his ruling group of associates and colleagues. Scholars debate why this regime endured so long and the extent to which it was or was not "Fascist." As to ideologies, Salazar's own education and beliefs were strongly influenced by his Catholic education for nine years in the Seminary at Viseu, by the decrees of Popes Leo X and Pius IX and by conservative, rural customs. Rather than one ideology, the former Coimbra University (q.v.) Economics Professor reflected various creeds including Portuguese nationalism, Integralism, Corporatist (q.v.) doctrines, various Catholic beliefs which were derived from Thomist teachings as well as the writings of the French ideologue Charles Maurras and his disciples. The spirit of Salazarism, if there is any truth to the notion of there being one typical ideology, is founded on a reaction against basic ideas from the French Revolution of individual liberty, fraternity and equality, against the revolutionary collectivist doctrines including Socialism and Communism, and against the excesses of politics and government during the ill-fated First Portuguese Republic (1910–1926). Salazar, nevertheless, was not only a man of thought but also a man of action. *See* CHURCH, CATHOLIC; CORPORATIVISM; INTEGRALISM; SALAZAR, ANTÓNIO DE OLIVEIRA.

SANTO ANTÓNIO DE PADUA (SAINT ANTHONY OF PADUA OR OF LISBON) (1195–1231). Franciscan saint, teacher and preacher, also known as Saint Anthony of Lisbon. Born in Lisbon (q.v.) and considered the Patron Saint of Portugal and of Lisbon, his feast day of June 13 is widely celebrated in the country. Santo António spent much of his life outside Portugal, teaching at Universities in Italy and France. He died at Padua and was canonized in 1232. He has been associated with many miracles and is known popularly as the "finder of lost articles," and appeared frequently in works of art as in popular crafts.

SÃO BENTO, PALACE OF AND SEAT OF GOVERNMENT. São Bento Palace in Estrela district of Lisbon in an earlier life was a convent (constructed 1598–1615). After 1834, Portugal's national legislature or *Cortes* was transferred to the old convent which thereafter was adapted and renovated. In common usage, the term "São Bento" refers to the seat of national government, much the way "Whitehall" in London or "Foggy Bottom" in Washington, D.C., describes the location of other national governments. In Portugal, though, São Bento houses not one but two branches of the national government: both the Legislative branch and part of the Executive. Since the foundation of the First Republic, then, São Bento has been the home of the Legislature and of the residence and office of the Prime Minister (or President of the Council of Ministers).

By the first decade of the 20th century, the legislative hall or chamber of São Bento was essentially the building of today. In a grand and imposing neo-classical style, the palace has housed all the legislative bodies whatever their names: in the Constitutional Monarchy, the House of Deputies and Peers; in the First Republic, the Senate and House of Deputies; in the *Estado Novo* (q.v.) Dictatorship, the National Assembly and Corporate Chamber; in Democratic (post-1974) Portugal, the Assembly of the Republic. While the building is largely pre-1910, the art and decorations are more recent. The halls, foyers, stairways and chambers are decorated with murals, frescoes and statuary, including the impressive oils of the 1920s in the murals by Columbano Bordalo Pinheiro which depict the pageant of Portugal's main legislators since 1821. Other art dates to the 1930s under the Dictatorship. Charmingly, the delegates' hall outside the main legislative chamber is known as the hall of "Lost Steps."

Behind the legislative halls, in another part of São Bento, lie the residence and offices of the Prime Minister, the official home of all heads of government beginning in the First Republic. Until the late 1980s, too, São Bento housed the country's main national archives, the National Archive of Torre do Tombo.

SÃO TOMÉ AND PRÍNCIPE. Comprising a former colony of Portugal, these two islands of volcanic origin are located in the Gulf of Guinea, West Africa. The Portuguese first found these tropical islands about 1471 and efforts to settle them began in 1486 on São Tomé and about 1500 on Príncipe Island. Portugal settled them with African slaves from the mainland. A significant portion of the Africans who were forced to work the coffee and cocoa plantations were from Angola and some were from the Cape Verde Islands (qq.v.). The early economy of the islands was dominated by sugar as plantations were established and were based on the systems pioneered earlier in Madeira (q.v.) and the Cape Verdes. In the 19th and 20th century, however, coffee and cocoa plantations were developed. The cocoa plantations which were owned largely by Portuguese from Portugal produced the raw material for chocolate and soon formed the principal wealth of this colony.

In the early 20th century, forced labor practices and other labor abuses on the Portuguese-owned plantations drew world attention through the famous writings of the British investigative reporter-writer, Henry W. Nevinson. Portugal's colonial rule there as well as in Angola and Mozambique (q.v.), whose excesses were now exposed in newspapers and books, also came under the scrutiny of leading humanitarian organizations in London and elsewhere. Though Portugal defended her colonial rule in this case, and made reform efforts, tragically extensive labor abuse in the islands persisted into the middle of the 20th century. The islands were not involved in a war of African insurgency. In 1975, Portugal granted independence to the archipelago, whose official language of government and instruction remains Portuguese.

SAUDADE. A feeling or sentiment said to be typically Portuguese which is a kind of nostalgia, yearning and melancholy longing. Though the word is almost untranslatable, one standard dictionary defined *saudade* as a sweet and soft remembrance of persons and things far away or long ago. A very common term in colloquial Portuguese, it expresses a sad feeling for an absent person or loved one. Philologists debate the word's precise origins. Some suggest that it derives from the Latin *Solitate,* while Aubrey Bell suggests that *saudade* derives from the Arabic word *saudawi,* or someone who is stricken with melancholy and a longing to be alone. *See* FADO.

SEBASTIANISM. Popular creed or belief, a Messianism, after the loss of King Sebastião in Morocco in 1578, that Portugal would be saved and made great again by a returning hero who would appear on a misty morning. Until the early 19th century,

various personalities who were imposters posed as a returning
Sebastian and sought to be recognized as conquering heroes.
Forms of Sebastianist belief have captured the imagination in
northeast Brazil (q.v.) as well. According to some historians,
Sebastianism was not limited to the 16th century or to
presumed royalty, but could find a popular following which
could attach to recent political figures in the 19th and 20th
centuries as well. There is a vast literature about Sebastianism
and its history. One of Portugal's most distinguished historians,
Dr. José Hermano Saraiva suggests that even today a Sebastianist feeling exists in a common tendency of persons who believe
that what one wants cannot happen, but at the same time hope
that it will happen and will happen independently of those
persons' efforts. Such a state of mind is related to the common
mood of Lisbon *fado* as well as to the notion of *saudade* (qq.v.).
See SEBASTIÃO, KING; FADO; SAUDADE.

SEBASTIÃO I, KING (1554–1578). The King of Portugal whose
disappearance and death in battle in Morocco in 1578 led to a
succession crisis and to Spain's (q.v.) annexation of Portugal in
1580 and the person after whom the cult and mythology of
"Sebastianism" (q.v.) is named. Sebastião succeeded to the
throne of Portugal at the tender age of three, upon the death of
his father King João III in 1557. With his great-uncle Cardinal
Henrique, he was the only other surviving legitimate male
member of the Aviz dynasty. The Spanish menace loomed on
Portugal's eastern horizons, as Phillip II of Spain gathered more
reasons to make good his own strong claims to the Portuguese
throne. A headstrong youth, Sebastião dreamed of glory in
battle against the Muslims and was certainly influenced by the
example of the feats of Phillip II's half-brother Don Juan of
Austria and the naval victory against the Turks at Lepanto in
1571. Sebastião's great project was a victory in Africa and he
ordered a major effort to raise a fleet and army to attack
Morocco. His forces landed at Tangier and Arzila and marched
to meet the Muslim armies. In early August 1578, at the battle
of Alcácer-Quivir (q.v.), Portugal's army was destroyed by
Muslim forces and the King himself was lost. Though he was
undoubtedly killed, his body was never found. The result of this
foolhardy enterprise changed the course of Portugal's history

and gave rise to the cult and myth that Sebastião survived and would return one foggy morning to make Portugal great once again. *See* SEBASTIANISM.

SINTRA, NATIONAL PALACE OF. Located off the main square in the town of Sintra, the National Palace is one of the country's oldest royal residences. Together with its rich mixture of architectural styles from different eras and cultures, the National Palace's long history of being the place where monarchs and councils made historic decisions makes the site today an especially appealing tourist point of interest. With its origins in a 14th century Gothic palace of the era of King Dinis (reign: 1279–1325) (q.v.), this monument was added on to and altered in the course of the 15th century. It was in this palace that King João I (q.v.) made the vital decision in 1415 to send an expedition to capture Ceuta in Morocco, the beginning of Portugal's overseas empire. The most important additions to the palace, however, came between 1505 and 1520 under King Manuel I and Manueline (qq.v.) style was added to the original Gothic. The two massive Gothic kitchen chimneys from an earlier era were incorporated and not changed. Into the Manueline style was blended a strong Moorish art element including decorative tiles or *azulejos* (q.v.) and an adapted interior Mosque which was converted into a Chapel. The National Palace contains the largest repository of the oldest *azulejos,* some dating to the 15th century, of any palace in Portugal. Among the unusual rooms must be counted the council room (with an ocean view), the Swan Room and the Magpie Room, with rare, painted ceilings. *See* SINTRA, TOWN OF.

SINTRA, TOWN OF. Located some 20 miles (48 kilometers) northwest of Lisbon, the charming town of Sintra possesses historic importance of an unusual type. The enduring beauty of Sintra's unique scenery, its micro-climate, its private and national palaces and houses and the views of other scenes from its mountain range comprise a special, diverse attraction to all who behold it. The town is dominated by the mountain range above it as well as the semi-tropical forests and plants surrounding it. While little of importance in politics occurred in this favorite summering place of royalty and nobility, of greater interest is the place itself and what did not happen here! After 1780, starting with the writings of the English Romantics Robert Southey and Lord Byron as well as the proto-Romantic writer and collector William Beckford, generations of English and other foreign writers and visitors placed Sintra and its surroundings on the map of Romantic places to visit and to cherish. Sintra has a special place in English travel literature. Perhaps the most famous single line is from Byron's long poem *Childe Harolde* where Sintra, in which Byron resided briefly, is depicted as a "Glorious Eden." Outside of Lisbon, there is no other place in the country that has been the subject of such an abundance of drawings, etchings, engravings, paintings and photographs as Sintra. In Portuguese 19th century literature, too, including the writings of Almeida Garrett and Eça de Queirós, Sintra is justly described and praised. *See* PENA, NATIONAL PALACE OF; SINTRA, NATIONAL PALACE OF.

SLAVERY AND SLAVE TRADE, PORTUGUESE. The Portuguese role in the Atlantic slave trade (ca. 1500–1850), next to Portugal's motives for empire and the nature of her colonial rule, remains one of the most controversial historical questions. The institution of slavery was conventional in Roman and Visigothic Portugal and the Church (q.v.) sanctioned slavery. The origins of an international traffic in enslaved African captives in the Atlantic are usually dated to after the year 1441, when the first black African slaves were brought to Portugal (Lagos) and sold, but there were activities a century earlier which indicated the beginnings. In the 1340s, under King Afonso IV, Portuguese had captured native islanders on voyages to the Canary Islands and later used them as slave labor in the sugar plantations of Madeira (q.v.). After 1500, and especially after the 1550s, when African slave-worked plantations became established in Brazil (q.v.) and other American colonies, the Atlantic slave trade became a vast international enterprise in which Portugal played a key role. But all the European maritime powers were involved in the slave trade from 1500 to 1800, including England, France (qq.v.) and Holland, those countries which eventually pressured Portugal to cease the slave trade in its empire.

No one knows the actual numbers of Africans enslaved in the nefarious business, but it is clear that millions of persons during more than three-and-a-half centuries were forcibly stolen from African societies and that the survivors of the terrible slave voyages helped build the economies of the Americas. Portugal's role in the trade was as controversial as the impact on Portuguese society. Comparatively large numbers of African slaves resided in Portugal, though the precise number remains a mystery, but by the last quarter of the 18th century when Dictator Pombal (q.v.) abolished slavery in Portugal the African racial element had been largely absorbed in Portuguese society. Great Portuguese fortunes were built on the African slave trade in Portugal, Brazil and Angola (q.v.), and the slave trade continued in the Portuguese empire until the 1850s and 1860s. The Angolan slave trade across the Atlantic was doomed after Brazil banned the import of slaves in 1850, under great pressure from Britain. As for slavery in Portugal's African empire, various forms of this institution, including forced labor, continued in Angola and Mozambique (q.v.) until the early 1960s. A curious vestige of the Portuguese role in the African slave trade over the centuries is found in the family name, found in Lisbon telephone books, of *Negreiro,* which means literally, "One who trades in (African) Negro slaves."

SOARES, MÁRIO ALBERTO NOBRE LOPES (1924–). Lawyer, staunch oppositionist to the Dictatorship, a founder of Portugal's Socialist Party, key leader of post-1974 Democratic Portugal and twice elected President of the Republic since 1985. Mário Soares was born on December 7, 1924, in Lisbon, the son of an educator and former cabinet officer of the ill-fated First Republic. An outstanding student, Soares received a degree in History and Philosophy from the University of Lisbon (1951) and his Law degree from the same institution (1957). A teacher and a lawyer, the young Soares soon became active in various organizations which opposed the Dictatorship starting in his student days and continuing into his association with the Socialist Party. He worked with the organizations of several oppositionist candidates for the Presidency of the Republic in 1949 and 1958 and as a lawyer defended a number of political figures against government prosecution in court. Soares was the family attorney for the family of General Delgado, murdered on the Spanish frontier by the regime's political police in 1965. Soares was signatory and editor of the "Program for the Democratization of the Republic" in 1961 and, in 1968, he was deported by the regime to São Tomé (q.v.), one of Portugal's African colonies.

In 1969, following the brief liberalization under new Premier Caetano (q.v.), Soares returned from exile in Africa and participated as a member of the opposition in general elections for the National Assembly. Though harassed by the political police, he was courageous in attacking Portugal's Dictatorship and its colonial policies in Africa. After the rigged election results were known, and no oppositionist deputy won a seat despite the Caetano "opening," Soares left for exile in France (q.v.). From 1969 to 1974, he resided in France, consulted with other political exiles and taught at a university. In 1973, at a meeting in West Germany, Soares participated in the (re)founding of the (Portuguese) Socialist Party.

The exciting, unexpected news of the April 25, 1974 Revolution (q.v.) reached Soares in France and soon he was aboard a train bound for Lisbon, where he was to play a major role in the difficult period of Revolutionary politics (1974–1975). During a most critical phase, the "hot summer" of 1975, when a civil war seemed in the offing, Soares' efforts to steer Portugal away from a Communist dictatorship and sustained civil strife were courageous and effective. He found allies in the moderate military and large sectors of the people. After the November 25, 1975 abortive Leftist coup, Soares played an equally vital role in assisting the stabilization of a pluralist democracy. Premier on several occasions during the era of post-Revolutionary adjustment (1976–1985), Soares continued his role as the respected leader of the Socialist Party. Following eleven hectic years of the Lusitanian political hurly-burly, Soares was eager for a change and some rest. Prepared to give up leadership of the factious Socialist Party and become a senior statesman in the new Portugal, Mário Soares ran for the Presidency of the Republic. Since 1985, he has been elected President of the Republic twice, both times with impressive majorities. *See* POLITICAL PARTIES.

SPAIN. Portugal's independence as a nation and sovereignty as a free people are based on being separate from Spain. Portugal's independence in a Peninsula where its only landward neighbor, Spain, is stronger, richer, larger and more populous, raises interesting historical questions. After centuries of war between Castile (and later unified Spain) and Portugal, how did Portugal maintain its sometimes precarious freedom? If the Basques, Catalans and Galicians succumbed to Castilian military and political dominance and were incorporated into greater Spain, how did little Portugal manage to survive the "Spanish menace?" Short answers to such questions are that a combination of factors enabled Portugal to keep free of Spain, despite the era of "Babylonian Captivity" (1580–1640). These include an intense Portuguese national spirit, foreign assistance in staving off Spanish invasions and attacks between the late 14th century and the mid-19th century, principally from the Anglo-Portuguese Alliance (q.v.) and some assistance from France (q.v.), historical circumstances regarding Spain's own tribulations and its decline in power after 1600, etc.

In Portugal's long history, Castile and Leon (later "Spain," as unified in the 16th century) acted as a kind of Iberian mother and step-mother (or father and step-father) and was present at Portugal's birth as well as at times when Portuguese independence was either in danger or lost. Portugal's birth as a separate state in the 12th century was in part a consequence of the King of Castile's granting the "County of Portucale" to a transplanted Burgundian Count in the late 11th century. For centuries Castile, Leon, Aragon and Portugal struggled for supremacy in the Peninsula, until the Castilian army met defeat in 1385 at Aljubarrota (q.v.) when Portugal's freedom was assured for nearly two centuries. Portugal and her overseas empire (q.v.) suffered considerably under rule by Phillipine Spain (1580–1640). Triumphant in the War of Restoration (q.v.) against Spain (1640–1668), Portugal came to depend on her foreign alliances to provide a counter-weight to a still menacing kindred neighbor. Under the Anglo-Portuguese Alliance, England (q.v.) (later Britain) managed to help Portugal thwart more than a few Spanish invasion threats in the next centuries. Rumors and plots of Spain consuming Portugal continued during the 19th century and even during the First Portuguese Republic's early years to 1914.

Following difficult diplomatic relations during Spain's subsequent Second Republic (1931–1936) and Civil War (1936–1939), Luso-Spanish relations improved significantly under the Dictatorships which ruled both states until the mid-1970s. Salazar's and Franco's (q.v.) authoritarian regimes signed non-aggression and other treaties, lent each other mutual support and periodically consulted one another on vital questions. During this era (1939–1974), there were relatively little trade, business and cultural relations between the two neighbors who mainly tended to ignore one another. Spain's economy developed more rapidly than Portugal's after 1950 and General Franco was quick to support the *Estado Novo* (q.v.) across the frontier if he perceived a threat to his fellow dictator's regime. In January 1962, for instance, Spanish army units approached the Portuguese frontier in case the abortive military coup at Beja (where a Portuguese oppositionist plot failed) threatened the Portuguese dictatorship.

Since Portugal's 1974–1975 Revolution and the death of General Franco and the establishment of democracy in Spain (1975–1978), Luso-Spanish relations have improved significantly. Portugal has experienced a great deal of Spanish investment, tourism, and other economic activities, since both Spain and Portugal became members of the European Community (q.v.) in 1986. Portugal remains determined not to be confused with Spain and whatever threat from across the frontier exists comes more from Spanish investment than from Spanish winds, marriages and armies. The fact remains that Luso-Spanish relations are more open and mutually beneficial than perhaps at any other time in history. *See* FRANCO, FRANCISCO.

SPÍNOLA, ANTÓNIO DE (1910–). Senior Army General, hero of Portugal's wars of African insurgency and first President of the Provisional Government after the coup of April 25, 1974. A career Army officer who became involved in politics after a long career of war service and administration overseas, Spínola's role in the 1974 coup and Revolution (q.v.) was somewhat analogous to that of General Gomes da Costa (q.v.) in the 1926 coup.

Spínola served in important posts as a volunteer in Portugal's intervention in the Spanish Civil War (1936–1939), a military observer on the Russian front with Third Reich armed forces in World War II and a top officer in the Republican National Guard. His chief significance in contemporary affairs, however, came following his military assignments and tours of duty in Portugal's colonial wars in Africa after 1961.

Spínola fought first in Angola, and later in Guinea (qq.v.), where during 1968–1973 he was both Commanding General of Portugal's forces and High Commissioner (administrator of the territory). His Guinean service tour was significant for at least two reasons: Spínola's dynamic influence upon a circle of younger career officers on his staff in Guinea, men who later conspired and planned the 1974 coup of the Armed Forces Movement (q.v.); and Spínola's experience of failure in winning the Guinea war militarily or finding a political means for compromise or negotiation with the Party for the Independence of Guinea and Cape Verde (PAIGC), the African insurgent movement that had fought a war with Portugal since 1963, largely in the forested tropical interior of the territory. Spínola became discouraged after failure to win permission to negotiate secretly for a political solution to the war with the PAIGC and was reprimanded by Prime Minister Caetano (q.v.).

After his return—not in triumph—from Guinea in 1973, Spínola was appointed Chief of Staff of the Armed Forces, but he resigned in a dispute with Lisbon. With the assistance of younger officers who also had African experience of costly but seemingly endless war, Spínola wrote a book *Portugal and The Future,* which was published in February 1974 despite official censorship and red tape. Next to the bible and editions of Camões' *The Lusiads,* Spínola's controversial book was briefly the bestselling work in Portugal's modern age. While not intimately involved with the budding conspiracy among career Army majors, captains and others, Spínola was prepared to head such a movement and the planners depended on his famous name and position as senior Army officer with the right credentials to win over both military and civil opinion when and where it counted. When the April 25, 1974 coup succeeded, Spínola was named head of the Junta of National Salvation and eventually Provisional President of Portugal. Among the military revolutionaries, though, there was wide disagreement about the precise goals of the Revolution and how to achieve them. Spínola's pathbreaking book, which when a surprised Marcello Caetano read it knew a revolution was "inevitable," had subtly proposed three new goals: the democratization of authoritarian Portugal; a political solution to the colonial African wars; and liberalization of the economic system. The officers' Armed Forces Movement (MFA) immediately proclaimed not coincidentally the same goals, but without specifying the means to attain them.

The officers who ran the newly emerging system fell out with Spínola over many goals, but especially over how to decolonize Portugal's besieged empire. Spínola proposed a gradualist policy which featured a free referendum or vote by all colonial voters to decide between a loose federation with Portugal or complete independence. MFA leaders wanted more or less immediate decolonization, a transfer of power to leading African movements and a pullout of Portugal's nearly 200,000 troops in three colonies. After a series of crises and arguments, Spínola resigned as President in September 1974. He conspired for a Conservative coup to oust the Leftists in power but the effort failed in March 1975 and Spínola was forced to flee to Spain and then to Brazil (qq.v.). Some years later, he returned to Portugal, lived in quiet retirement and could be seen enjoying horseback riding. In the early 1980s, he was promoted to the rank of Marshal, in retirement. *See* ARMED FORCES MOVEMENT; EMPIRE, PORTUGUESE OVERSEAS.

- T -

TAGUS, RIVER. The Tagus (*Rio Tejo* in Portugal, *Rio Tajo* in Spain) is the longest river in the Iberian Peninsula. It rises in east-central Spain, east of Madrid, and flows west across Spain to the Portuguese border, for about 25 miles (60 kilometers) forming a section of the Luso-Spanish border, then turns southwest and enters the Atlantic at Lisbon (q.v.). The Tagus Estuary is an important harbor resource. About 10 miles (24 kilometers) above Lisbon (q.v.), the Tagus burgeons into a 7 mile (16 kilometer) wide lagoon which narrows at

Lisbon to a channel of some 2 miles (5 kilometers) wide and 8 miles (18 kilometers) long, blocked in part by a sand bar. The Tagus is navigable as far as the town of Abrantes, roughly 100 miles (240 kilometers) up. In tradition and history, this river acts as a kind of dividing line between north and south Portugal, each with different regions and features. *See* LISBON.

TENTH OF JUNE. An official Portuguese national holiday which is called "Camões Day" or "Portugal Day" in official literature. It commemorates the death on June 10, 1578, of Portugal's national epic poet, Luís de Camões (q.v.), after the Moroccan disaster of the loss of Portugal's King Sebastian (q.v.) and his army to Muslim forces in North Africa. The Tenth of June has become the principal national independence day of Portugal, a time when Portuguese in Portugal and in overseas Portuguese communities from New Bedford, Massachusetts, to Macau, China, to Caracas, Venezuela, celebrate national independence and history. A day also when traditionally various honors and awards for the year are conveyed by the national leaders in ceremonies and when citizens in parades mark the principal national independence day. *See* CAMÕES, LUÍS DE.

TIMOR, EAST. Colony of Portugal since the 16th century, with an area of 18,989 square miles (40,000 square kilometers), which is located on the eastern portion of the island of Timor in the Indonesian archipelago. Since 1975, it is a possession of the Republic of Indonesia, though its legal status as a colony of Portugal is debated in international circles.

In the 16th century the Portuguese established trading posts on the island, but for centuries few Portuguese settled there and the "colony" remained isolated and neglected. After the Dutch won control of Indonesia, there was a territorial dispute with Portugal as to who "owned" what on the island of Timor. In 1859, this question was decided as the Dutch and Portuguese governments formally divided the island into a Dutch portion (west) and the Portuguese colony (east) and established the frontier. From the late 19th century to World War I, Portugal consolidated her control of East Timor by means of military campaigns against the Timorese tribes. While there were a few missionaries and merchants from Portugal, besides the colonial officials, few Portuguese ever settled there.

East Timor's geographic location close to the north coast of Australia and its sharing of one island in the Dutch colony catapulted East Timor into world affairs early in World War II. To forestall a Japanese invasion of Timor, a joint Dutch-Australian expedition landed on December 17, 1941; the Portuguese authorities neither resisted nor cooperated. In February 1942, when Japanese troops landed in Timor, the small allied force fled to the hills and later was evacuated to Australia. Japan occupied all of Timor and the remainder of the Dutch East Indies until their surrender in September 1945. Portugal soon reassumed control.

After the April 25, 1974 coup in Lisbon, East Timorese nationalist parties hoped for rapid decolonization and independence with Lisbon's cooperation. But, on November 28, 1975, before a preoccupied Portugal could work out a formal transfer of power, the Revolutionary Front for Independent East Timor (FRETILIN), then in control of the former colony's capital, declared independence, and, on December 7, 1975, Indonesian armed forces swiftly invaded, occupied and annexed East Timor. In the following years, a tragic loss of life occurred. Portugal has refused to recognize Indonesia's sovereignty over East Timor and still claims legal sovereignty before the United Nations. As Indonesia has persistently and brutally suppressed Timorese nationalist resistance, world media attention has focused on this still remote island. In the United Nations, the tragic East Timor question remains a hotly debated issue. *See* EMPIRE, PORTUGUESE.

TOMÁS, ADMIRAL AMÉRICO DE DEUS RODRIGUES (1894–1987). Tomás was the last President of the Republic of the *Estado Novo* (q.v.) Dictatorship (1958–1974). While he was selected by Salazar (q.v.) for his exceptional qualities of loyalty to the system's principles and to the Dictator, the last period of the regime, a time of crisis, tested those very characteristics. In the crisis of September 1968, when Salazar was suddenly incapacitated, Tomás selected Salazar's successor, Dr. Marcello Caetano (q.v.). Later, when Caetano faltered and wished to resign his besieged office, it was Tomás' intransigence which worked to make Caetano go on.

A career Naval officer who graduated from the Naval School in 1916, Tomás rose steadily through Naval ranks to top positions, including Minister of the Navy. Salazar chose him to be the regime's Presidential candidate in the controversial 1958 elections because he considered Tomás to be the most reliable, honest and hardworking of the regime's military officers of the day. Twice Tomás was re-elected in the managed Presidential elections of 1965 and 1972, as pressures on the regime mounted. After the April 25, 1974 military coup by the Armed Forces Movement (qq.v.), Tomás, along with Caetano, his now reluctant Premier, was sent into exile on Madeira Island and later to Brazil (qq.v.). Despite demands from Leftist forces for the arrest and prosecution of Tomás, the new Lisbon government never initiated a legal case against him. Tomás was allowed to return from his Brazilian exile in July 1978 and to settle in Cascais, outside Lisbon. In 1980, he was granted a State pension, but, despite numerous requests, he was not restored to his rank and membership in the Navy. He died peacefully at home at age 92, outliving by 11 years even the Dictator Salazar.

TORDESILLAS, TREATY OF (June 7, 1494). Following the voyage to the West Indies by Columbus in Spain's (q.v.) service, a treaty between Spain and Portugal which, in effect, divided the known world between the two Iberian states. A line of demarcation was set 370 leagues west of the Cape Verde Islands (q.v.) which gave Portugal claim to Brazil (q.v.) yet to be discovered. Lands found by either country in the bounds of the other had to be surrendered. Portugal's lands were to the east of the line, Spain's to the west. A commission of representatives of the states' pilots, mariners and astrologers would establish the line. This commission was assigned the task of sailing two caravels to the west within ten months until they found land or had established the line. Bickering over the issue of how to determine the line of the Treaty of Tordesillas continued until at least 1777.

TORRES VEDRAS, BATTLE OF (October 9–November 14, 1810). A hilly area near the village of Torres Vedras, north of Lisbon and site of the place where prepared positions of the Portuguese and English forces of the Duke of Wellington (q.v.) withstood repeated French attacks under Masséna. Blocking the way to Lisbon, Wellington's defensive preparations were successful as were the factors of English and Portuguese liaison and a fighting spirit. After his failure before the Lines of Torres Vedras, due to the English and Portuguese fortified works, Masséna hesitated and sent to Napoleon for instructions. The French commander, however, was greatly weakened due to food shortages and to the fact that the supply lines with Spain (q.v.) were now cut. Therefore, before Napoleon could answer his messages, Masséna was forced to begin his withdrawal to Spain. Masséna withdrew from Portugal in April 1811 and, with the abandonment of a French garrison at Almeida on the frontier, France's (q.v.) occupation of Portugal was at an end. The remainder of the Peninsular Wars then moved to Spain.

TWENTY-FIFTH OF APRIL. Since 1974, an official national holiday in Portugal. In the early morning hours of April 25, 1974, the Armed Forces Movement (MFA) began its military operations against the Dictatorship in the Lisbon area. Signals for action included the playing of two songs on a popular radio station's (*Rádio Renascença*) midnight program broadcast. The songs were *"Depois do Adeus"* and *"Grândola, Vila Morena."* The latter song, sung on the record made by composer-singer José Afonso, had been banned by government censorship and was usually played only clandestinely. The military coup process proceeded during the period from midnight to about 4:30 p.m. on the afternoon of April 25th, a rainy day, and met relatively little resistance from the Dictatorship's few remaining staunch defenders. Most of the drama was played out in the streets of Lisbon as MFA tanks, armored cars and troops took positions and demanded the surrender of neutral or loyal forces. After Premier Caetano (q.v.) had taken refuge in the Republican National Guard's (GNR) Carmo barracks, traditionally a place of sanctuary for government incumbents in previous military coup attempts, Caetano surrendered to the insurgent military forces. He was later flown to exile in Madeira, with President Tómas, and then to Brazil (qq.v.). This date marks the end of the *Estado Novo* (q.v.) and the beginning of Democratic Portugal. *See* ARMED FORCES MOVEMENT.

TWENTY-EIGHTH OF MAY. During the Dictatorship (1926–1974), May 28th was an important national holiday celebrated by the regime as marking the day of the 1926 military coup led by General Gomes da Costa (q.v.) which overthrew the first parliamentary Republic. During that 48-year period, the regime employed this celebration as means to impress the citizenry with its armed strength and support, to show solidarity among regime stalwarts and to unify regime ranks. Traditionally, the regime organized a military parade in Lisbon (q.v.) on the major Avenida de Liberdade from Praça Pombal to Praça Rossio. In regime propaganda, the 28th of May symbolized the beginning of the so-called "National Revolution" of the Conservative, nationalist, Corporatist authoritarian system led by Premier Salazar and later by Premier Caetano (qq.v.) until it was overthrown in 1974. *See* ESTADO NOVO.

- U -

ULTIMATUM, THE ENGLISH. A painful and, for Portugal, embarrassing, diplomatic incident with England (q.v.) during the "Scramble for Africa." On January 11, 1890, England presented the Lisbon government with an ultimatum which stated that unless Portugal withdrew her armed forces from what is today a section of Malawi in central-east Africa England would consider breaking the ancient Anglo-Portuguese Alliance (q.v.) and dispatching naval units to Mozambique (q.v.) and possibly to Portugal itself. The center of the conflict was disputed claims over an area to the west of northern Mozambique, a region in which England claimed to have special interests. Portugal requested international arbitration of the dispute, but England refused and presented the ultimatum. At the time, Portugal had an armed force in the disputed sector and was claiming sovereignty.

The English Ultimatum led to the fall of the Lisbon government of the day, which submitted to the ultimatum and withdrew Portugal's forces, and to unprecedented public agitation over the question. The Anglo-Portuguese Alliance came under great strain, though it was mended and renewed with the 1899 Treaty of Windsor (q.v.). The Monarchy was badly damaged by the national humiliation, and the Republican Party gained supporters. There is a vast literature on this incident. Portugal's current national anthem was inspired by it. *See* PORTUGUESA, A; ANGLO-PORTUGUESE ALLIANCE.

UNIÃO NACIONAL. The officially-sanctioned political movement of regime loyalists during the *Estado Novo* (q.v.) Dictatorship. Founded in 1930, the "National Union," whose name may have been modeled in part on the "Patriotic Union" of Spain's Primo de Rivera Dictatorship (1923–1930), was not a mass political party, but a movement whose purpose was to support the policies and aims as well as the control of the Dictatorship. The strategy of the founders was that an organization like the *União Nacional* would unite diverse groups in one movement, including warring Monarchists and Republicans, and would replace a political party system. After 1935, when all political parties and other associations such as the Masons were banned by the government, the National Union was the only legal political "movement." In all future "elections" under the Dictatorship this organization sponsored all regime candidates. Only beginning with the 1942 municipal elections, under severe restrictions, were opposition candidates allowed to run against the National Union slates. Membership in the *União Nacional* for a long period was virtually compulsory for most Government employees. *See* ESTADO NOVO.

UNITED STATES OF AMERICA (USA). Portugal and the United States established full and formal diplomatic relations in 1791 and the first commercial treaty between them was signed in 1840. The two very different countries have been linked by geography and by Portuguese immigration to the United States. Both share the status of being Atlantic powers. Significant Portuguese immigration to the eastern seaboard, especially to coastal New England, began in the first half of the 19th century but the numbers of Lusitanian immigrants reached their peak only after 1910. While there was relatively little trade between the two countries until after 1880, Portugal's diplomats briefly toyed with the notion of using the United States as a counterweight ally to her oldest ally, England (q.v.), especially during the era of bitter territorial and trade disputes between England and Portugal over tropical Africa after 1850.

It was during the 20th century, however, that Luso-American diplomatic relations assumed a new importance and again the Atlantic connection played a key role. On two occasions during World Wars, in 1917–1918 and 1944–1945, the United States armed forces used the Azores Islands (q.v.) for air and naval bases. In 1951, Portugal and the USA signed the first major Azores base agreements, at first as part of America's Cold War defense strategy needs, and the Azores Base question has assumed an essential role in the diplomatic relationship between the two countries. American trade and investment in Portugal increased significantly since the 1940s and, by 1980, the United States had become one of Portugal's main trade partners. By the 1990s, this relationship experienced some changes, as Portugal's membership in the European Community (EC) (q.v.) strengthened the trade positions of EC members such as Britain, Germany, France and Spain (qq.v.). Luso-American cultural relations, including the increasing diffusion of the knowledge of English in Portugal, became closer. Among the factors responsible for this were the presence of a larger American community in Portugal, American investment, the Fulbright exchange program, and American language schools whose activity suggested that English taught in British language schools in Portugal no longer held a clear monopoly. *See* AZORES ISLANDS; INTRODUCTION, POPULATION AND EMIGRATION.

- V -

VICENTE, GIL (ca. 1465–ca. 1537). Sixteenth century Portuguese playwright, perhaps the nation's greatest, who was also a talented goldsmith, musician, actor and dramatist. Born in humble circumstances, Gil Vicente rose to become an important figure who was recognized and celebrated in the royal court of his day. His first play or *auto* was performed in 1502 and his last piece was produced in 1536. Vicente's work was influenced not only by the religious plays of late medieval Portugal, but by work from contemporary Humanism and the Renaissance.

There were at least four basic aspects of Vicentine plays: dramatization of rural folklore; social satire; imaginative analysis of nature; and religious themes. What was remarkable about Vicente, besides his great versatility (he was the goldsmith who produced the gold monstrance of Belém in Jerónimos Monastery) and brilliance, was that he was popular with both the people and the elite and was a masterful dramatist in a country which has lacked extraordinary dramatic traditions. Some of his plays were censored by the Inquisition (q.v.) after his death, and it was only during the 19th century Romantic era that Portuguese writers sought a revival of his reputation.

VIEIRA, FATHER ANTÓNIO DE (1608–1697). One of the most talented and influential individuals and one of the greatest speakers and prose writers of early modern Portugal, Vieira was a Jesuit preacher, writer, missionary, advisor to Kings and diplomatic negotiator. At age eight he went to Brazil (q.v.) and was educated there in a Jesuit College. Like Francisco Manuel de Melo (q.v.), his Jesuit-educated contemporary, Vieira participated in the great crises and conflicts of his day including the ongoing war between the Inquisition and Portugal's New Christians (qq.v.), the loss and partial recovery of parts of Portugal's still extensive overseas empire, the rise to the Portuguese throne of the Braganza dynasty, the restoration of Portugal's independence from Spain (q.v.) in 1640 and the subsequent struggle to retain that independence under adverse circumstances.

One of Father Vieira's major efforts was his campaign to have the Portuguese Inquisition relax its policy of confiscation of New Christian capital and property and to convince converted Jews in Portugal and Portuguese Jews in exile to provide capital in Portugal's efforts to reinforce its defenses against many threatened Spanish invasions during 1640–1668, when Spain finally officially recognized Portugal's independence in a treaty. Such monies were also employed in defending Portugal's empire (q.v.) and helping to drive out enemies who had occupied portions of Portugal's dominions abroad.

Father Vieira spent an important part of his career in Brazil as a Jesuit missionary and administrator and was famous for defending the freedom and rights of Amerindians against settlers. A great sermonizer who possessed a strong Messianic belief and grounding in the prophecies of the Old Testament, Vieira became an influential advisor to the Portuguese Kings as well as a diplomat assigned important tasks abroad. Vieira preached sermons in which he proclaimed that the awaited Messiah who would restore Portugal to world power status in the future was not King Sebastião (q.v.), who died in 1578 in battle against the Muslims in Morocco, but his King João (q.v.) of Braganza, an assertion which lost some credibility following the King's death in 1656.

Among Father Vieira's prolific writings, his most noted are his collected *Sermons* in 15 volumes, *Letters,* his *História do Futuro* and his famous defense against accusations when on trial before the Portuguese Inquisition, the *Defesa perante o Tribunal do Santo Ofício.*

VIRIATUS. Ancient Lusitanian hero who led Lusitanian resistance against Roman rule in Lusitania from ca. 154–135 BC. In Roman-ruled Hispania or Iberia, Lusitania (q.v.) was one of the westernmost provinces. Viriatus was a hunter and shepherd who lived in the mountainous areas of Lusitania between the Tagus and Douro (qq.v.) rivers. A ferocious fighter and fearless leader, Viriatus successfully held off Roman occupation and defeated Roman forces for years. Betrayed by friends who sold out to the Romans, Viriatus was murdered while he slept. In Portuguese tradition, Viriatus became a mythical figure who was a symbol of Portuguese resistance to foreign threats. Under the Dictatorship, his name and example were invoked to promote loyalty to the government and national independence. "The Legion of Viriatus" was the name the regime gave to its corps of so-called volunteer soldiers who fought for Franco's (q.v.) Nationalists in the Spanish Civil War (1936–1939).

- W -

WAR OF RESTORATION (1641–1668). After the Revolution of December 1, 1640, when King João IV (q.v.) of Braganza overthrew Spanish rule and declared Portugal independent, Portugal and Spain fought a war which decided the fate of little

Portugal. The War of Restoration was fought by Spanish armies and by Portuguese armies, assisted by foreign mercenaries and by the oldest ally, England (q.v.). Portugal's 1640 Revolution and the war against Spain to maintain her reclaimed independence were supported as well by France (q.v.) during the era 1640–1659. After 1659, France gave no more assistance to Lisbon and cut diplomatic relations. Portugal's great friend during this War, which was fought largely near the Luso-Spanish frontier or in Portugal in the flat Alentejo province, with no natural barriers to Spanish invasion, was ally England. This crucial alliance was re-established in the Anglo-Portuguese treaties of 1642, 1654 and 1661. Various truce and peace treaties, too, were signed with Holland, which was willing to side with Portugal, or at least be neutral, against Spain. Catalonia's prolonged rebellion against Spanish (Castilian) rule during Portugal's struggle played an important role in weakening Spain's effort to recover Portugal. At Ameixial, on June 8, 1663, a decisive battle in the War occurred and resulted in the defeat of the Spanish army and its withdrawal from Portugal. The Luso-Spanish Peace Treaty of 1668 (q.v.) concluded the War. See PEACE TREATY OF 1668.

"WAR OF THE BROTHERS" (1831–1834). Civil War in Portugal fought between the forces of Absolutist Monarchy and Constitutionalist Monarchy. Each side was headed and represented by a royal brother, King Miguel I, who usurped the throne of young Maria II, and King Pedro IV (qq.v.), formerly emperor Pedro I of Brazil, who abdicated to restore his daughter Maria to the throne her uncle Miguel had purloined. In the end, the forces of Pedro triumphed, those of Miguel lost and Miguel went into exile in Austria. See CARLOTA JOAQUINA, QUEEN; MARIA II, QUEEN; MIGUEL I, KING; PEDRO IV, KING.

WELLINGTON, DUKE OF (ARTHUR WELLESLEY) (1769–1852). The British general who helped liberate Portugal from French occupation under Napoleon's armies (1808–1811), turn back three French invasions and enable Portugal to reassert her independence as a nation-state. Born in Ireland, Arthur Wellesley became the most talented and honored soldier of several generations during the first half of the 19th century. He attended England's famed public school, Eton, and entered the British army and first served in the Low Countries in the 1790s and then in campaigns in British India and the 1807 Copenhagen expedition. When the British government decided to send an expedition to oppose Napoleon's occupation of Portugal, Wellesley was appointed commander of the force which landed at the mouth of the Mondego River on August 1, 1808. For the next three years, the famous Lieutenant General led Anglo-Portuguese forces against the three French invasions and by 1811 had defeated the French. Wellington's forces proceeded across the frontier into Spain (q.v.) where, for the next two years, the allied forces fought victoriously against the French. Wellington received a number of honors, titles and decorations from Portugal for his heroic efforts; after the final expulsion of French forces under Masséna, in 1810, Portugal's Government granted Wellington among other honors the title of Viscount of Vimieiro and the medal, the Grand Cross of the Tower and the Sword (*Torre e Espada*). See BUÇACO, BATTLE OF; TORRES VEDRAS, BATTLE OF.

WINDSOR, TREATIES OF. Various Anglo-Portuguese treaties bear the name of Windsor. Among others were the treaties of 1386 and 1899. Signed at Windsor, England (q.v.), on May 9, 1386, the former treaty confirmed the Alliance Treaty between England and Portugal of 1383 and committed both signatories to defend the other against all enemies and to participate in a "perpetual" league, friendship and confederation. The 1899 Treaty of Windsor (a misnomer since it was signed in London) followed the outbreak of the Anglo-Boer War in South Africa. Portugal pledged to allow the movement of British forces through its east-African colony of Mozambique (q.v.) to South Africa and to prevent arms reaching the Boers through the same colony. At the same time, there was a reaffirmation of the ancient Anglo-Portuguese Alliance (q.v.), as spelled out in articles of the 1642 and 1661 Anglo-Portuguese treaties; by this was signified a mutual defense treaty for both countries. Especially vital for Portugal, concerned about secret negotiations between Britain and Germany over the possible breakup of Portugal's African empire due to Portugal's bankruptcy, was the 1899 Treaty's reconfirmed pledge on Britain's part that Britain would defend Portugal as well as her overseas empire against all enemies "future and present." *See* ANGLO-PORTUGUESE ALLIANCE.

- X -

XAVIER, SAINT FRANCIS (1506–1551). Jesuit missionary and preacher in Asia, known as the "Apostle of the Indies" and the "Apostle of Japan," one of the most prominent and admired saints in the Catholic tradition. Born a Basque in Navarre, Spain, Xavier studied at the University of Paris and became one of the first Jesuits following his friendship and association with St. Ignatius Loyola. He became a Jesuit in Italy and, in 1541, was named by the Pope "Apostolic Nuncio to the East." After an arduous 13-month journey he reached Goa, Portuguese India (q.v.), which became the base for his personal preaching and conversion crusade in Asia. He spread the Gospel and converted thousands in India, Malaysia, Malacca, and Japan for a full decade of tireless effort. Prematurely, he died exhausted in China on the eve of an effort to preach in that kingdom. He was buried in Goa, India, in 1551 and his body remained in an incorrupt state for a long period and became an important Catholic shrine and center of devotion. In 1622, he was canonized by Pope Gregory XV and Pius XI declared him "Patron of all Foreign Missions" in our century. *See* CHURCH, CATHOLIC.

- Z -

ZÉ POVINHO. The Portuguese "everyman" or "common person," Zé Povinho (literally in Portuguese, "Joe Little People," Zé being a common abbreviation for "José" or "Joe") originated as a cartoon character created in 1875 by the artist Rafael Bordalo Pinheiro. "Zé Povinho" is a variation of "Zé-dos-anzois" ("Joe of the Fish-Hooks"), representing the ordinary Portuguese fisherman. The character was representative of the rural masses, the common people, and was intended to be in sharp contrast to the slick, sophisticated, spoiled urban Portuguese of Lisbon (q.v.).

Pinheiro's cartoon character's traits included peasant simplicity, candor, long-suffering patience and credulity. As Pinheiro drew Zé Povinho, he was a short, bearded, swarthy figure, his heavy features wreathed in smiles; he was dressed in a white open shirt, dark trousers and a hat. While the name, the idea and the appearance of this cartoon character were meant to depict the majority of Portuguese of Pinheiro's day—largely rural, peasant, illiterate masses—more than one hundred years later Zé Povinho still appears regularly in the print media and books both in Portugal and in Portuguese language newspapers among overseas Portuguese communities in the world. Joe Little People's appearance changes little and in some Portuguese language periodicals in the United States and Canada his critical function in political discussions remains, namely to indicate the weaknesses of the government of the day.

BIBLIOGRAPHY

INTRODUCTION

For a small country perched on the edge of Western Europe but with an early history which began more than 2,000 years ago, there is a vast bibliography extant in many languages. Since general reference works with bibliography on Portugal are few, I have listed both principal and some minor works while maintaining selectivity. While favoring works in English, I have also made an effort to include a variety of Portuguese language works which are counted as significant if not always classic.

It is appropriate that most of the works cited in some sections of the Bibliography are in English, but this pattern should be put in historical perspective. Since the late 1950s, the larger proportion of foreign language works on Portugal and the Portuguese have been in English. But this was not the case before World War II. As a whole, there were more studies in French, with a smaller number in German, Italian and Spanish, than in English. Most of the materials published today on all aspects of this topic continue to be in Portuguese, but English language works have come to outnumber the other non-Portuguese language studies. In addition to books useful to a variety of students, I have taken care to include a selection of classic works of use to the visitor, tourist and foreign resident of Portugal as well as to those interested in overseas Portuguese communities.

Readers will note that for the most part publishers' names are omitted from all Portuguese citations as well as from a number of French works. There are several reasons for this. First, in many of the older sources the publishers no longer exist and are difficult to trace. Second, the names of the publishers have been changed in some cases and are also difficult to trace. Third, in many older books and periodicals printers' names but not publishers were cited and identifying the publishers is virtually impossible.

The organization of the Bibliography is as follows:

1. Bibliographies
2. Periodicals Relating to Portugal
3. General References: Guides to Archives and Libraries
4. General References: Statistical
5. General References: Encyclopedias and Dictionaries
6. General References: Historical, Legal, Political, Country Studies
7. General References: Culture, Literature, Language
8. Travel and Tourist Guides on Portugal
9. History of Portugal
      Ancient and Medieval (2000 BC–1415 AD)
      Imperial and Early Modern (1415–1822)
      Constitutional Monarchy and Liberalism (1822–1910)
      Parliamentary, Republican Portugal (1910–1926)
      Authoritarian Portugal (1926–1974)
10. Physical Features: Geography, Geology, Fauna and Flora
11. Foreign Travelers and Residents' Accounts of Portugal
12. Portuguese Cartography, Discoveries, Navigation
13. Portugal and Her Overseas Empires (1415–1975)
14. Portuguese Migration and Communities Abroad
15. Portugal's Atlantic Islands (Azores, Madeiras)
16. Anglo-Portuguese Alliance (1373–present)
17. Anthropology, Sociology, Rural and Urban Society
18. Arts, Architecture, Urban Planning; Music
19. Portuguese Literature in English Translation
20. Portuguese and Portuguese-American Cooking; Cuisine
21. Gardens and Gardening of Portugal and Madeira
22. Education, Science, Health and Medical History
23. Portuguese Feminism and Women's Studies
24. Religion and Catholic Church
25. Agriculture, Viticulture and Fishing
26. Economy, Industry and Development
27. Government and Politics Since 1974
28. Contemporary Portugal Since 1974

1. BIBLIOGRAPHIES

Academia Portuguesa de História. *Guia Bibliográfica Histórica portuguesa,* vol. I–?. Lisbon, 1954–?

Bell, Aubrey F. G. *Portuguese Bibliography.* New York, 1922.

186 / Bibliography

Borchardt, Paul. *La Bibliographie de l'Angola, 1500–1900.* Brussels, 1912.

Duffie, Bailey W. "A Bibliography of the Principal Published Guides to Portuguese Archives and Libraries," *Proceedings of the International Colloquium on Luso-Brazilian Studies.* Nashville, 1953.

Gallagher, Tom. *Dictatorial Portugal, 1926–1974: A Bibliography.* Durham, NH: International Conference Group on Portugal, 1979.

Greenlee, William B. "A Descriptive Bibliography of the History of Portugal." *Hispanic American Historical Review,* XX (August 1940): 491–516.

Gulbenkian, Fundação Calouste. *Boletim Internacional de Bibliografia Luso-Brasileira,* vols, 1–15. Lisbon, 1960–1974.

Junta De Investigações Científicas Do Ultramar. *Bibliografia Da Junta De Investigações Científicas Do Ultramar Sobre Ciências Humanas E Sociais.* Lisbon: Junta de Investigações Científicas Do Ultramar, 1975.

Kettenring, Norman E. (comp.). *A Bibliography of Theses and Dissertations on Portuguese Topics Completed in the United States and Canada, 1861–1983.* Durham, NH: International Conference Group on Portugal, 1984.

Lomax, William. *Revolution In Portugal: 1974–1976. A Bibliography.* Durham, NH: International Conference Group on Portugal, 1978.

McCarthy, Joseph M. *Guinea-Bissau and Cape Verde Islands: A Comprehensive Bibliography.* New York: Garland, 1977.

Portuguese Studies Newsletter, Nos. 1–23 (1976–1990). Durham, NH: International Conference Group on Portugal.

Portuguese Studies Review, I, 1 (1991–). Durham, NH: International Conference Group on Portugal.

Rogers, Francis Millet and David T. Haberly. *Brazil, Portugal and*

Other Portuguese-Speaking Lands: A List of Books Primarily in English. Cambridge, MA: Harvard University Press, 1968.

Santos, Manuel dos. *Bibliografia geral ou descrição bibliográfica de livros tantos de autores portugueses como brasileiros e muitos outras nacionalidades, impressos desde o século XV até à actualidade.* 2 vols. Lisbon, 1914–25.

Silva, J. Donald. *A Bibliography on the Madeira Islands.* Durham, NH: International Conference Group on Portugal, 1987.

University of Coimbra, Faculty of Letters. *Bibliografia Anual de História de Portugal,* vol. 1– [sources published beginning in 1989–] Coimbra: Grupo de História; Faculdade de Letras; Universidade de Coimbra, 1992– .

Unwin, P. T. H. (comp.). *Portugal,* vol. 71, World Bibliographical Series. Oxford, UK and Santa Barbara, CA: Clio Press, 1987.

Viera, David J., et al. (comp.). *The Portuguese in the United States (Supplement to the 1976 Leo Pap Bibliography).* Durham, NH: International Conference Group on Portugal, 1990.

Welsh, Doris Varner (comp.). *A Catalogue of the William B. Greenlee Collection of Portuguese History and Literature and the Portuguese Materials in the Newberry Library.* Chicago, IL: Newberry Library, 1953.

2. PERIODICALS RELATING TO PORTUGAL

Africa Report. New York. Monthly or Bi-monthly.

Africa Today. Denver, CO. Quarterly.

American Historical Review. Washington, D.C. Quarterly.

Almanaque do Exército. Lisbon, 1912–1940.

Anais da Académia Portuguesa da História. Lisbon.

Anais Da Assembleia Nacional e Da Câmara Corporativa. Lisbon.

Análise Social. Lisbon. Quarterly.

Anglo-Portuguese News. Monte Estoril and Lisbon. Bi-weekly.

Anuário Católico de Portugal. Lisbon.

Architectural Digest. New York. Monthly.

Arquivo das Colónias. Lisbon. 1917–1933.

Arquivo Histórico Portuguez. Lisbon.

Avante! Lisbon. Portuguese Communist Party. Daily.

Boletim da Academia Internacional da Cultura Portuguesa. Lisbon.

Boletim da Agência Geral das Colónias. Lisbon.

Boletim de Estudos Operários. Lisbon.

Boletim do Instituto Histórico da Ilha Terceira. Angra do Heroismo, Terceira, Azores Islands. Semi-Annual.

Boletim da Sociedade de Geografia de Lisboa. Lisbon Quarterly; Bi-monthly.

Boletim Geral do Ultramar. Lisbon.

Bracara Augusta. Braga.

British Historical Society of Portugal. Annual Report and Review. Lisbon.

Brotéria. Lisbon. Quarterly.

Bulletin des Études Portugaises. Paris. Quarterly.

Bulletin de l'Institut Français au Portugal. Lisbon.

Cadernos do Noroeste. Braga, University of Minho. Semi-annual.

Camões Center Quarterly. New York.

Capital (A). Lisbon. Daily newspaper.

Colóquio/Artes. Lisbon. Gulbenkian Foundation. Quarterly.

Colóquio/Letras. Lisbon. Gulbenkian Foundation. Quarterly.

Conimbriga. Coimbra.

Cultura. London. Quarterly.

Dia (0). Lisbon. Daily newspaper.

Diário da Assembleia Nacional e Constituente. Lisbon. 1911.

Diário da Câmara de Deputados. Lisbon. 1911–1926.

Diário do Governo. Lisbon. 1910–1974.

Diário de Lisboa. Lisbon. Daily newspaper.

Diário de Notícias. Lisbon. Daily newspaper of record.

Diário do Senado. Lisbon. 1911–1926.

Economia. Lisbon. Quarterly.

Economia e Sociologia. Lisbon. Quarterly.

Economist (The). London. Weekly magazine.

Estudos Contemporâneos. Lisbon.

Expresso. Lisbon. Weekly newspaper.

Facts and Reports. Amsterdam. Collected press clippings.

Finisterra. Lisbon. Quarterly.

Flama. Lisbon. Monthly magazine.

Garcia de Orta. Lisbon. Quarterly.

Hispania. USA. Quarterly.

Hispanic American Historical Review. Chapel Hill, NC. Quarterly.

Iberian Studies. Nottingham, UK. Quarterly or Semi-annual.

Illustração Portugueza. Lisbon. 1911–1930s. Magazine.

Instituto (O). Coimbra. Annual.

Itinerário. Leiden (Netherlands). 1976– . Semi-annual.

Jornal (O). Lisbon. Weekly newspaper.

Jornal de Letras (O). Lisbon. Weekly culture supplement.

Journal of the American Portuguese Culture Society. New York. 1966–1981. Semi-annual or annual.

Journal of Modern History. Chicago, IL. Quarterly.

Ler História. Lisbon. Quarterly.

Lusitania Sacra. Lisbon. Quarterly.

Luso-Brazilian Review. Madison, WI. 1964– . Semi-annual.

Ordem do Exército. Lisbon. 1926–1974. Monthly.

Penélope. Lisbon. Semi-annual.

Portugal. Annuário Estatístico do Ultramar. Lisbon. 1950–1974.

Portugal em África. Lisbon. 1894–1910. Bi-monthly.

Portuguese & Colonial Bulletin. London. 1961–1974. Quarterly.

Portuguese Studies. London. 1985– . Annual.

Portuguese Studies Newsletter. Durham, NH, 1976–1990. Semi-annual.

Portuguese Studies Review. Durham, NH, 1991– . Semi-annual.

Primeiro do Janeiro. Oporto. Daily newspaper.

República (A). Lisbon. Daily newspaper.

Revista da Faculdade de Direito da Universidade de Lisboa. Lisbon. Quarterly.

Revista da Faculdade de Letras. Lisbon. Quarterly.

Revista de Guimarães. Guimarães. Semi-annual.

Revista da Universidade de Coimbra. Coimbra. Quarterly.

Revista Internacional de Estudos Africanos. Lisbon. Semi-annual.

Revista Lusitana. Lisbon. Quarterly.

Revista Militar. Lisbon. Quarterly.

Revista Portuguesa de História. Coimbra. Quarterly.

Sábado. Lisbon. Weekly news magazine.

Seara Nova. Lisbon. 1921– . Bi-monthly.

Século (O). Lisbon. Daily Newspaper.

Selecções do Readers Digest. Lisbon. Monthly.

Sociedade e Território. Revista de estudos urbanos e regionais. Oporto, 1986– . Quarterly.

Studia. Lisbon. Quarterly.

Studium Generale. Oporto. Quarterly.

Tempo (O). Lisbon. Daily newspaper.

Tempo e o Modo (O). Lisbon. 1968–1974. Quarterly.

Trabalhos da Sociedade Portuguesa de Antropologia. Oporto. Semi-annual.

Translation. New York. Quarterly.

Ultramar. Lisbon. 1960–1974. Quarterly.

Vida Mundial. Lisbon. Weekly news magazine.

3. GENERAL REFERENCES: GUIDES TO PORTUGUESE ARCHIVES AND LIBRARIES

Axelson, Eric. "Report on the Archives and Libraries of Portugal," in Axelson, Eric. *Portuguese in South-East Africa, 1488–1600.* Johannesburg, SA: C. Struik, 1973: 247–263.

Boxer, C. R. *The Portuguese Seaborne Empire 1415–1825.* London: Hutchinson, 1969: 392–413.

Brooks, George E. "Notes on Research Facilities in Lisbon and the Cape Verde Islands." *International Journal of African Historical Studies,* 6 (1973): 304–314.

Cardozo, Manoel. "Portugal [Archives and Libraries]," in Daniel H. Thomas and Lynn M. Case (eds.). *New Guide to the Diplomatic Archives of Western Europe.* Philadelphia: University of Pennsylvania Press, 1975: 256–274.

Chilcote, Ronald H. "Documenting Portuguese Africa." *Africana Newsletter* (Stanford, CA), I (Autumn 1963): 16–36.

Denuce, J. "Une visite aux archives de Lisbonne et de Seville." *Revue de l'Instruction Publique en Belgique,* 49 (1906): 94–100.

Diffie, Bailey W. "Bibliography of the Principal Guides to Portuguese Archives and Libraries." *Actas do Colóquio Internacional de Estudos Luso-Brasileiras de 1950 (Washington),* Nashville, TN: Vanderbilt University Press, 1953: 181–188.

Iria, Alberto. *Inventário geral dos códices do Arquivo Histórico Ultramarino.* Lisbon, 1966.

Jadin, L. "Recherches dans les Archives et Bibliothéques d'Italie et du Portugal sur l'Ancien Congo . . . " *Bulletin des Séances de l'Académie Royale des Sciences d'Outre-Mer,* II, 6 (1956): 951–990.

Pescatello, Ann. *"Relatório* [Report] from Portugal: The Archives and Libraries of Portugal and Their Significance for the Study of Brazilian History." *Latin American Research Review,* 5, 2 (1970): 17–52.

Rau, Virginia. "Arquivos de Portugal: Lisboa," in *The Proceedings of the International Colloquium on Luso-Brazilian Studies.* Nashville, TN: Vanderbilt University Press, 1953: 189–231.

Ryder, A. F. C. *Materials for West African History in Portuguese Archives.* London: Athlone Press, University of London, 1965.

Serrão, Joel, Maria da Silva Leal, and Miriam Halpern Pereira (eds.). *Roteiro de fontes da História Portuguesa Contemporânea. Arquivo Nacional da Torre do Tombo.* Volumes I and II. Lisbon, 1984.

Silva, Jaime H. da. *Guide to Archives in Portugal, the Azores and Madeira Islands.* Durham, NH: International Conference Group on Portugal; Essays in Portuguese Studies, Number 7, 1993.

Silva Leal, Maria da and Miriam Halpern Pereira (eds.). *Arquivo e Historiografia. Colóquio sobre as Fontes de História Contemporânea Portuguesa.* Lisbon, 1988.

Wheeler, Douglas L. "Ajuda Library/Biblioteca Da Ajuda [Lisbon, Portugal]." *Portuguese Studies Newsletter,* 7 (Winter/Spring 1980–81): 1–2.

————. "Archival Materials and Manuscripts on United States History in Portugal and the Azores Islands," in Lewis Hanke (ed.). *Guide to the Study of United States History Outside the U.S. 1945–1980.* White Plains, NY: Kraus International Publications; American Historical Association; University of Massachusetts, Amherst, 1985: 346–356.

————. "The Archives of Portugal: A Guide to an Intelligence Treasure Trove." *International Journal of Intelligence and Counterintelligence,* 4, 4 (Winter 1990): 539–550.

4. GENERAL REFERENCES: STATISTICAL

Agência Geral do Ultramar. *Portugal. Overseas Provinces: Facts and Figures.* Lisbon, 1965.

————. *Províncias ultramarinas portuguesas: dados informativos.* Lisbon, 1962–66.

Anuário Estatístico. Lisbon: Instituto Nacional de Estatística, 1875–present.

Anuário Estatístico. II. Províncias Ultramarinas, 1969. Lisbon: Instituto Nacional de Estatística, 1971.

Ayala, José Aldana. *Compêndio Geographico-Estadistico de Portugal y sus Posesiones Ultramarinas.* Madrid, 1855.

Balbi, Adriano. *Essai Statistique sur le Royaume de Portugal et d'Algarve.* Paris, 1822.

Estatísticas Agrícolas. Lisbon: Instituto Nacional de Estatística, 1965–present.

Estatísticas Industriais. Lisbon: Instituto Nacional de Estatística, 1967–present.

Estatísticas de Saúde. Lisbon, 1970–present.

Gaspar, Jorge (ed.). *Portugal Em Mapas E Em Números.* Lisbon: Livros Horizonte, 1990 ed.

McNitt, Harold A. (comp.). *Selected Agricultural and Trade Statistics for the European Community, Greece, Spain and Portugal, 1967–79.* Washington, DC: U.S. Department of Agriculture; Statistical Bulletin no. 692, 1982.

Organisation for Economic Co-operation and Development (OECD). *Portugal. OECD Economic Surveys.* Paris: OECD, 1979–present.

Pery, Geraldo. *Geographia e Estatistica de Portugal e Colonias.* Lisbon, 1875.

Portugal. Lisbon: Instituto Nacional de Estatistica, 1969; annual volumes.

5. GENERAL REFERENCES; ENCYCLOPEDIAS AND DICTIONARIES

Azevedo, Cândido De (ed.). *Classe Política Portuguesa. Estes Políticos Que Nos Governam.* Lisbon: 1989.

Enciclopédia Luso-Brasileira da Cultura. 30 vols. to date. Lisbon, 1963–1991.

Grande Enciclopédia Portuguesa e Brasileira. 40 vols. Lisbon and Rio de Janeiro: 1924–1960.

Secretaria de Estado da Informação e Turismo. *Orgânica Governamental, Sua Evolução, E Elencos Ministeriais Constituidos Desde 5 De Outubro De 1910 à 31 De Março De 1972.* Lisbon: 1972.

Serrão, Joel (ed.). *Dicionário De História De Portugal.* 5 vols. Lisbon: 1963–1971.

————. *Pequeno Dicionário De História De Portugal.* Lisbon: 1987.

6. GENERAL REFERENCES: GENERAL HISTORIES, LEGAL, POLITICAL STUDIES, AREA AND COUNTRY STUDIES.

Almeida, Fortunato de. *História de Portugal.* 6 vols. Coimbra, 1922–1929.

Ameal, João. *História de Portugal. Das Orígens Até 1940.* Oporto, 1958, 4th ed.

Birot, Pierre. *Le Portugal.* Paris, 1949.

Bourdon, Albert-Alain. *Histoire du Portugal.* Paris: Presses Universitaires de France, 1970.

Bradford, Sarah. *Portugal.* London: Thames & Hudson, 1973.

Caetano, Marcello. *História Breve das Constituições Portuguesas.* Lisbon, 1974. 4th ed.

————. *Lições de História do Direito Português.* Coimbra, 1962.

Eppstein, John. *Portugal: The Country and Its People.* London: Queen Anne Press, 1967.

Garcia, José Manuel. *História de Portugal: Uma Visão Global.* Lisbon, 1989. 4th ed.

Kaplan, Marion. *The Portuguese. The Land and Its People.* New York: Viking, 1992.

Keefe, Eugene K. (et al.). *Area Handbook for Portugal.* Washington, DC: American University, 1977 ed.

Koebel, William. *Portugal: Its Land and People.* London: Constable, 1909.

Livermore, Harold V. *A History of Portugal.* Cambridge, UK: Cambridge University Press, 1947.

————. *A New History of Portugal.* Cambridge, UK: Cambridge University Press, 1976 ed.

————. *Portugal and Brazil: An Introduction.* Oxford, UK: Oxford University Press, 1953.

————. *A Short History of Portugal.* Edinburgh, UK: Edinburgh University Press, 1973.

Martinez, Pedro Soares. *História Diplomática de Portugal.* Lisbon, 1986.

Naval Intelligence Division. *(Handbook for) Spain and Portugal,* Vol. II. London: Admiralty, Naval Intelligence Division, 1942.

Nowell, Charles E. *A History of Portugal.* New York: Van Nostrand, 1953.

————. *Portugal.* Englewood Cliffs, NJ: Prentice-Hall, 1973.

Oliveira Marques, A. H. de. *História de Portugal.* 2 vols. Lisbon, 1972–1990, various eds.

————. *History of Portugal.* 2 vols. New York: Columbia University Press, 1972; 1976 ed. in one volume.

Oliveira Martins, J. *História de Portugal.* 2 vols. Lisbon, 1880 and later editions.

Opello, Walter C., Jr. *Portugal: From Monarchy to Pluralist Democracy.* Boulder, CO: Westview, 1991.

Pajot, Lalé. *Le Portugal.* Paris: Pichon and Durand, 1971.

Pattee, Richard. *Portugal and the Portuguese World.* Milwaukee: Bruce, 1957.

Payne, Stanley G. *A History of Spain and Portugal.* 2 vols. Madison, WI: University of Wisconsin Press, 1973.

Peres, Damião (ed.). *História de Portugal.* 9 vols. Barcelos and Coimbra, Monumental Edition, 1928–1985.

Raibaud, A. *Petite histoire du Portugal. Des Origines à 1910.* Nice, 1964.

Saraiva, José Hermano. *História Concisa de Portugal.* Lisbon, 1978 and later eds.

Selvagem, Carlos. *Portugal Militar.* Lisbon, 1931.

Sérgio, António. *A Sketch of the History of Portugal.* Lisbon, 1928.

Serrão, Joel and A. H. de Oliveira Marques (eds.). *Nova História De Portugal.* 10 vols. Lisbon, 1987– .

Trend, J. B. *Portugal.* London: Ernest Benn, 1957.

Veríssimo Serrão, José. *História De Portugal.* 10 vols. Lisbon, 1980–1991.

Vieira, Nelson H. (ed.). *Roads to Today's Portugal: Essays on Contemporary Portuguese Literature, Art and Culture.* Providence, RI: Gávea-Brown, 1983.

7. GENERAL REFERENCES: CULTURE, LITERATURE, LANGUAGE

Bell, Aubrey F. G. *The Oxford Book of Portuguese Verse: XIIth Century-XXth Century.* Oxford: Oxford University Press, 1925; 2nd ed. by B. Vidigal, 1952.

———. *Portuguese Literature.* Oxford: Oxford University Press, 1922, 1st ed.; 1970, 2nd ed. Ed. by B. Vidigal.

Cidade, Hernani. *Lições de Cultura e Literatura Portuguesa.* 3 vols. Lisbon, 1960–62.

Figueiredo, Fidelino. *História literária de Portugal.* Coimbra, 1944.

Gentile, Georges Le. *La Littérature Portugaise.* Rev. ed. Paris, 1951.

Longland, Jean. *Contemporary Portuguese Poetry. A Bilingual Selection.* Irvington-on-Hudson: Harvey House, 1966.

Prado Coelho, Jacinto do. *Dicionário das Literaturas Portuguesa, Galega e Brasileira.* Oporto, 1978, 3rd ed.

Rossi, Giuseppe C. *Storia della letteratura portuguesa.* Florence, 1953.

Saraiva, António José. *História da cultura em Portugal.* 3 vols. Lisbon, 1950–60.

———. *História da Literatura Portuguesa.* Lisbon, 1990 ed.

——— and Óscar Lopes. *História da Literatura Portuguesa.* Oporto and Coimbra, 1978, 10th ed.

Seguier, Jaime de (ed.). *Dicionário Prático Ilustrado.* Oporto: Lello, 1961 and later eds.

Simões, João Gaspar. *História da poesia portuguesa.* 2 vols. Lisbon: 1955–56 and later eds.

———. *História da poesia portuguesa do século XX.* Lisbon: 1959 and later eds.

Stern, Irwin (ed.-in-chief). *Dictionary of Brazilian Literature.* Westport, CT: Greenwood Press, 1988.

8. TRAVEL AND TOURIST GUIDES ON PORTUGAL

Adragão, José Victor. *The Algarve. The Land, The Sea and Its People.* Lisbon, 1988.

Ballard, Sam and Jane Ballard. *Pousadas of Portugal. Unique Lodgings in State-owned Castles, Palaces, Mansions and Hotels.* Boston: Harvard Common, 1986.

Bridge, Ann and Susan Lowndes Marques. *The Selective Traveller in Portugal.* London: Chatto & Windus, 1968.

Ellingham, Mark et al. *The Rough Guide to Portugal.* Boston: Routledge, 1984.

Hogg, Anthony. *Travellers' Portugal.* London: Solo Mio, 1983.

Kite, Cynthia and Ralph Kite. *Portuguese Country Inns & Pousadas.* New York: Warner Books; Karen Brown's Country Inn Series, 1988.

Lowndes, Susan (ed.). *Fodor's Portugal 1991.* New York: Fodor's, 1990.

Proença Raúl and Sant'anna Dionísio (eds.). *Guía De Portugal. I. Generalidades. Lisboa E. Arredores.* Lisbon: Fundação Calouste Gulbenkian, 2nd ed. 1983 of original 1924 ed.

Robertson, Ian. *Portugal. Blue Guide.* London: Benn; New York: Norton, 1988 ed.

Tucker, Alan (ed.). *The Penguin Guide to Portugal 1990.* New York: Viking/Penguin, 1990.

Villier, Franz. *Portugal.* Paris, 1957.

Wright, Carol. *Lisbon.* London: Dent, 1981.

―――. *Portugal on Your Own.* New York: Hippocrene Books, 1986.

Wright, David and Patrick Swift. *Algarve: A Portrait and Guide.* New York: Scribners, 1973.

―――. *Lisbon: A Portrait and Guide.* New York: Scribners, 1971.

―――. *Minho and North Portugal: A Portrait and Guide.* New York: Scribners, 1968.

9. HISTORY OF PORTUGAL

ANCIENT AND MEDIEVAL (2000 BC–1415 AD)

Alarção, Jorge de. *Roman Portugal. Volume I. Introduction.* Warminster, UK: 1988.

Almeida, Fortunato de. *História de Portugal.* Vol. I. Coimbra, 1922.

Arnaut, Salvador Dias. *A Crise Nacional dos fins do século XVI.* Vol. I. Coimbra, 1960.

Baião, António, Hernani Cidade, and Manuel Múrias (eds.). *História de Expansão Portuguesa no Mundo.* 3 vols. Lisbon, 1937–40.

Caetano, Marcello. *Lições de História do Direito Português.* Coimbra, 1962.

Cortesão, Jaime. *Os Factores Democráticos no Formação de Portugal.* Lisbon, 1960.

David, Pierre. *Études Historiques sur la Galice et le Portugal du VI au XII siécle.* Paris: 1947.

Diffie, Bailey W. *Prelude to Empire: Portugal Overseas before Henry the Navigator.* Lincoln: University of Nebraska Press, 1960.

Dutra, Francis A. "Portugal: To 1279." *Dictionary of the Middle Ages.* Vol. X: 35–48. New York: Scribner, 1987.

———. "Portugal: 1279–1481." *Dictionary of the Middle Ages.* Vol. X: 48–56. New York: Scribner, 1987.

Erdmann, Carl. "Der Kreuzzugsgedanke in Portugal." *Historische Zeitschrift,* 141, 1 (1929): 25–53.

Gama Barros, Henrique de. *História de Administração Pública em Portugal nos séculos XII à XV.* 11 vols. Lisbon, 1945–51.

Godinho, Vitorino Magalhães. *A Economia dos Descobrimentos Henriquinos.* Lisbon, 1962.

Gonzaga de Azevedo, Luís. *História de Portugal.* 6 vols. Lisbon, 1939–44.

Herculano, Alexandre. *História de Portugal.* 8 vols. Lisbon, 1940, 9th ed.

Lencastre e Tavora, Luíz Gonzaga. *O Estudo da Sigilografia Medieval Portuguesa.* Lisbon, 1990.

Livermore, H. V. *The Origins of Spain and Portugal.* London: Allen & Unwin, 1971.

Lopes, David. "Os Árabes nas obras de Alexandre Herculano." *Boletim da Segunda Classe.* Lisbon: Academia Real das Sciências, III (1909–1910).

MacKendrick, Paul. *The Iberian Stones Speak.* New York: Funk & Wagnalls, 1969.

Martinez, Pedro Soares. *História Diplomática De Portugal* [chapter I, 1143–1415]. Lisbon, 1986.

Oliveira Marques, A. H. de. *Daily Life in Portugal in the Middle Ages.* Madison: University of Wisconsin Press, 1971.

————. *Ensaios de História Medieval Portuguesa.* Lisbon, 1980.

————. *Guía do Estudante de História Medieval Portuguesa.* Lisbon, 1985, 3rd ed.

————. *Hansa e Portugal na Idade Média.* Lisbon, 1959.

————. *Introduçao à História da Agricultura em Portugal.* Lisbon, 1968.

————. "Introduçao à História da Cidade Medieval Portuguesa." *Bracara Augusta,* XXV, 92–93 (January–December 1981): 367–387.

————. *Portugal Na Crise Dos Séculos XIV e XV . . . . Vol. IV of Serrão and Oliveira Marques, Nova História de Portugal.* Lisbon, 1987.

Peres, Damião de (ed.). *História de Portugal.* Vols. I, II. Barcelos, 1928–1929.

Rau, Virginia. *Sesmárias Medievais Portuguesas.* Lisbon, 1946.

————. *Subsídios para o estudo das Feiras Medievais Portuguesas.* Lisbon, 1943.

Ribeiro, Orlando. "Portugal, formação de." *Dicionário da História de Portugal.* Vol. III. Lisbon, 1966: 432–451.

Rogers, Francis M. *The Travels of the Infante Dom Pedro of Portugal.* Cambridge, MA: Harvard University Press, 1961.

Russell, P. E. *The English Intervention in Spain and Portugal in the Time of Edward III and Richard II.* Oxford: Oxford University Press, 1955.

Savory, H. N. *Spain and Portugal. The Prehistory of the Iberian Peninsula.* New York: Thames and Hudson, 1968.

Silva, Armando Coelho Ferreira. *A Cultura Castreja no Noroeste de Portugal.* Pacos de Ferreira, 1986.

Varagnac, André. *O Homem antes da Escrita (Pre-história).* Lisbon, 1963.

IMPERIAL AND EARLY MODERN (1415–1822)

Azevedo, J. Lúcio de. *Épocas de Portugal Económico.* Lisbon, 1929.

————. *História de António de Vieira.* 2 vols. Lisbon, 1918–20.

Borges de Macedo, Jorge. "Pombal." *Dicionário de História de Portugal.* Vol. III (Lisbon, 1968): 415–423.

————. *Problemas de História de Indústria Portuguesa no Século XVIII.* Lisbon, 1963.

Boxer, C. R. *Four Centuries of Portuguese Expansion, 1415–1825: A Succinct Survey.* Johannesburg, SA: Witwaterstrand University Press, 1961.

————. *João de Barros: Portuguese Humanist and Historian of Asia.* New Delhi, India: Xavier Centre, 1981.

————. *The Portuguese Seaborne Empire 1415–1825.* London: Hutchinson, 1969.

Cheke, Marcus. *Dictator of Portugal: A Life of the Marquis of Pombal, 1699–1782.* London: Sidgwick & Jackson, 1938.

Cunha, Luís da. *Testamento Político.* Lisbon, 1820.

Duncan, T. Bentley. *Uneasy Allies: Anglo-Portuguese Commercial, Diplomatic and Maritime Relations, 1642–1662*. Chicago, IL: Unpublished Ph.D. Dissertation, History Department, University of Chicago, 1967.

Dutra, Francis A. "Membership in the Order of Christ in the Seventeenth Century." *The Americas,* 27 (1970): 3–25.

Ericeira, Luís de Meneses [Count of]. *História de Portugal Restaurado.* 4 vols. Oporto, 1945.

Fisher, H. E. S. "Anglo-Portuguese Trade, 1700–70." *Economic History Review,* XVI, 2 (1963): 219–233.

———. *The Portugal Trade: A Study of Anglo-Portuguese Commerce, 1700–1770.* London: Methuen, 1971.

Francis, A. D. *The Methuens and Portugal, 1691–1708.* Cambridge: Cambridge University Press, 1966.

———. *Portugal, 1715–1808.* London: Tamesis, 1985.

———. *The Wine Trade.* London: Black, 1972.

Hanson, Carl A. *Economy and Society in Baroque Portugal, 1668–1703.* Minneapolis, MN: University of Minnesota Press, 1981.

Herculano, Alexandre. *History of the Origin and Establishment of the Inquisition in Portugal.* New York: AMS Press, 1968 reprint.

Kendrick, T. D. *The Lisbon Earthquake.* London: Methuen, 1956.

Livermore, H. V. "The Privileges of an Englishman in the Kingdom and Dominions of Portugal." *Atlante,* II (1954): 57–77.

Macauley, Neil. *Dom Pedro: The Struggle for Liberty in Brazil and Portugal, 1798–1834.* Durham, NC: Duke University Press, 1986.

Macauley, Rose. *They Went to Portugal.* London: Jonathan Cape, 1946.

———. *They Went to Portugal, Too.* London: Carcanet, 1990.

Magalhães Godinho, Vitorino. *A Economia dos descobrimentos henriquinos.* Lisbon, 1962.

————. *Estructura da Antiga Sociedade Portuguesa.* Lisbon, 1975.

————. "Portugal and Her Empire" in *New Cambridge Modern History* (Cambridge University Press), vol. V (1961): 384–397; vol. VI (1961): 509–540.

————. *Prix et Monnaies au Portugal.* Paris, 1955.

Mauro, Frédéric. *Le Portugal et l'Atlantique au XVII siécle (1570–1670).* Paris: SEVPEN, 1960.

Maxwell, Kenneth. *Conflicts and Conspiracies: Brazil and Portugal, 1750–1808.* Cambridge, UK: Cambridge University Press, 1973.

————. "Pombal and the Nationalization of the Luso-Brazilian Economy." *Hispanic American Historical Review,* XLVIII (November 1968): 608–631.

Oliveira, António de. *A Vida Económica e Social de Coimbra de 1537 à 1640.* 2 vols. Coimbra, 1971–72.

Prestage, Edgar. "The Mode of Government in Portugal during the Restoration [1640–1668] Period." In Edgar Prestage (ed.). *Melange d'Etudes Portugaises Offerts a M. Georges Le Gentil.* Lisbon, 1949: 265–270.

————. *Portuguese Pioneers.* London: Black, 1933.

————. *The Royal Power and the Cortes in Portugal.* Watford, UK: Voss & Michael, 1927.

Rabassa, Gregory. "Padre António Vieira: Portugal's Amazing Polymath." *Camões Centre Quarterly,* 2, 3–4 (Autumn and Winter 1990): 27–32.

Rau, Virginia. *D. Catarina de Bragança, Rainha de Inglaterra.* Lisbon, 1944.

Ricard, Robert. "Prophecy and Messianism in the Works of António Vieira." *The Americas,* 37 (1960): 357–388.

Roche, T. W. E. *Philippa: Dona Filipa of Portugal.* London: Phillimore, 1971.

Rogers, Francis M. *The Travels of the Infante Dom Pedro of Portugal.* Cambridge, MA: Harvard University Press, 1961.

Roth, Cecil. *A History of the Marranos.* Philadelphia, PA: Jewish Publication Society of America, 1932.

―――. "The Religion of the Marranos." *Jewish Quarterly Review,* 22 (1931): 1–33.

Saraiva, António José. *Inquisição e Cristãos-Novos.* Oporto, 1969.

―――. *A Inquisição Portuguesa.* Lisbon, 1969 and later eds.

Schneider, Susan. *O Marquês De Pombal E O Vinho Do Porto. Dependência e subdesenvolvimento em Portugal no século XVIII.* Lisbon, 1980.

Shaw, L. M. E. *Trade, Inquisition and the English Nation in Portugal, 1640–1690.* London: Carcanet, 1989.

Shillington, V. M. and A. B. W. Chapman. *The Commercial Relations of England and Portugal.* London: Routledge, 1907.

Sideri, Sandro. *Trade and Power: Informal Colonialism in Anglo-Portuguese Relations.* Rotterdam: Rotterdam University Press, 1970.

Smith, John Athelstone [Conde de Carnota]. *Marquis of Pombal.* London, 1872. 2nd ed.

Verlinden, Charles. "Virginia Rau and the Economic History of Portugal." *Journal of European Economic History,* 4 (1975): 243–245.

Walford, A. R. *The British Factory in Lisbon.* Lisbon, 1940.

Zuquete, Afonso E. M. *Nobreza de Portugal.* 3 vols. Lisbon, 1960.

CONSTITUTIONAL MONARCHY AND LIBERALISM (1822–1910)

Baptista, Jacinto. *O Cinco de Outubro.* Lisbon, 1965.

Brandão, Raúl. *Memórias.* 3 vols. Lisbon, 1969 ed.

Cabral, Manuel Villaverde. *O desenvolvimento do capitalismo em Portugal no século XIX.* Lisbon, 1981.

Caetano, Marcello. *História Breve das Constituções portuguesas.* Lisbon, 1971 ed.

Carnota, Conde da. *Memoirs of Marshal, the Duke of Saladanha, with Selections from His Correspondence.* 2 vols. London: John Murray, 1880.

Carvalho, Joaquim de. *Estudos sobre a cultura portuguesa do século XIX.* Coimbra, 1955.

Cheke, Marcus. *Carlota Joaquina, Queen of Portugal.* London: Sidgwick and Jackson, 1947.

França, José-Augusto. *Zé Provinho na Obra de Rafael Bordalo Pinheiro.* Lisbon, 1975.

Fuschini, Augusto. *Liquidações políticas.* Lisbon, 1896.

Godinho, Vitorino Magalhães. *Estrutura da Antiga Sociedade Portuguesa.* Lisbon, 1975 ed.

Hammond, Richard J. *Portugal and Africa, 1815–1910: A Study in Uneconomic Imperialism.* Stanford, CA: Stanford University Press, 1966.

Homem, Amadeu Carvalho. *A Propaganda Republicana (1870–1910).* Coimbra, 1990.

Livermore, H. V. *Portugal: A Short History.* Edinburgh, UK: Edinburgh University Press, 1973.

Machado, Álvaro Manuel. *A Geração de 70-uma revolução cultural e literária.* Lisbon, 1986 ed.

Martins, Joaquim Pedro de Oliveira. *Portugal Contemporâneo.* 3 vols. Lisbon, 1953 ed.

Medina, João. *Eça Político.* Lisbon, 1974.

Pereira, Miriam Halpern. *Livre Câmbio e Desenvolvimento Económico, Portugal na segunda metade do século XIX.* Lisbon, 1971.

————. *Revolução, Finanças, Dependência Externa (de 1820 à convenção de Gramido).* Lisbon, 1979.

Peres, Damião (ed.). *História de Portugal. Volume III.* Barcelos, 1935 ed.

Rorick, David. *Maria da Fonte. History and Myth.* M. A. Thesis, History Department, Sonoma State University, Sonoma, CA, 1984.

Sá, Vítor de. *Perspectivas do Século XIX.* Lisbon, 1964.

Serrão, Joel. "Liberalismo." In Joel Serrão (ed.). *Dicionário de História de Portugal.* Vol. II. Lisbon, 1965: 732–741.

————. *Sampaio Bruno. O homem e o pensamento.* Lisbon, 1958.

————. *Do Sebastianismo ao Socialismo.* Lisbon, 1975 ed.

————. *Temas Oitocentistas.* 2 vols. Lisbon, 1959–62.

Silbert, Albert. *Do Portugal de Antiga Regime ao Portugal Oitocentista.* Lisbon, 1972.

Teles, Basílio. *Do Ultimatum ao 31 de Janeiro.* Lisbon, 1968 ed.

PARLIAMENTARY, REPUBLICAN PORTUGAL (1910–1926)

Antunes, José Freire. *A Cadeira do Sidónio Pais.* Lisbon, 1980.

Arriaga, Manuel de. *Na primeira presidência da República Portugueza: Um rápido relatório.* Lisbon, 1916.

Bell, Aubrey, F. G. *In Portugal.* London, 1912.

————. *Portugal of the Portuguese.* London: Pitman, 1915.

Bragança-Cunha, V. de. *Revolutionary Portugal, 1910–1936.* London: Swift, 1937.

Brandão, Raúl. *Memórias.* 3 vols. In Brandão, *Obras Completas.* Lisbon, 1969.

Burity, Braz [Pseudonym of Joaquim Madureira]. *A Forja da Lei.* Coimbra, 1915.

Cabral, Manuel V. "The Aesthetics of Nationalism: Modernism and Authoritarianism in Early 20th Century Portugal." *Luso-Brazilian Review* (Madison, WI), 26, 1 (Summer 1989): 15–43.

————. *Portugal Na Álvorada Do Século XX.* Lisbon, 1979.

Campos, Ezequiel. *Política.* Oporto, 1924.

Cardia, Sottomayor (ed.). *Seara Nova. Antologia. Pela Reforma da República (1, 2) 1921–1926.* 2 vols. Lisbon, 1971–72.

Carqueja, Bento. *O Futuro de Portugal. Portugal Apos À Guerra.* Oporto, 1920.

————. *O Povo de Portugal.* Oporto, 1916.

Chagas, João. *Diário, 1914–1918.* 3 vols. Lisbon, 1929–30.

Cortesão, Jaime. *Memórias da Grande Guerra.* In *Obras Completas de Jaime Cortesão.* Lisbon, 1969.

Cunha Leal, Francisco. *As Minhas Memórias.* 3 vols. Lisbon, 1966–68.

Derou, Jean. *Les Relations Franco-Portugaises (1910–1926).* Paris: Publications de la Sorbonne, 1986.

Fazenda, Pedro. *A Crise Política.* Lisbon, 1926.

Ferrão, Carlos. *História De 1ª República.* Lisbon, 1976.

Ferreira, David. "5 De Outubro de 1910." In Joel Serrão (ed.). *Dicionário de História De Portugal*, III (1968): 264–267.

————. *História Política da Primeira República Portuguesa (1910–1915)*. 2 vols. Lisbon, 1973.

Ferreira Martins, Gen. Luís (ed.). *Portugal na Grande Guerra*. 2 vols. Lisbon, 1945.

Gomes da Costa, Gen. Manuel. *Memórias*. Lisbon, 1930.

Lorenzo, Felix. *Portugal (cinco años de republica)*. Madrid, 1915.

Machado, Bernardino. *Depois de 21 de Maio*. Lisbon, 1922.

Machado Santos, António. *1907–1910. A revolução portugueza. Relatório*. Lisbon, 1911.

Madureira, Arnaldo. *0 28 De Maio*. Lisbon, 1982.

Magno, David. *Livro da Guerra de Portugal na Flandres*. Oporto, 1920.

————. *A Situação Portuguesa*. Oporto, 1926.

Marques Guedes, Armando. *Cinco Meses no governo*. Oporto, 1926.

Martins, Rocha. *Memórias sobre Sidónio Pais*. Lisbon, 1921.

Medeiros, Fernando. *A Sociedade E A Economia Portuguesas Nas Orígens Do Salazarismo*. Lisbon, 1978.

Medina, João. *"Oh! a República! . . . ," Estudos sobre o Republicanismo e a Primeira República Portuguesa*. Lisbon, 1990.

———— (ed.). *História Contemporânea De Portugal: Primeira República*. 2 vols. Lisbon, 1986.

Mónica, Maria Filomena. "Uma Aristocracia Operária: Os Chapeleiros (1870–1913)." *Análise Social*, 60, 2nd series (1979).

Montalvor, Luís de (ed.). *História de Regimen Republicano em Portugal*. 2 vols. Lisbon, 1930–32.

Oliveira, César. *O Operariado E A República Democrática, 1910–1914.* Oporto, 1972.

Oliveira Marques, A. H. de. *Guía De História Da 1ª República Portuguesa.* Lisbon, 1981 ed.

————. *História De 1ª República Portuguesa: As Estruturas De Base.* 2 vols. Lisbon, 1973–74.

————. "The Portuguese 1920s: A General Survey." *Iberian Studies,* 2 (1973): 32–40.

————. *A Primeira República Portuguesa. Alguns aspectos estruturais.* Lisbon, 1975 ed.

————. *O Terceiro Governo Afonso Costa-1917.* Lisbon, 1977.

Pabón, Jesus. *La Revolución Portuguesa.* 2 vols. Madrid, 1945–46. [Portuguese edition: Lisbon, 1961]

Paxeco, Óscar. *Os Que Arrancaram Em 28 De Maio.* Lisbon, 1937.

Peres, Damião (ed.). *História De Portugal. Ediçao Monumental. Supplemento.* Oporto, 1954.

Pessoa, Fernando. *A Memória do Presidente-Rei Sidónio Pais.* Lisbon, 1928.

Relvas, José. *Memórias Políticas.* 2 vols. Lisbon, 1977–78.

Schwartzman, Kathleen C. "Lucros, investimentos e coligações políticas na I República." *Análise Social,* XVIII, 72–74 (1982): 741–758.

Serrão, Joel. *Liberalismo, socialismo e republicanismo.* Lisbon, 1979.

Silva, António Maria da. *O Meu Depoimento.* 2 vols. Mem Martins, 1978–82.

Telo, António José. *Decadência E Queda Da I República Portuguesa.* 2 vols. Lisbon, 1980–84.

Torre (Gomez), Hipólito de la and J. Sanchez Cervello. *Portugal En El*

Siglo XX. Madrid: Ediciones Istmo: Colección La Historia en sus textos, 1992.

Valente, Vasco Pulido. *O Poder e o Povo: A Revolução de 1910.* Lisbon, 1974.

————. "A República e as classes trabalhadores (Outubro 1910– Agosto 1911)." *Análise Social,* IX, 34 (1972): 293–316.

Veríssimo Serrão, Joaquim. *História De Portugal. Volume XI. A Primeira República (1910–1926): História Política, Religiosa, Militar e Ultramarina.* Lisbon, 1989.

————. *História De Portugal. Volume XII. História Diplomática, Social, Económica e Cultural.* Lisbon, 1990.

Vincent-Smith, John. "Britain and Portugal, 1910–1916." London: Ph.D. dissertation, History, University of London, 1971.

Wheeler, Douglas L. "Nightmare Republic: Portugal, 1910–1926." *History Today* (London), 32 (September 1981): 5–10.

————. "The Portuguese Revolution of 1910." *Journal of Modern History,* 44 (June 1972): 172–194.

————. *Republican Portugal. A Political History, 1910–1926.* Madison, WI: University of Wisconsin Press, 1978.

Young, George. *Portugal Old and Young: An Historical Study.* Oxford, Clarendon Press, 1917.

AUTHORITARIAN PORTUGAL (MILITARY DICTATORSHIP AND "ESTADO NOVO") (1926–1974)

Antunes, José Freire (ed. and comp.). *Os Americanos E Portugal. Vol. I. Os anos de Ricard Nixon, 1969–1974.* Lisbon, 1986.

————. *Cartas Particulares À Marcello Caetano.* 2 vols. Lisbon, 1985–86.

Aquino, Acácio Tómas de. *O Segredo das Prisões Atlânticas.* Lisbon, 1978.

Araquistain, Luis. "Dictatorship in Portugal." *Foreign Affairs,* 7 (October 1928): 41–53.

Assac, Jacques Ploncard. *Salazar.* Paris: La Table Ronde, 1967.

Baklanoff, Eric N. "The Political Economy of Portugal's Old Regime: Growth and Change Preceding the 1974 Revolution." *World Development,* 7, 8–9 (August–September 1979): 799–812.

Barreno, Maria Isabel, Maria Teresa Horta and Maria Velho da Costa. *The Three Marias: New Portuguese Letters.* New York: Doubleday, 1975.

Blume, Norman. "SEDES: An Example of Opposition in a Conservative Authoritarian State." *Government and Opposition,* 12 (Summer 1977): 351–366.

Braga da Cruz, Manuel. "O Integralismo nas orígens do Salazarismo." *Análise Social,* XVIII (1982): 1409–1419.

————. *Monárquicos e Republicanos no Estado Novo.* Lisbon, 1986.

————. "Notas para uma caracterização política do salazarismo." In Gabinete de Investigações Sociais. *Análise social. A Formação de Portugal Contemporâneo: 1900–1980.* Vol. I, 72–74 (April–December 1981): 773–794.

————. "A Oposição Eleitoral ao Salazarismo." *Revista de História das Ideias,* V (1983).

————. *A orígem da democracia-cristã em Portugal e o Salazarismo.* Lisbon, 1979.

Cabral, Manuel V. "Sobre o fascismo e o seu avento em Portugal." *Análise Social,* XII, 48 (1976), 873–915.

Caetano, Marcello. *Depoimento.* São Paulo, 1974.

————. *História Breve das Constituições Portugueses.* Lisbon, 1974.

————. *As Minhas Memórias de Salazar.* Lisbon, 1977.

————. *A Missão Dos Dirigentes.* Lisbon, 1966, 4th ed.

Campinos, Jorge. *A Ditadura Militar, 1926–1933*. Lisbon, 1975.

Carrilho, Maria. *Forças Armadas e Mudança Política em Portugal no Século XX*. Lisbon, 1985.

————, et al. *Portugal na Segunda Guerra Mundial. Contributos para uma reavaliação*. Lisbon, 1989.

Carvalho, Otelo Saraiva de. *Alvorada em Abril*. Lisbon, 1977.

Costa Pinto, António et al. *O Fascismo Em Portugal*. [Proceedings of Conference, Lisbon, March 1980]. Lisbon, 1982.

————. "The Radical Right and the Military Dictatorship in Portugal: The National May 28 League (1928–1933)." *Luso-Brazilian Review*, 23, 1 (Summer 1986): 1–15.

————. "O Salazarismo No Recente Investigação Sobre o Fascismo Europeu . . . " *Análise Social*, XXV (1990): 695–713.

Delgado, Humberto. *The Memoirs of General Delgado*. Ed. by Iva Delgado. London: Cassell, 1964; Portuguese ed. Lisbon, 1990.

Duarte Silva, A. E. et al. *Salazar E O Salazarismo*. Lisbon, 1989.

Egerton, F. C. C. *Salazar, Rebuilder of Portugal*. London: Hodder & Stoughton, 1943.

Ferraz, Artur Ivens. *A Asenção de Salazar. Memórias de Ivens Ferraz*. Lisbon, 1988.

Ferro, António (ed.). *Portugal. Breviário Da Pátria Para Os Ausentes*. Lisbon, 1946.

————. *Salazar: O Homem E A Sua Obra*. Lisbon, 1933; English edition: *Salazar: Portugal and Her Leader*. London: Faber & Faber, 1939, and editions in other languages.

Figueiredo, António. "The Case Against Portugal." In Philip Mason (ed.). *Angola. A Symposium. Views of a Revolt*. Oxford: Oxford University Press, 1962: 46–57.

————. *Portugal and Its Empire: The Truth*. London: Gollancz, 1961.

———. *Portugal. Fifty Years of Dictatorship.* Harmondsworth, UK: Penguin, 1975.

Fox, Ralph. *Portugal Now.* London, 1937.

Fryer, Peter and Patricia McGowan Pinheiro. *Oldest Ally. A Portrait of Salazar's Portugal.* London: Dobson, 1961.

Gallagher, Tom. "Controlled Repression in Salazar's Portugal." *Journal of Contemporary History,* 14, 3 (July 1979): 385–403.

———. "From Hegemony to Opposition: The Ultraright before and after 1974." In L. S. Graham and D. L. Wheeler (eds.). *In Search of Modern Portugal.* Madison, WI: University of Wisconsin Press, 1983: 81–103.

———. "The Mystery Train: Portugal's Military Dictatorship 1926–32." *European Studies Review,* 11 (1981): 325–354.

———. *Portugal: A Twentieth Century Interpretation.* Manchester, UK and Dover, NH: Manchester University Press, 1983.

Galvão, Henrique. *Carta Aberta ao Dr. Salazar.* Lisbon, 1975.

———. *Santa Maria: My Crusade for Portugal.* London: Weidenfeld and Nicholson, 1961.

Garnier, Christine. *Vacances avec Salazar.* Paris, 1952; American edition: *Salazar in Portugal: An Intimate Portrait.* New York, 1954.

Georgel, Jacques. *O Salazarismo.* Lisbon, 1985.

Gouveia, Fernando. *Memórias de um Inspector da PIDE.* Lisbon, 1979.

Graham, Lawrence S. "The Military in Politics: The Politicization of the Portuguese Armed Forces." In L. S. Graham and H. M. Makler (eds.). *Contemporary Portugal*: 221–256.

———. "Portugal: The Bureaucracy of Empire." *LADAC Occasional Papers,* series 2, 9 (1973): Austin, TX: Institute of Latin American Studies.

———. *Portugal: The Decline and Collapse of an Authoritarian Order.* Beverly Hills, CA: Sage, 1975.

———— and Harry M. Makler (eds.). *Contemporary Portugal. The Revolution and Its Antecedents.* Austin, TX: University of Texas Press, 1979.

———— and Douglas L. Wheeler (eds.). *In Search of Modern Portugal. The Revolution and Its Consequences.* Madison, WI: University of Wisconsin Press, 1983.

Guyomard, George. *La Dictature Militaire au Portugal.* Paris, 1927.

Kay, Hugh. "A Catholic View." In Philip Mason (ed.) *Angola. A Symposium. Views of a Revolt.* Oxford: Oxford University Press, 1962: 80–103.

————. *Salazar and Modern Portugal.* New York: Hawthorne, 1970.

Leeds, Elizabeth. *Labor Export, Development and the State: The Political Economy of Portuguese Emigration.* Ph.D. dissertation, Department of Political Science. Cambridge, MA: Massachusetts Institute of Technology, 1984.

Lewis, Paul H. "Salazar's Ministerial Elite, 1932–1968." *Journal of Politics,* 40 (August 1987): 622–647.

Lins, Álvaro. *Missão em Portugal.* Lisbon, 1974.

Linz, Juan. "Foreword." In L. Graham and H. Makler (eds.). *Contemporary Portugal.* Austin, TX: University of Texas Press, 1979: xii–xi.

Lucena, Manuel. *A evolução do sistema corporativo português.* 2 vols. Lisbon, 1976.

————. "The Evolution of Portuguese Corporatism under Salazar and Caetano." In L. Graham and H. Makler (eds.). *Contemporary Portugal.* Austin, TX: University of Texas Press, 1979: 47–88.

Magalhães Godinho, Vitorino. *O Socialismo e o Futuro da Peninsula.* Lisbon, 1969.

Makler, Harry M. *A "Elite" Industrial Portuguesa.* Lisbon, 1969.

————. "The Portuguese Industrial Elite and Its Corporative Relations." *Economic Development and Cultural Change,* 24, 3 (April 1976): 495–526.

Martins, Hermínio. "Introduction: *tristes durées.*" In R. Feijó, H. Martins and J. de Pina-Cabral (eds.). *Death in Portugal: Studies in Portuguese Anthropology and Modern History.* Oxford: Journal of the Anthropological Society of Oxford, 1983.

————. "Opposition in Portugal." *Government and Opposition,* 4 (Spring 1969): 250–263.

————. "Portugal." In S. J. Woolf (ed.). *European Fascism.* New York: Vintage, 1969: 302–336.

McCarthy, Mary. "Letter from Lisbon." *The New Yorker,* XXX, 51 (February 5, 1955): 80–96.

Medina, João. *Ditadura: O "Estado Novo."* 2 vols. in his *História Contemporânea De Portugal.* Lisbon, 1986.

————. *Salazar E Os Fascistas. Salazarismo e Nacional-Sindicalismo. A história dum conflito 1932/1935.* Lisbon, 1978.

————. *Salazar em França.* Lisbon, 1977.

Ministério dos Negócios Estrangeiros (ed.). *Dez Anos de Política Externa (1936–1947). A Nação Portuguesa e a Segunda Guerra Mundial.* 12 vols. and in progress. Lisbon, 1964– .

Mónica, Maria Filomena. *Educação e Sociedade no Portugal de Salazar.* Lisbon, 1978.

Nogueira, Alberto Franco. *História de Portugal, 1933–1974. II Supplemento.* Oporto, 1981.

————. *Um político confessa-se (Diário: 1960–1968).* Oporto, 1987. 3rd ed.

————. *Salazar.* 6 vols. Coimbra and Oporto, 1978–85.

Nunes, Leopoldo. *A Ditadura Militar.* Lisbon, 1928.

Oliveira, César. *Portugal e a II República de Espanha, 1931–1936.* Lisbon, 1985.

———. *Salazar E A Guerra Civil De Espanha.* Lisbon, 1988, 2nd ed.

Oliveira Marques, A. H. de. *História de Portugal.* 2 vols. Lisbon: 1980 and later eds.

———. *History of Portugal.* 1 in 2 vols. New York: Columbia University Press, 1976 ed.

———. *A Liga de Paris E A Ditadura Militar, 1927–1928.* Lisbon, 1976.

——— (ed.). *A Literatura Clandestina Em Portugal, 1926–1932.* 2 vols. Lisbon, 1990.

———. *A Maçonaria Portuguesa e o Estado Novo.* Lisbon, 1975.

Pattee, Richard. *Portugal and the Portuguese World.* Milwaukee: Bruce, 1957.

Payne, Stanley G. *A History of Spain and Portugal. Volume 2.* Madison, WI: University of Wisconsin Press, 1973.

———. "Salazarism: 'Fascism' or 'Bureaucratic Authoritarianism'?" In *Estudos de história portuguesa: Homenagem à A. H. de Oliveira Marques.* Lisbon, 1983.

Pereira, José Pacheco. *Conflitos sociais nos campos do sul de Portugal.* Mem Martins, 1978.

———. *A Preparação Ideológica da Intervenção Militar de 28 de Maio de 1926.* Oporto, 1978.

———. "Problemas da história do P. C. P." In A. Costa Pinto et al. *O Fascismo Em Portugal* [Proceedings of Conference, University of Lisbon, March 1980]. Lisbon, 1982: 269–285.

Pires, José Cardoso. *Dinossauro Excelentíssimo.* Lisbon, 1972.

Porch, Douglas. *The Portuguese Armed Forces and the Revolution.* London: Croom Helm, 1977.

Presidência do Conselho de Ministros. *Correspondência de Pedro Teotónio Pereira para Oliveira Salazar vol. 1 (1931–1939)*. 2 vols. Lisbon, 1987–89.

――――. *Correspondência Entre Mário De Figueiredo E Oliveira Salazar.* Lisbon, 1986.

――――. *Discriminação Política No Emprego No Regime Fascista.* Lisbon, 1982.

――――, Comissão do Livro Negro Sobre o Regime Fascista ["Black Book" series], *Eleições No Regime Fascista.* Lisbon, 1979.

――――. *Os Estudantes No Regime Fascista.* Lisbon, 1983.

――――. *Livros Proibidos No Regime Fascista.* Lisbon, 1981.

――――. *A Política De Informação No Regime Fascista.* 2 vols. Lisbon, 1980.

――――. *Presos Políticos No Regime Fascista.* 5 vols. Lisbon, 1981–87.

――――. *Proibição Da "Time" No Regime Fascista* [Time magazine number of July 23, 1946, with Dr. Salazar on cover]. Lisbon, 1982.

――――. *Relatórios Para Oliveira Salazar, 1931–1939.* Lisbon, 1981.

――――. *Repressão Política E Social No Regime Fascista.* Lisbon, 1986.

――――. *Trabalho, Sindicatos E Greves No Regime Fascista.* Lisbon, 1984.

Queiroga, Captain Fernando. *Portugal Oprimido.* Lisbon, 1974.

Raby, David L. *Fascism and Resistance in Portugal. Communists, Liberals and the Military Dissidents in the Opposition to Salazar, 1941–1974.* Manchester and New York: Manchester University Press, 1988.

――――. "Populism and the Portuguese Left: From Delgado to Otelo." In L. S. Graham and D. L. Wheeler (eds.). *In Search of Modern Portugal.* Madison, WI: University of Wisconsin Press, 1983: 61–80.

Raby, Dawn Linda. "The Portuguese Presidential Election of 1949: A Successful Government Maneuver?" *Luso-Brazilian Review,* 27, 1 (Summer 1990): 63–77.

Rêgo, Raúl. *Diário Político.* Lisbon, 1969, 1st ed; 1974, 2nd ed.

————. *Horizontes Fechados.* Oporto, 1970.

————. *Horizontes Fechados/Páginas de Política.* Lisbon, 1974. 3rd ed.

Ribeiro, Aquilino. *Quando os Lobos Uivam.* Lisbon, 1958; English ed: Trans. by Patricia McGowan Pinheiro; London, Cape, 1963.

————. *Volfrâmio.* Lisbon, 1944.

Robinson, Richard A. H. *Contemporary Portugal: A History.* London and Boston: Allen & Unwin, 1979.

Rocha, José António De Oliveira. *The Portuguese Administrative State.* Ph.D. dissertation, Department of Political Science. Columbia, SC: University of South Carolina, 1986.

Rosas, Fernando. *O Estado Novo Nos Anos Trinta. 1928–1938.* Lisbon, 1986.

————. *Portugal Entre A Paz E A Guerra . . . 1939–1945.* Lisbon, 1990.

————. *O Salazarismo E A Aliança Luso-Britânica.* Lisbon, 1988.

Rudel, Christian. *Salazar.* Paris: Mercure de France, 1969.

Sá Carneiro, Francisco. *A Liberalização bloqueada.* Lisbon, 1972.

————. *Uma Tentativa de Participação política.* Lisbon, 1971.

————. *Vale a Pena ser Deputado?* Fundão, 1973.

Salazar, António de Oliveira. *Discursos E Notas Políticas.* [Speeches, Broadcasts, Notes and Statements, 1928–1966]. 6 vols. Coimbra, 1935–1966. Several editions.

————. *Doctrine and Action: Internal and Foreign Policy of the New Portugal, 1928–1939.* Transl. by Robert Edgar Broughton. London: Faber & Faber, 1939.

————. *Entrevistas. 1960–1966.* [Interviews] Coimbra, 1967.

————. "Realities and Trends of Portugal's Policies." *International Affairs,* XXXIX, 2 (April 1963): 169–183.

————. *The Road for the Future.* [Speeches, statements of policy made during 1928–1962]. Lisbon, 1963.

————. *Salazar. Pensamento e doutrina política. Textos anthológicos.* [Anthology of speeches, writings, interviews granted, 1914–1968] Edited by Mendo C. Henriques and Gonçalo de Sampaio e Melo. Lisbon, 1989.

Santana, Emílio. *História de um Atentado. O atentado contra Salazar.* Lisbon, 1976.

Schmitter, Philippe C. *Corporatism and Public Policy in Authoritarian Portugal.* London and Beverly Hills, CA: Sage, 1975.

————. "The Impact and Meaning of Elections in Authoritarian Portugal, 1933–74. In G. Hermet et al. (eds.). *Elections Without Choice.* Basingstoke, UK: Macmillan, 1978.

————. "Liberation by Golpe: Retrospective Thoughts on the Demise of Authoritarian Rule in Portugal." *Armed Forces and Society,* 2 (Nov. 1975): 5–33.

————. "The 'Régime d'exception' That Became the Rule: Forty-Eight Years of Authoritarian Domination in Portugal." In L. S. Graham and H. M. Makler (eds.). *Contemporary Portugal. The Revolution and Its Antecedents.* Austin, TX: University of Texas Press, 1979: 3–46.

———— and Gerhard Lehmbruch (eds.). *Trends Towards Corporatist Intermediation.* Beverly Hills, CA: Sage, 1979.

Shelton, Richard L. *Development of the Communist Party of Portugal, 1921–1976.* Ph.D. dissertation, Department of History, St. Louis, MO: St. Louis University, 1984.

Silva, José. *Memórias de um operário.* Vol. 2. Oporto, 1971.

Soares, Mário. *Escritos Políticos.* Lisbon, 1969.

————. *Portugal Bailloné.* Paris, 1972; Portuguese edition: *Portugal Amordaçado,* Lisbon, 1974; English edition: *Portugal's Struggle for Liberty.* Translated by Mary Gawsworth. London: Allen & Unwin, 1975.

Spínola, António de. *Portugal e o Futuro.* Lisbon, 1974; English edition: Johannesburg: Perskor, 1974.

Teixeira, Luís [Sampaio]. *Perfil de Salazar.* Lisbon, 1938.

Teixeira, Nuno Severiano. "From Neutrality to Alignment: Portugal in the Foundation of the Atlantic Pact." *EUI: Working Papers in History.* Florence, Italy: European University Institute, 1991.

Telo, António José. *Portugal na Segunda Guerra.* Lisbon, 1987.

Teotónio Pereira, Pedro. *Memórias.* 2 vols. Lisbon, 1972–73.

Vasco, Nuno. *Vigiados e perseguidos.* Lisbon, 1977.

Veríssimo, Serrão. *Marcello Caetano. Confidências No Exílio.* Lisbon, 1985.

Vintras, R. E. *The Portuguese Connection: The Secret History of the Azores Base.* London: Bachman & Turner, 1974.

West, S. George. *The New Corporative State of Portugal.* [Inaugural lecture, King's College, London, Feb. 1937] London: New Temple Press, 1937.

Wheeler, Douglas L. "And Who Is My Neighbor? A World War II Hero of Conscience for Portugal." *Luso-Brazilian Review,* 26, 1 (Summer 1989): 119–139.

————. "António de Oliveira Salazar (1889–1970)." In *Research Guide to European Historical Biography,* vol. 3, Washington, DC: Beacham, 1992.

———. "António de Oliveira Salazar (1889–1970)." In Jacques Frémontier (ed.). *Les Hommes d'Siécle XX. Les Dictateurs.* Paris: Mazenod, 1978.

———. *A Ditadura Militar Portuguesa, 1926–1933.* Mem Martins, 1988.

———. "Days of Wine and Carnations: The Portuguese Revolution of [April 25] 1974." *Bulletin. New Hampshire Council on World Relations,* XX (July 1974): 1–10.

———. "The Military and the Portuguese Dictatorship, 1926–1974." In S. Graham and H. M. Makler (eds.). *Contemporary Portugal: The Revolution and Its Antecedents.* Austin, TX: University of Texas Press, 1979: 191–219.

———. "The Price of Neutrality: Portugal, the Wolfram Question, and World War II." *Luso-Brazilian Review* [two part article], 12, 1–2 (Summer 1986; Winter 1986): 107–127.

———. *Republican Portugal: A Political History, 1910–1926.* Madison, WI: University of Wisconsin Press, 1978. Portuguese edition: *História Política de Portugal, 1910–1926.* Mem Martins, 1985.

———. "In the Service of Order: The Portuguese Dictatorship's Political Police (PVDE; PIDE) and the British, German and Spanish Intelligence [Services]." *Journal of Contemporary History,* 24, 2 (January 1983): 1–25.

———. "Thaw in Portugal." *Foreign Affairs,* 48, 4 (July 1970): 769–781.

———. "The Third Pig: From Theory to Grubby Fact in Reassessing the Estado Novo." In B. F. Taggie and R. W. Clement (eds.). *Iberia & the Mediterranean.* Warrensburg, MO: Central Missouri State Press, 1989: 145–168.

——— and René Pélissier. *Angola.* New York: Praeger and London: Pall Mall, 1971; reprinted: Westport, CT: Greenwood Press, 1977.

Wiarda, Howard J. *Corporatism and Development. The Portuguese Experience.* Amherst, MA: University of Massachusetts Press, 1977.

———. "The Corporatist Tradition and the Corporative System in Portugal." In L. S. Graham and H. M. Makler (eds.). *Contemporary Portugal. The Revolution and Its Antecedents.* Austin, TX: University of Texas Press, 1979: 89–122.

———. "Toward a Framework for the Study of Political Change in Iberic-Latin Tradition: The Corporative Model." *World Politics,* 25 (January 1973): 206–235.

10. PHYSICAL FEATURES: GEOGRAPHY, GEOLOGY, FAUNA AND FLORA

Birot, Pierre. *Le Portugal. Étude de géographie régionale.* Paris, 1950.

Delgado, D. G. *The Climate of Portugal and Notes on Its Health Resorts.* Coimbra, 1914.

Drain, Michel. *Geographie de la péninsule ibérique.* Paris, 1964.

Embleton, Clifford. *Geomorphology of Europe.* London: Macmillan, 1984.

Freund, Bödo. *Portugal: Länderprofile, Geographische Struktüren.* Stuttgart: Klett, 1981.

Girão, Aristides de ·Amorim. *Atlas de Portugal.* Coimbra, 1958, 2nd ed.

———. *Condições geográficos e históricas de autonomia política de Portugal.* Coimbra, 1935.

———. *Divisão regional, divisão agrícola e divisão administrativa.* Coimbra, 1932.

Houston, J. M. *The Western Mediterranean World. An Introduction to Its Regional Landscapes.* London: Longmans, 1964.

Polunin, Oleg and B. E. Smythies. *Flowers of South-west Europe: A Field Guide.* London: Oxford University Press, 1973.

Ribeiro, Orlando. *Ensaios de Geografia Humana e Regional.* Lisbon, 1970.

————. *A geografia e a divisão regional do país.* Lisbon, 1970.

————. *Portugal,* Volume V of *Geografia de España y Portugal.* Barcelona, 1955.

————. *Portugal, O Mediterrâneo e o Altântico.* Coimbra, 1945.

Stanislawski, Dan. *The Individuality of Portugal.* Austin, TX: The University of Texas Press, 1959.

————. *Portugal's Other Kingdom: The Algarve.* Austin, TX: University of Texas Press, 1963.

Tait, William C. *The Birds of Portugal.* London: Witherby, 1924.

Taylor, Albert William. *Wild Flowers of Spain and Portugal.* London; Chatto & Windus, 1972.

Way, Ruth. *A Geography of Spain and Portugal.* London: Methuen, 1962.

11. FOREIGN TRAVELERS AND RESIDENTS' ACCOUNTS OF PORTUGAL

Andersen, Hans Christian. *A Visit to Portugal 1866.* London: Peter Owen, 1972.

Beckford, William. *Italy, with Sketches of Spain and Portugal.* Paris: Baudry's European Library, 1834.

————. *The Journal of William Beckford in Portugal and Spain 1787–1788* [ed. by Boyd Alexander] London: Hart-Davies, 1954.

————. *Recollections of an Excursion to the Monasteries of Alcoboca and Batalha.* Fontwell, UK: Centaur Press, 1972.

Bell, Aubrey F. G. *In Portugal.* London: Bodley Head, 1912.

Chaves, Castelo Branco. *Os livros de viagens em Portugal no século XVIII e a sua projecção europeia.* Lisbon, 1977.

Costigan, Arthur William. *Sketches of Society and Manners in Portugal.* London: T. Vernon, 1787.

Crawfurd, Oswald. *Portugal Old and New.* London: Kegan, Paul, 1880.

————. *Round the Calendar in Portugal.* London: Chapman & Hall, 1890.

Darymple, William. *Travels through Spain and Portugal in 1774.* London: J. Almon, 1777.

Dumouriez, Charles Francois Duperrier. *An Account of Portugal as It Appeared in 1766.* London: C. Law, 1797.

Fielding, Henry. *Jonathan Wild and the Journal of a Voyage to Lisbon.* London: J. M. Dent, 1932.

Gibbons, John. *I Gathered No Moss.* London: Robert Hale, 1939.

Gordon, Jan and Cora Gordon. *Portuguese Somersault.* London: Harrap, 1934.

Huggett, Frank. *South of Lisbon: Winter Travels in Southern Portugal.* London: Gollancz, 1960.

Hume, Martin. *Through Portugal.* London: Richards, 1907.

Jackson, Catherine Charlotte, Lady. *Fair Lusitania.* London: Bentley, 1874.

Kelly, Marie Noele. *This Delicious Land Portugal.* London: Hutchinson, 1956.

Kempner, Mary Jean. *Invitation to Portugal.* New York: Atheneum, 1969.

Kingston, William H. G. *Lusitanian Sketches of the Pen and Pencil.* 2 vols. London: Parker, 1845.

Latouche, John [Pseudonym of Oswald Crawfurd]. *Travels in Portugal*. London: Ward, Lock & Taylor, ca. 1874.

Link, Henry Frederick. *Travels in Portugal and France and Spain . . .* London: Longman & Rees, 1801.

Macauley, Rose. *They Went to Portugal*. London: Jonathan Cape, 1946.

————. *They Went to Portugal, Too*. Manchester: Carcanet Books, 1990.

Merle, Iris. *Portuguese Panorama*. London: Ouzel, 1958.

Murphy, J. C. *Travels in Portugal*. London: 1795.

Quillinan, Dorothy [Wordsworth]. *Journal of a Few Months in Portugal with Glimpses of the South of Spain*. 2 vols. London: Moxon, 1847.

Sitwell, Sacheverell. *Portugal and Madeira*. London: Batsford, 1954.

Smith, Karine R. *Until Tomorrow: Azores and Portugal*. Snohomish, WA: Snohomish Publishing, 1978.

Thomas, Gordon Kent. *Lord Byron's Iberian Pilgrimage*. Provo, UT: Brigham Young University Press, 1983.

Twiss, Richard. *Travels through Portugal and Spain in 1772–1773*. London: 1775.

Watson, Gilbert. *Sunshine and Sentiment in Portugal*. London: Arnold, 1904.

Wheeler, Douglas L. "A[n American] Fulbrighter in Lisbon, Portugal, 1961–62." *Portuguese Studies Review*, I (1991): 9–16.

12. PORTUGUESE CARTOGRAPHY (MAPS, MAPMAKING), DISCOVERIES AND NAVIGATION

Albuquerque, Luís de. *Curso de História de Naútica*. Coimbra, 1972.

————. *Os Descobrimentos Portugueses*. Lisbon, 1985.

——. *Introdução a história dos descobrimentos.* Mem Martins, 1983. 3rd ed.

——. *Navegadores, viajantes e aventureiros portugueses. Séculos XV e XVI.* Lisbon, 1984.

——. *Portuguese Books on Nautical Science from Pedro Nunes to 1650.* Lisbon, 1984.

Boorstin, Daniel. *The Discoverers.* New York: Random House, 1983.

Boxer, C. R. *The Portuguese Seaborne Empire, 1415–1825.* London: Hutchinson, 1969.

Cortesão, Armando and Avelino Teixeira de Mota. *Cartografia Portuguesa Antiga.* Lisbon: 1960.

——. *História da Cartografia Portuguesa.* 2 vols. Coimbra, 1969–70.

——. *Portugalia Monumenta Cartográfica.* 6 vols. Lisbon, 1960–62.

Cortesão, Jaime. *Os descobrimentos portugueses* (ed. by V. Magalhães Godinho and Joel Serrão). 2 vols. Lisbon, 1960.

——. *Descobrimentos precolombanos dos portugueses.* Lisbon, 1966.

——. *A expansão dos Portugueses no período henriquinho.* Lisbon, 1965.

——. *L'expansion des portugais dans l'historie de la civilisation.* Brussels, 1930.

Costa, Abel Fontoura da. *A Marinharia dos Descobrimentos.* Lisbon, 1960. 3rd ed.

Costa Brochado, Idalino F. *Descobrimento do Atlântico.* Lisbon, 1958. English ed., 1959–60.

Coutinho, Admiral Gago. *A naútica dos descobrimentos.* 2 vols. Lisbon, 1951–52.

Crone, G. R. *Maps and Their Makers.* New York: Capricorn Books, 1966.

Dias, José S. da Silva. *Os descobrimentos e a problemática cultural do Século XVI.* Lisbon, 1982, 2nd ed.

Godinho, Vitorino Magalhães (ed.). *Documentos sobre a expansão portuguesa* [to 1460]. 3 vols. Lisbon, 1945–54.

Guedes, Max and Gerald Lombardi (eds.). *Portugal. Brazil. The Age of Atlantic Discoveries.* Lisbon: Bertrand; Milan: Ricci; Brazilian Culture Foundation, 1990. [Catalogue of New York Public Library Exhibit, Summer 1990.]

Harley, J. B. and David Woodward. *The History of Cartography. Volume 1: Cartography in Prehistoric, Ancient and Medieval Europe and Mediterranean.* Chicago: University of Chicago Press, 1987.

Leite, Duarte. *História dos Descobrimentos. Colectânea de esparsos.* 2 vols. Lisbon, 1958–61.

Ley, Charles. *Portuguese Voyages, 1498–1663.* London: Dent, 1953.

Marques, J. Martins da Silva. *Descobrimentos portugueses.* 2 vols. Lisbon, 1944–1971.

Morison, Samuel Eliot. *The European Discovery of America: The Northern Voyages, A.D. 500–1600.* New York: Oxford University Press, 1971.

————. *Portuguese Voyages to America in the Fifteenth Century.* Cambridge: Harvard University Press, 1974.

Mota, Avelino Teixeira da. *Mar, Além-Mar-Estudos e Ensaios de História e Geografia.* Lisbon, 1972.

Nemésio, Vitorino. *Vida e Obra do Infante D. Henrique.* Lisbon, 1959.

Parry, J. H. *The Discovery of the Sea.* New York: Dial, 1974.

Penrose, Boies. *Travel and Discovery in the Renaissance, 1420–1620.* Cambridge, MA: Harvard University Press, 1952.

Peres, Damião. *História dos Descobrimentos Portugueses.* Oporto 1943.

Prestage, Edgar. *The Portuguese Pioneers.* London, 1933. New ed.: New York: Barnes & Noble, 1967.

Rogers, Francis M. *Precision Astrolabe. Portuguese Navigators and Transoceanic Aviation.* Lisbon, 1971.

Velho, Álvaro. *Roteiro {Navigator's Route} da Primeira Viagem de Vasco da Gama (1497–1499).* Lisbon: 1960.

13. PORTUGAL AND HER OVERSEAS EMPIRES (1415–1975)

Abshire, David M. and Michael A. Samuels (eds.). *Portuguese Africa. A Handbook.* New York: Praeger, 1969.

Albuquerque, J. Moushino de. *Moçambique.* Lisbon, 1898.

Alexandre, Valentim. *Orígens do Colonialismo Português Moderno (1822–1891).* Lisbon, 1979.

Axelson, Eric A. *Congo to Cape: Early Portuguese Explorers.* New York: Harper & Row, 1974.

———. *Portugal and the Scramble for Africa, 1875–1891.* Johannesburg: Witwaterstrand University Press, 1967.

———. *Portuguese in South-East Africa, 1488–1699.* Cape Town: Struik, 1973.

———. "Prince Henry and the Discovery of the Sea Route to India." *Geographical Journal* (UK), 127, 2 (June 1961): 145–158.

———. *South-East Africa, 1488–1530.* London: Longmans, 1940.

Azevedo, Mário. *Historical Dictionary of Mozambique.* Metuchen, NJ: Scarecrow Press, 1991.

Bender, Gerald J. *Angola under the Portuguese. The Myth Versus Reality.* Berkeley, CA: University of California Press, 1978.

———. "The Limits of Counterinsurgency [in the Angolan War, 1961–72]." *Comparative Politics,* (1972): 331–360.

Bhila, H. H. K. *Trade and Politics in a Shona Kingdom. The Manyika and Their Portuguese and African Neighbours, 1875–1902.* Harlow, UK: Longman, 1990.

Birmingham, David. *The Portuguese Conquest of Angola.* Oxford: Clarendon Press, 1965.

Bottineau, Yves. *Le Portugal Et Sa Vocation Maritime.* Paris: Boccard, 1977.

Boxer, C. R. *The Christian Century in Japan.* Berkeley: University of California Press, 1951.

————. *Fidalgos in the Far East—Fact and Fancy in the History of Macau.* Berkeley: University of California Press, 1948.

————. *Four Centuries of Portuguese Expansion, 1415–1825: A Succinct Survey.* Johannesburg: Witwaterstrand University Press, 1961.

————. *The Golden Age of Brazil, 1695–1750.* Berkeley: University of California Press, 1962.

————. *The Portuguese Seaborne Empire 1415–1825.* London: Hutchinson, 1969.

————. *Portuguese Society in the Tropics.* Madison, WI: University of Wisconsin Press, 1965.

————. *Race Relations in the Portuguese Colonial Empire, 1415–1825.* Oxford: Clarendon Press, 1963.

————. *Salvador de Sá and the Struggle for Brazil and Angola, 1602–1688.* London, 1952.

———— and Carlos de Azevedo (eds.). *Fort Jesus and the Portuguese in Mombasa.* London: Hollis and Carter, 1960.

Broadhead, Susan H. *Historical Dictionary of Angola.* Metuchen, NJ: Scarecrow Press, 1992. 2nd ed.

Burton, Richard. *Goa and the Blue Mountains.* London: Bentley, 1851.

Cabral, Luís. *Crónica da Libertação.* Lisbon, 1984.

Caetano, Marcello. *Colonizing Traditions, Principles and Methods of the Portuguese.* Lisbon, 1951.

————. *Portugal E A Internacionalização Dos Problemas Africanos.* Lisbon, 1965. 3rd ed.

Castro, Armando. *O Sistema Colonial Português em África (meados do Século XX).* Lisbon, 1978.

Chaliand, Gerard. "The Independence of Guinea-Bissau and the Heritage of [Amilcar] Cabral." In *Revolution in the Third World.* Harmondsworth: Penguin, 1978.

Chilcote, Ronald H. *Portuguese Africa.* Englewood Cliffs, NJ: Prentice-Hall, 1967.

Clarence-Smith, Gervase. *Slaves, Peasants and Capitalists in Southern Angola 1840–1926.* Cambridge, UK: Cambridge University Press, 1979.

————. *The Third Portuguese Empire 1825–1975. A Study in Economic Imperialism.* Manchester, UK: Manchester University Press, 1985.

Davies, Shann. *Macau.* Singapore: Times Editions, 1986.

Dias, C. Malheiro (ed.). *História da colonização portuguesa no Brasil.* 3 vols. Oporto, 1921–24.

Diffie, Bailey W. and George Winius. *Foundations of the Portuguese Empire, 1415–1580.* Minneapolis, MN: Minnesota University Press, 1977.

Disney, Anthony R. *Twilight of the Pepper Empire: Portuguese Trade in Southwest India in the Early Seventeenth Century.* Cambridge, MA: Harvard University Press, 1978.

Duffy, James. *Portugal in Africa.* Cambridge, MA: Harvard University Press, 1962.

————. *Portuguese Africa.* Cambridge, MA: Harvard University Press, 1959.

————. "The Portuguese Territories." In Colin Legum (ed.). *Africa. A Handbook to the Continent.* New York: Holmes & Meier, 1967.

————. *A Question of Slavery.* Oxford: Oxford University Press, 1967.

————. *Shipwreck and Empire: Being an Account of Portuguese Maritime Disaster in a Century of Decline.* Cambridge, MA: Harvard University Press, 1955.

Felgas, Hélio. *Guerra em Angola.* Lisbon, 1961.

————. *História do Congo Português.* Carmona, Angola, 1958.

Galvão, Henrique and Carlos Selvagam. *O Império Ultramarino Português.* 3 vols. Lisbon, 1953.

Godinho, Vitorino Magalhães. "Portugal and Her Empire." In *The New Cambridge Modern History.* Vol. V (1961): 384–397; Vol. VI (1963): 509–540.

Hammond, Richard J. "Economic Imperialism: Sidelights on a Stereotype." *Journal of Economic History,* XXI, 4 (1961): 582–598.

————. *Portugal and Africa, 1815–1910: A Study in Uneconomic Imperialism.* Stanford: Stanford University Press, 1966.

Harris, Marvin. *Portugal's African Wards.* New York: American Committee on Africa, 1957.

————. "Portugal's Contribution to the Underdevelopment of Africa and Brazil." In Ronald H. Chilcote (ed.). *Protest & Resistance in Angola & Brazil. Comparative Studies.* Berkeley: University of California Press, 1972: 209–223.

Henderson, Lawrence W. *Angola. Five Centuries of Conflict.* Ithaca, NY: Cornell University Press, 1979.

Hilton, Anne. *The Kingdom of Kongo.* Oxford: Clarendon Press, 1985.

Hower, Alfred and Richard Preto-Rodas (eds.). *Empire in Transition: The Portuguese World in the Time of Camões.* Gainesville, FL: University Presses of Florida, 1985.

Isaacman, Allen. *Mozambique: The Africanization of a European Institution: The Zambezi Prazos, 1750–1902.* Madison, WI: University of Wisconsin Press, 1972.

―――. "The Prazos da Coroa 1752–1830: A Functional Analysis of the Political System." *STUDIA* (Lisbon), 26 (1969): 149–178.

―――. *The Tradition of Resistance in Mozambique. Anti-Colonial Activity in the Zambesi Valley 1850–1921.* Berkeley: University of California Press, 1976.

Jardim, Jorge. *Sanctions Double-Cross. Oil to Rhodesia.* Lisbon, 1978.

Kea, Ray A. *Settlements, Trade and Politics in the Seventeenth Century Gold Coast.* Baltimore: Johns Hopkins University Press, 1982.

Livingstone, Charles and David Livingstone. *Narrative of an Expedition to the Zambezi and Its Tributaries.* New York: 1866.

Livingstone, David. *Missionary Travels and Researches in South Africa.* London, 1857.

Lobban, Richard and Joshua Forrest. *Historical Dictionary of the Republic of Guinea-Bissau.* Metuchen, NJ: Scarecrow Press, 1988, 2nd ed.

―――― and Marilyn Halter. *Historical Dictionary of Cape Verde.* Metuchen, NJ: Scarecrow Press, 1988, 2nd ed.

Martin, Phyllis M. *Historical Dictionary of Angola.* Metuchen, NJ: Scarecrow Press, 1980, 1st ed.

Martins, Rocha. *História das Colónias Portuguesas.* Lisbon, 1933.

Marvaud, Angel. *Le Portugal et Ses Colonies.* Paris, 1912.

Mason, Philip (ed.). *Angola. A Symposium. Views of a Revolt.* Oxford: Oxford University Press, 1961.

Melo, João de (ed.). *Os Anos Da Guerra 1961–1975. Os Portugueses em África.* 2 vols. Lisbon, 1988.

Miller, Joseph C. *Way of Death. Merchant Capitalism and the Angolan Slave Trade, 1730–1830.* Madison, WI: University of Wisconsin Press, 1988.

Ministry of Foreign Affairs, Portugal. *Portugal Replies in the United Nations.* Lisbon, 1970.

————. *Vinte Anos de Defesa do Estado Português de Índia.* Lisbon, 1967.

Mondlane, Eduardo. *The Struggle for Mozambique.* Harmondsworth, UK: Penguin, 1969.

Moreira, Adriano. *Política Ultramarina.* Lisbon, 1956.

————. *Portugal's Stand in Africa.* New York: University Publishers, 1962.

Múrias, Manuel (ed.). *História da expansão portuguesa no mundo.* 2 vols. Lisbon, 1937–42.

————. *Short History of Portuguese Colonization.* Lisbon, 1940.

Negreiros, António de Almada. *Les Colonies Portugaises.* Paris, 1907.

Newitt, Malyn. *Portugal in Africa. The Last Hundred Years.* London: Longmans, 1981.

————. *Portuguese Settlement on the Zambesi. Exploration, Land Tenure and Colonial Rule in East Africa.* New York: Holmes & Meier, 1973.

Nogueira, Alberto Franco. *Diálogos Interditos. A Política Externa Portuguesa E A Guerra De África.* 2 vols. Lisbon, 1979.

————. *História De Portugal. 1933–1974. II Suplemento.* Oporto, 1981.

————. *Um político confessa-se (Diário: 1960–1968).* Oporto, 1987. 3rd ed.

————. *Salazar. Vol. V. A Resistência (1958–1964).* Oporto, 1984.

————. *The United Nations and Portugal. A Study of Anti-Colonialism.* London: Sidgwick and Jackson, 1963.

Nowell, Charles E. "Portugal and the Partition of Africa." *Journal of Modern History*, XIX, 1 (1947): 1–17.

Okuma, Thomas. *Angola in Ferment. The Background and Prospects of Angolan Nationalism.* Boston: Beacon, 1962.

Pattee, Richard. *Portugal and the Portuguese World.* Milwaukee: Bruce, 1957.

Pélissier, René. *La Colonie Du Minotaure. Nationalismes Et Revoltes En Angola (1926–1961).* Orgeval (France): Pélissier, 1978.

———. *Les Guerres Grises. Résistance Et Révoltes en Angola (1845–1941).* Orgeval: Pélissier, 1977.

———. *História de Moçambique. Vol. II.* Lisbon, 1988.

———. *Naissance De La Guinée; Portugais Et Africains Senegambie (1841–1936).* Orgeval: Pélissier, 1989.

———. *Naissance Du Mozambique: Tome 1, Tome 2, Résistance Et Révoltes Anticoloniales (1854–1981).* Orgeval: Pélissier, 1984. 2 vols.

Prestage, Edgar. *The Portuguese Pioneers.* London: Black, 1933.

Ranger, T. [Terence] O. "Revolt in Portuguese East Africa: The Makombe Rising of 1917." *St. Anthony's Papers.* Carbondale, IL: Southern Illinois University Press, 15 (1963).

Remy. *Goa, Rome of the Orient.* Trans. from the French by Lancelot Sheppard. London, 1957.

Ricard, Robert. *Études sur l'Histoire du Portugais au Maroc.* Coimbra, 1955.

Richards, J. M. *Goa.* London: Hurst, 1982.

Rodney, Walter. *A History of the Upper Guinea Coast, 1545–1800.* New York: Oxford University Press, 1970.

Rodrigues, José Honório. *África e Brasil: Outro Horizonte.* Rio de Janeiro, 1961.

Rogers, Francis M. *The Obedience of a King of Portugal.* Minneapolis: University of Minnesota Press, 1958.

————. *The Quest for Eastern Christians: Travels and Rumors in the Age of Discovery.* Minneapolis: University of Minnesota Press, 1962.

————. "Valentim Fernandes, Rodrigo de Santaella, and the Recognition of the Antilles as 'Opposite India.'" *Boletim da Sociedade de Geografia de Lisboa,* series 75 (July–September 1957): 279–309.

Russell-Wood, A. J. "Colonial Brazil." In David W. Cohen and Jack Greene (eds.). *Neither Slave nor Free.* Baltimore: Johns Hopkins University Press, 1972: 84–133.

————. *Fidalgos and Philanthropists: The Santa Casa da Misericordia of Bahia, 1550–1755.* Berkeley: University of California Press, 1968.

————. *From Colony to Nation: Essays on the Independence of Brazil.* Baltimore: Johns Hopkins University Press, 1975.

————. "Local Government in Portuguese America: A Study in Cultural Divergence." *Comparative Studies in Society and History,* 16 (1974): 187–231.

Salazar, António de Oliveira. *Goa and the Indian Union.* Lisbon, 1954.

————. "Portugal, Goa and the Indian Union." *Foreign Affairs* (New York), 34, 3 (April, 1956): 418–431.

————. "Realities and Trends of Portugal's Policies." *International Affairs* (London), XXXIX, 2 (April 1963): 169–183.

Saldanha, C. F. *A Short History of Goa.* Goa, 1957.

Sanceau, Elaine. *Good Hope, the Voyage of Vasco da Gama.* Lisbon, 1967.

————. *Henry the Navigator.* New York: Norton, 1947.

————. *Indies Adventure: The Amazing Career of Afonso de Albuquerque . . .* London: Blackie, 1936.

——. *Knight of the Renaissance: A Biography of Dom João de Castro* . . . London: Hutchinson, n.d.

——. *The Land of Prester John.* New York: Knopf, 1944.

——. *The Perfect Prince: Dom João II.* Oporto, 1959.

——. *Portugal in Quest of Prester John.* London: Hutchinson, 1943.

——. *The Reign of the Fortunate King {Manuel I}, 1495–1521.* Hamden, CT: Archon, 1969.

Schwartz, Stuart G. *Sovereignty and Society in Colonial Brazil.* Berkeley: University of California Press, 1973.

Serra, Carlos (ed.). *História de Moçambique.* 2 vols. Maputo (Mozambique): Tempo, 1982–83.

Silva, Botelho da (ed. and comp.). *"Dossier" Goa. {General Manuel} Vassalo e Silva. A Recusa do Sacrifício Inútil.* Lisbon, 1975.

Silva Cunha, J. M. da. *Questões Ultramarinos e Internacionais.* Lisbon, 1960.

Silva Rego, A. da. *História das missões do padroado português do Oriente: Índia (1500–1542) I vol.* Lisbon, 1949.

——. *Portuguese Colonization in the Sixteenth Century: A Study of Royal Ordinances.* Johannesburg: Witwaterstrand University Press, 1957.

——. *O Ultramar Português No Século XIX (1834–1910).* Lisbon, 1966.

Sousa Dias, Gastão. *Os Portugueses em Angola.* Lisbon, 1959.

Sykes, John. *Portugal and Africa: The People and the War.* London: Hutchinson, 1971.

Vail, Leroy and Landeg White. *Capitalism and Colonialism in Mozambique. A Study of Quelimane District.* Minneapolis: Minnesota University Press, 1980.

Verlinden, Charles. *The Beginnings of Modern Colonization.* Ithaca, NY: Cornell University Press, 1970.

————. "Italian Influence on Iberian Colonization." *Hispanic American Historical Review,* 33 (1953): 199–211.

Vogel, Charles. *Le Portugal et Ses Colonies.* Paris, 1860.

Vogt, John. *Portuguese Rule on the Gold Coast 1469–1682.* Athens, GA: University of Georgia Press, 1979.

Wheeler, Douglas L. "African Elements in Portugal's Armies in Africa (1961–1974)." *Armed Forces and Society* (Chicago), 2, 2 (Feb. 1976): 233–250.

————. "Anti-Imperialism Traditions in Portugal, Yesterday and Today." *Boston University Graduate Journal,* XII, 2 (Spring 1964): 125–137.

————. "The First Portuguese Colonial Movement, 1835–1875." *Iberian Studies* (Keele, UK), I, 1 (Spring 1975): 25–27.

————. "Gungunhana." In Norman R. Bennett (ed.). *Leadership in Eastern Africa, Six Political Biographies.* Boston: Boston University Press, 1968: 165–220.

————. "Gungunyane the Negotiator." *Journal of African History,* IX, 4 (1968): 585–602.

————. "Nineteenth Century African Protest in Angola: Prince Nicolas of Kongo (1830?–1860)." *African Historical Studies* (Boston), I (1968): 40–59.

————. "Portugal in Angola: A Living Colonialism?" In C. Potholm and R. Dale (eds.). *Southern Africa in Perspective.* New York: Free Press, 1972: 172–182.

————. "The Portuguese Army in Angola." *Journal of Modern African Studies* (Cambridge, UK), 7, 3 (Oct. 1969): 425–439.

————. "The Portuguese and Mozambique: The Past Against the Future." In John A. Davis and James K. Baker (eds.). *Southern Africa in Transition.* New York: Praeger, 1966: 180–196.

————. *The Portuguese in Angola, 1836–1891: A Study in Expansion and Administration.* Boston: Boston University, Department of History, Unpublished Doctoral dissertation, 1963.

————. "Portuguese Colonial Governors in Africa, 1870–1974." In L. H. Gann and Peter Duignan (eds.). *African Proconsuls. European Governors in Africa.* New York: Free Press, 1978: 415–426; and "J. Mousinho de Albuquerque (1855–1902)" and "J. Norton de Matos (1867–1955)": 427–444; 445–463.

————. "The Portuguese Exploration Expeditions and Expansion in Angola, 1877–1883." In Academia de Marinha and Instituto de Investigação Científica Tropical, *Vice Almirante A. Teixeira Da Mota. In Memoriam. Volume I.* Lisbon: 1987: 267–276.

————. "The Portuguese Withdrawal from Africa, 1974–1975; The Angolan Case." In John Seiler (ed.), *Southern Africa Since the Portuguese Coup.* Boulder, CO: Westview, 1980: 3–21.

————. "Rebels and Rebellions in Angola, 1672–1892." In Mark Karp (ed.). *African Dimensions. Essays in Honor of William O. Brown.* Boston: Boston University Press, 1975: 81–93.

————. "Thaw in Portugal." *Foreign Affairs,* 48, 4 (July 1970): 769–781.

———— and René Pélissier. *Angola.* London: Pall Mall and New York: Praeger, 1971; reprinted, Westport, CT: Greenwood, 1977.

Whiteway, R. W. *The Rise of the Portuguese Power in India, 1497–1550.* London: Constable, 1899.

Winius, George D. *The Black Legend of Portuguese India.* New Delhi: New Concept, 1985.

————. *The Fatal History of Portuguese Ceylon: Transition to Dutch Rule.* Cambridge, MA: Harvard University Press, 1971.

————. "The Portuguese Asian 'Decadência' Revisited." In Alfred Hower and Richard Preto-Rodas (eds.). *Empire in Transition.* Gainesville, FL: University Presses of Florida, 1980: 106–117.

14. PORTUGUESE MIGRATION AND COMMUNITIES ABROAD

Alpalhão, João António and Victor M. Pereira da Rosa. *Da Emigração a Aculturação: Portugal Insular e Continental no Quebeque.* Lisbon, 1983.

————. *A Minority in a Changing Society.* Lisbon, 1988.

————. "The Portuguese in a Changing Society." In J. L. Eliott (ed.). *Two Nations, Many Cultures: Ethnic Groups in Canada.* Scarborough, Ontario: Prentice-Hall, 1983.

Alves, Marcial. *Os Portugueses no Mundo.* Lisbon, 1983.

Anderson, Grace M. and David Higgs (eds.). *A Future to Inherit: Portuguese Communities in Canada.* Toronto: McClelland and Steward, 1976.

Arroteia, Jorge Carvalho. *A emigração Portuguesa-suas orígens e distribuição.* Lisbon, 1983.

Brettell, Caroline B. "Emigrar Para Voltar. A Portuguese Ideology of Return Migration." *Papers in Anthropology,* 20 (1979): 1–20.

————. "Nineteenth and Twentieth Century Portuguese Emigration. A Bibliography." *Portuguese Studies Newsletter,* 3 (Fall–Winter, 1977–1978).

————. *Men Who Migrate, Women Who Wait. Population and History in a Portuguese Parish.* Princeton: Princeton University Press, 1986.

————. *We Have Already Cried Many Tears: The Stories of Three Portuguese Migrant Women.* Cambridge, MA: Schenkman Publishing Co., 1982.

Carvalho, Eduardo de. *Os portugueses na Nova Inglaterra.* Rio de Janeiro, 1931.

Caspari, Andrea. "The Return Orientation among Portuguese Migrants in France." In E. de Sousa Ferreira and W. C. Opello, Jr. (eds.). *Conflict and Change in Portugal, 1974–1984.* Lisbon, 1985: 193–203.

Clausse, Guy. "L'Immigration Portugaise Au Luxembourg: Quelques Réflexions." *Réflets economiques luxembourgeois*, XXIX (1983): 39–51.

Felix, John Henry and Peter F. Senecal. *The Portuguese in Hawaii.* Honolulu, HI: Authors' edition, 1978.

Ferreira, Eduardo de Sousa. *As orígens e formas de emigração.* Lisbon, 1976.

Giles, Wenona. *Motherhood and Wage Labour in London, England. Portuguese Migrant Women and the Politics of Gender.* Ph.D. dissertation, Department of Anthropology. Toronto: University of Toronto, 1987.

Higgs, David (ed.). *Portuguese Migration in Global Perspective.* Ontario: Multicultural Society, 1990.

Klimt, Andrea. *Portuguese Migrants in Germany: Class, Ethnicity and Gender.* Ph.D. dissertation, Department of Anthropology. Stanford, CA: Stanford University, 1987.

Lavigne, Gilles. *Les ethniques et la ville: L'aventure des immigrants portugais à Montreal.* Montreal: Preamble, 1987.

Leder, Hans Howard. *Cultural Persistence in a Portuguese-American Community.* New York: Arno, 1980.

Lewis, J. R. and A. M. Williams. "Emigrants and Retornados: A Comparative Analysis of the Economic Impact of Return Migration in the Região Centro." In E. D. Sousa Ferreira and W. C. Opello, Jr. (eds.). *Conflict and Change in Portugal, 1974–1984.* Lisbon, 1985: 227–250.

Martins, J. Oliveira. *Fomento Rural e emigração portuguesa.* Lisbon, 1956.

Nazareth, J. Manuel. "Família e Emigração em Portugal." *Economia e Sociedade* (Lisbon), 23 (1977): 31–50.

Nunes, Maria Luisa. *A Portuguese Colonial in America: Belmira Nunes Lopes. The Autobiography of a Cape Verdean-American.* Pittsburgh, PA: Latin American Literary Review Press, 1982.

Pap, Leo. *The Portuguese-Americans.* Boston: Twayne, 1981.

Pereira, Miriam Halpern. *A Política Portuguesa Da Emigraçao, 1850–1930.* Lisbon, 1981.

Pereira da Rosa, Victor M. and Salvato V. Trigo. "Elementos para uma Caracterização da Família Imigrante Portuguesa na África do Sul." *Économia e Sociologia,* 41 (1986): 61–71.

————. *Portugueses e Moçambicanos no Apartheid: Da Ficção à Realidade.* Lisbon, 1986.

Purves, James. "Portuguese in Bermuda." *Bermuda Historical Quarterly,* 3 (1946): 133–142.

Ribeiro, F. G. Cassola. *Emigração Portuguesa.* Lisbon, 1986.

Rocha-Trinidade, Maria Beatriz da and Jorge Arroteia. *Bibliografia da Emigração Portuguesa.* Lisbon, 1984.

————. "Emigração." In *Dicionário Illustrado Da História De Portugal.* (1985): 205–207.

————. *A Emigração.* Lisbon, 1986.

————. "Espaços de herança cultural portuguesa-gentes, factos, políticas." *Análise Social* (Lisbon), XXIV (1988): 313–351.

————. "Prólogo." In E. Mayonne Dias (ed.). *Portugueses na América do Norte.* Los Angeles: UCLA, 1984: 7–12.

————. "La Sociologie des Migrations au Portugal." *Current Sociology,* 32, 2 (Summer 1984): 175–198.

————. "Towards Reintegration of Emigrants." In E. de Sousa Ferreira and Guy Clausse (eds.). *Closing the Migratory Cycle: The Case of Portugal.* Saarbrücken and Ft. Lauderdale: Breitenbach, 1985: 183–194.

Rogers, Francis M. *Americans of Portuguese Descent: A Lesson in Differentiation.* Beverly Hills, CA: Sage, 1974.

Serrão, Joel. *A Emigração Portuguesa.* Lisbon, 1974, 1st ed.

————. *Testemunhos sobre a Emigração Portuguesa. Antologia.* Lisbon, 1976.

Silva, F. Emídio da. *A Emigração Portuguesa.* Lisbon, 1917.

Silva, Manuela et al. *Retorno, Emigração e Desenvolvimento Regional em Portugal.* Lisbon, 1984.

Simões, Mário Pinto. *O Emigrante Português-Processos de Adaptação (o exemplo da Suíça).* Oporto, 1985.

Simões, Nuno. *O Brasil e a Emigração Portuguesa.* Coimbra, 1934.

Sousa Ferreira, Eduardo de and Guy Clausse (eds.). *Closing the Migratory Cycle: The Case of Portugal.* Saarbrucken and Ft. Lauderdale, FL: Verlag Breitenbach, 1986.

Viera, David et al. *Portuguese in the United States. A Bibliography (Supplement to the 1976 Leo Pap Bibliography). Essay Number 6 in Essays in Portuguese Studies.* Durham, NH: International Conference Group on Portugal, 1989.

Warrin, Donald. "Portuguese Immigrants in Nevada: An Historical Sketch," *UPEC Life* [União Portuguesa Do Estado Da California], LXXXIII, 1 (Spring 1989).

Williams, Jerry. *And Yet They Come. Portuguese Immigration from the Azores to the United States.* New York: Center for Migration Studies, 1982.

15. PORTUGAL'S ATLANTIC ISLANDS (AZORES AND MADEIRAS)

Bannerman, David A. and W. Mary Bannerman. *Birds of the Atlantic Islands.* Vol. III. Edinburgh: Oliver & Boyd, 1966.

Biddle, Anthony J. Drexel. *The Madeira Islands.* 2 vols. London: Hurst and Blackett, 1900.

Bryans, Robin. *The Azores.* London: Faber & Faber, 1963.

————. *Madeira, Pearl of the Atlantic.* London: Robert Hale, 1959.

Cooke, Rupert Croft. *Madeira.* London: Putnam, 1961.

Cossart, Noel. *Madeira—the Island Vineyard.* London: Christie's, 1984.

Da Silva, Fernando Augusto and Carlos Azevedo de Menezes. *Elucidário Madeirense.* 3 vols. Funchal, 1940.

Duncan, T. Bentley. *Atlantic Islands in the Seventeenth Century: Madeira, the Azores and the Cape Verdes in Seventeenth Century Commerce and Navigation.* Chicago: University of Chicago Press, 1972.

Gregory, Desmond. *The Beneficent Usurpers. A History of the British in Madeira.* Rutherford, NJ: Fairleigh Dickinson University Press, 1988.

Guill, James H. *A History of the Azores Islands.* Menlo Park, CA: Author's Edition, 1972.

Instituto Histórico Da Ilha Terceira [Azores]. *Os Açores E O Atlântico (Séculos XIV–XVII)* [Proceedings of International Colloquium, August 1983]. Angra do Heroismo, Terceira Island, Azores, 1984.

Koebel, William Henry. *Madeira Old and New.* London: Griffiths, 1909.

Mee, Jules. *Histoire de la découverte des Iles Açores.* Ghent, 1901.

Peres, Damião. *A Madeira sob os donatórios-Séculos XV e XVI.* Funchal, 1914.

Rogers, Francis M. *Atlantic Islanders of the Azores and Madeiras.* North Quincy, MA: Christopher House, 1979.

Serpa, Caetano Valadão. *A Gente Dos Açores. Identificaçao-Emigração E Religiosidade. Séculos XVI–XX.* Lisbon: 1978.

Silva, J. Donald. *A Bibliography {works in English} on the Madeira Islands.* Durham, NH: International Conference Group on Portugal; University of New Hampshire: Essays in Portuguese Studies, Number 5, 1987.

———. "With Columbus in Madeira." *Portuguese Studies Review* (Durham, NH), I, 1 (Spring–Summer 1991).

Wheeler, Douglas L. "The Azores and the United States (1787–1987): Two Hundred Years of Shared History." In *Boletim do Instituto Histórico da Ilha Terceira,* XLV (1988): 55–71.

16. THE ANGLO-PORTUGUESE ALLIANCE (1373–PRESENT)

Almada, José de. *A Aliança Inglesa.* 2 vols. Lisbon, 1947.

———. *Para a história da aliança luso-britânica.* Lisbon, 1955.

Atkinson, William C. *British Contributions to Portuguese and Brazilian Studies.* London: British Council, 1974.

Bourne, Kenneth. *The Foreign Policy of Victorian England 1830–1902.* Oxford: Oxford University Press, 1970.

British Broadcasting Corporation (BBC). *600 Years of Anglo-Portuguese Alliance.* London: BBC, 1973.

British Community Council of London. *Souvenir Brochure Commemorating the 600th Anniversary of the Anglo-Portuguese Treaty of Alliance and Friendship, 1373–1973.* Lisbon, 1973.

Cabral, Manuel Villaverde. *Portugal na Álvorada do Século XX.* Lisbon, 1979.

Caetano, Marcello. "L'alliance Anglo-Portuguese: histoire et situation actuelle." *Chronique de politique etrangére* (Paris), XX, 6 (1967): 695–708.

———. "Aliança Inglesa." *Enciclopédia Luso-Brasileira da Cultura,* Vol. I (1963): 1270–1271.

———. *Portugal e a Internacionalização dos Problemas Africanos.* Lisbon, 1971.

Crollen, Luc. "Portugal," In O. De Raeymaeker et al. *Small Powers in Alignment*. Leuven, Belgium: Leuven University Press, 1974: 27–96.

———. *Portugal, the U.S. and NATO*. Leuven, Belgium: Leuven University Press, 1973.

Cunha Leal, Francisco. *Portugal e Inglaterra*. Corunna, 1932.

Davidson, Basil. "The Oldest Alliance Faces a Crisis." In Philip Mason (ed.). *Angola. A Symposium. Views of a Revolt*. London: Oxford University Press, 1962: 138–160.

Duff, Katherine. "The War and the Neutrals." In Arnold and Veronica Toynbee (eds.). *Survey of International Affairs*. London: Chatham House, 1956.

Duffy, James. *A Question of Slavery*. Oxford: Clarendon Press, 1967.

Epstein, John. "The Anglo-Portuguese Alliance, 1373–1973." *World Survey* (London), 54 (June 1973): 18 p.

Ferreira, José Medeiros. *Estudos de Estratégia e Relações Internacionais*. Lisbon, 1981.

Ferreira Martins, General L. *A Cooperação Anglo-Portuguesa na Grande Guerra de 1914–18*. Lisbon, 1942.

———. *O Poder Militar Da Gran-Bretanha E A Aliança Anglo-Lusa*. Coimbra, 1939.

Fisher, H. E. S. *The Portugal Trade: A Study of Anglo-Portuguese Commerce 1700–1770*. London: Methuen, 1971.

Francis, A. D. *The Methuens and Portugal 1691–1708*. Cambridge: Cambridge University Press, 1966.

———. *Portugal 1715–1808*. London: Tamesis, 1985.

———. *The Wine Trade*. London: Black, 1972.

Freitas, A. Barjona de. *A Questão Ingleza*. Lisbon, 1891.

Gallagher, Tom. "Anglo-Portuguese Relations Since 1900." *History Today* (London), 35 (1986): 39–45.

Glover, Michael. "A Particular Service: [Marshal] Beresford's Peninsular War." *History Today* (London), 36 (1986): 34–38.

Gonçalves, Caetano. *A Aliança Luso-Britânica e o Domínio Colonial Português*. Lisbon, 1917.

Guedes, Armando Marques. *A Aliança Inglesa. Notas de História diplomática, 1383–1943*. Lisbon, 1943.

Halpern Pereira, Miriam. *Revolução, finanças, dependência externa*. Lisbon, 1979.

Howorth, A. H. D'Araujo Scott. *A Aliança Luso-Britânica E A Segunda Guerra Mundial*. Lisbon, 1956.

Kay, Hugh. *Salazar and Modern Portugal*. New York: Hawthorne, 1970.

Lawrence, L. *Nehru Seizes Goa*. New York: Pageant, 1963.

Livermore, H. V. "The Anglo-Portuguese Alliance: Historical Perspective." *600 Years of Anglo-Portuguese Alliance*. Lisbon: BBC, 1973: 7–15.

Macedo, Jorge Borges de. *História Diplomática Portuguesa-Constantes e Linhas de Força*. Lisbon, 1987.

Manoel, J. de Câmara. *Portugal e Inglatterra*. Lisbon, 1909.

Martinez, Pedro S. *História Diplomática de Portugal*. Lisbon, 1986.

Medlicott, W. N. *The Economic Blockade, Vol. II*. London: His Majesty's Stationery Office, 1952.

Ortigão, Ramalho. *John Bull*. Lisbon, 1887.

Prestage, Edgar. *Chapters in Anglo-Portuguese Relations*. London: Voss & Michael, 1935.

————. *Diplomatic Relations of Portugal with France, England and Holland from 1646 to 1668.* Watford, UK: Voss & Michael, 1925.

Read, Jan. "A True League: Portugal and Britain, 1373–1973." *History Today,* 23, 10 (July 1973): 486–494.

Russell, Peter E. *The English Intervention in Spain and Portugal in the Time of Edward III and Richard II.* Oxford: Oxford University Press, 1955.

Sarmento, J. E. Morães. *The Anglo-Portuguese Alliance and Coast Defense.* London, 1908.

Serrão, Joel. "O Ultimatum [January 1890]." *Dicionário de História de Portugal.* Vol. IV (1971): 219–224.

Shafaat, Ahmed Khan (ed.). *Anglo-Portuguese Negotiations Relating to Bombay, 1660–1667.* Oxford: Oxford University Press, 1922.

Sideri, Sandro. *Trade and Power. Informal Colonialism in Anglo-Portuguese Relations.* Rotterdam: Rotterdam University Press, 1970.

Sousa, Carlos Hermenegildo de. *A Aliança Anglo-Portuguesa.* Lisbon, 1943.

Stone, Glyn A. "The Official British Attitude to the Anglo-Portuguese Alliance, 1910–45." *Journal of Contemporary History* (London), 10, 4 (Oct. 1975): 729–746.

Teixeira, Nuno Severiano. *O Ultimatum Inglês. Política Externa no Portugal do 1890.* Lisbon, 1990.

Teles, Basílio. *Do Ultimatum ao 30 de Janeiro.* Oporto, 1905.

Vieira de Castro, Luís. *D. Carlos I. (Elementos de História Diplomática).* Lisbon, 1941. 2nd ed.

Vincent-Smith, John. "Britain, Portugal and the First World War." *European Studies Review,* 4, 3 (1974).

————. "The Portuguese Economy and the Anglo-Portuguese Commercial Treaty of 1916." *Iberian Studies* (Keele, UK), III, 2 (Autumn 1974): 49–54.

———. "The Portuguese Republic and Britain, 1910–14." *Journal of Contemporary History,* 10, 4 (Oct. 1975): 707–727.

———. *As Relações Políticas Luso-Britânicas 1910–1916.* Lisbon, 1975.

Vintras, R. E. *The Portuguese Connection. A Secret History of the Azores Base.* London: Bachman & Turner, 1974.

Viriato (Pseudon.). *A Aliança Inglesa.* Lisbon, 1914.

Walford, A. R. *The British Factory in Lisbon and Its Closing Stages Ensuring upon the Treaty of 1810.* Lisbon, 1940.

Wheeler, Douglas L. "19th Century: Anglo-Portuguese Alliance and the Scramble for Africa." In BBC, *600 Years of Anglo-Portuguese Alliance.* London: BBC, 1973: 40–43.

———. *The Portuguese in Angola, 1836–1891: A Study in Expansion and Administration.* Unpublished Ph.D. Dissertation, History Department, Boston University, 1963.

———. "The Price of Neutrality: Portugal, the Wolfram Question and World War II." *Luso-Brazilian Review* (Madison, WI), 34, 1, 2 (Summer 1986; Winter 1986): 107–127; 97–111.

Wordsworth, William. *William Wordsworth's Convention of Cintra: A Facsimile of the 1809 Tract.* [Introduction by Gordon Kent Thomas] Provo, UT: Brigham Young University Press, 1983.

Young, George. *Portugal Old and Young.* Oxford: Oxford University Press, 1917.

17. ANTHROPOLOGY, SOCIOLOGY, RURAL AND URBAN SOCIETY

Brettell, Caroline B. "The Absence of Men." *Natural History,* 96, 2 (Feb. 1987): 52–61.

———. "Male Migrants and Unwed Mothers: Illegitimacy in a Northwestern Portuguese Town." *Anthropology,* 9, 1–2 (1985): 87–110.

————. *Men Who Migrate, Women Who Wait: Population and History in a Portuguese Parish.* Princeton: Princeton University Press, 1986.

————. "The Portuguese." In *Encyclopedia of World Cultures.* New Haven: Human Relations Area Files, 1990.

————. "The Priest and His People: The Contractual Basis for Religious Practice in Rural Portugal." In Ellen Badone (ed.). *Religious Orthodoxy and Popular Faith in European Society.* Princeton: Princeton University Press, 1990: 55–75.

Brogger, Jan. *Pre-bureaucratic Europeans: A Study of a Portuguese Fishing Community.* Oxford: Oxford University Press, 1989.

Cabral, Manuel Villaverde. "Portuguese Perspectives." *Sociologia Ruralis* [Journal of European Rural Sociology], XXIV, 1 (1986); number devoted to rural Portugal today.

Chaney, Rick. *Regional Emigration and Remittances in Developing Countries: The Portuguese Experience.* New York: Praeger, 1986.

Cutileiro, José. *A Portuguese Rural Society.* Oxford: Oxford University Press, 1971.

Deschamps, Paul. *Histoire Sociale du Portugal.* Paris, 1959.

————. *Portugal: La Vie Social Actuelle.* Paris, 1935.

Dias, Jorge. *Ensaios Etnológicos.* Lisbon, 1961.

————. *The Portuguese Contribution to Cultural Anthropology.* Johannesburg: Witwaterstrand University Press, 1964.

————. *Rio do Onor-comunitarismo agropastoral.* Oporto, 1953.

————. *Vilarinho Da Furna: Uma Aldeia Comunitária.* Lisbon, 1981. rev. ed.

Downs, Charles. *Community Organization, Political Change and Urban Policy: Portugal, 1974–1976.* Ph.D. dissertation, Department of Sociology. Berkeley, CA: University of California, 1980.

————. *Os Moradores à Conquista da Cidade.* Lisbon, 1978.

————. "Residents' Commissions and Urban Struggles in Revolutionary Portugal." In L. S. Graham and D. L. Wheeler (eds.). *In Search of Modern Portugal: The Revolution and Its Consequences.* Madison, WI: University of Wisconsin Press, 1983.

Espírito Santo, Moise. *Communidade Rural ao Norte do Tejo.* Lisbon, 1980.

Feijó, Rui, H. Martins and João de Pina Cabral (eds.). *Death in Portugal.* Oxford: Journal of the Anthropological Society of Oxford, 1983.

Feijó, Rui Graça. "State, Nation and Regional Diversity in Portugal: An Overview." In Richard Herr and John H. Polt (eds.). *Iberian Identity. Essays on the Nature of Identity in Portugal and Spain.* Berkeley: Institute of International Studies, University of California, 1989: 37–47.

Feio, Mariano. *Les Bas Alentejo et l'Algarve.* Lisbon, 1949.

Ferreira de Almeida, João. *Classes sociais nos campos.* Lisbon, 1986.

Fonseca, Ramiro da. *O Livro da Saúde e da Doença.* Lisbon, 1979.

Gallop, Rodney. *Portugal: A Book of Folk-Ways.* Cambridge, UK: Cambridge University Press, 1936. Reprinted, 1961.

Hoefgen, Lynn. *The Integration of Returnees from the Colonies into Portugal's Social and Economic Life.* Ph.D. dissertation, Department of Anthropology. Gainesville, FL: University of Florida, 1985.

Ingerson, Alice Elizabeth. *Corporatism and Class Consciousness in Northwestern Portugal.* Ph.D. dissertation, Department of Anthropology. Baltimore: Johns Hopkins University, 1984.

Jenkins, Robin. *The Road to Alto.* London: Pluto Press, 1979.

Lawrence, Denise. "Menstrual Politics: Women and Pigs in Rural Portugal." In T. Buckley and A. Gottlieb (eds.). *Blood Magic: The Anthropology of Menstruation.* Berkeley: University of California Press, 1988: 117–136.

―――――. "Suburbanization of House Form and Gender Relations in a Rural Portuguese Agro-Town." *Architecture and Behavior*, 4, 3 (1988): 197–212.

Martins, Hermínio. "Portugal." In Margaret S. Archer and Salvador Giner (eds.). *Contemporary Europe: Class, Status and Power*. New York: St. Martins, 1971.

Mattoso, José. *Identificação de um país*. Lisbon, 1985.

Merten, Peter. *Anarchismüs und Arbeiterkämpf in Portugal*. Hamburg: Liberatare Association, 1981.

Monteiro, Paulo. *Terra que ja foi terra. Análise Sociológica de nove lugares agro-pastorais da Serra da Lousã*. Lisbon, 1985.

Nataf, Daniel. *Social Cleavages and Regime Formation in Contemporary Portugal*. Ph.D. dissertation, Department of Political Science. Los Angeles: UCLA, 1987.

Nazareth, J. Manuel. "Família e Emigração em Portugal: Ensaio Exploratório." *Economia e Socialismo*, 23 (1977): 31–50.

O'Neill, Brian Juan. "Dying and Inheriting in Rural Tras-os-Montes." *Journal of the Anthropological Society of Oxford*, 14 (1983): 44–74.

―――――. *Social Inequality in a Portuguese Hamlet. Land, Late Marriage, and Inheritance, 1870–1978*. Cambridge: Cambridge University Press, 1987.

Pacheco, Helder. *Tradições Populares de Portugal*. Lisbon, 1985.

Pardoe, Julia. *Traits and Traditions of Portugal*. 2 vols. London, 1832.

Pereira Neto, João Baptista. "Social Evolution in Portugal since 1945." In Raymond S. Sayers (ed.). *Portugal and Brazil in Transition*. Minneapolis: University of Minnesota Press, 1968: 212–227.

Pina-Cabral, João de. "Sociocultural Differentiation and Regional Identity in Portugal." In R. Herr and J. H. Polt (eds.). *Iberian Identity*. Berkeley: Institute of International Studies, 1989: 3–18.

————. *Sons of Adam, Daughters of Eve: The Peasant World-View of the Alto Minho.* Oxford: Clarendon Press, 1986.

Poinard, Michel. *La Retour des Traveilleurs Portugais.* Paris: La Documentation Francaise, 1979.

Reed, Robert Roy. *Managing the Revolution: Revolutionary Promise and Political Reality in Rural Portugal.* Ph.D. dissertation, Department of Anthropology. Bloomington, IN: Indiana University, 1988.

Riegelhaupt, Joyce F. "Festas and Padres: The Organization of Religious Action in a Portuguese Parish." *American Anthropologist,* 75 (1973): 835–852.

————. "Peasants and Politics in Salazar's Portugal: The Corporate State and Village 'Nonpolitics.'" In H. Makler and L. S. Graham (eds.). *Contemporary Portugal: The Revolution and Its Antecedents.* Austin, TX: University of Texas Press, 1979: 167–190.

————. "Saloio Women: An Analysis of Informal and Formal Political and Economic Roles of Portuguese Peasant Women." *Anthropological Quarterly,* 40, 3 (July 1967): 109–126.

————. *In the Shadow of the City: Integration of a Portuguese Village* [São João das Lampas, nr, Cascais]. Ph.D. dissertation, Department of Anthropology. New York: Columbia University, 1964.

Rodrigues, Julieta E. S. de Almeida. *Continuity and Change in Urban Portuguese Women's Roles: Emerging New Household Structures.* Ph.D. dissertation, Department of Sociology. New York: Columbia University, 1979.

Rowland, Robert. "Demographic Patterns and Rural Society in Portugal." *Sociologica Ruralis.* 26, 1 (1986): 36–47.

Sanchis, Pierre. *Arraial. La Fête d'un Peuple: Les Pélerinages Populaires au Portugal.* Paris, 1976.

Siegel, Bernard J. "Conflict, Parochialism and Social Differentiation in Portuguese Society." *Journal of Conflict Resolution,* V, 1 (March 1961): 35–42.

————. "Social Structure and Medical Practitioners in Rural Brazil and Portugal." *Sociologia* (São Paulo), 20, 4 (Oct. 1958): 463–476.

Smith, T. Lynn. "The Social Relationships of Man to the Land in Portugal." *Sociologia,* 25, 4 (Dec. 1963): 319–343.

Sousa Santos, Boaventura. "Estado e sociedade na semiperíferia do sistema mundiale: o caso português." *Análise Social,* 87–89 (1985): 869–902.

————. "Social Crisis and the State." In Kenneth Maxwell (ed.). *Portugal in the 1980s: Dilemmas of Democratic Consolidation.* Westport, CT: Greenwood, 1986: 167–195.

Vasconcellos, Joaquim Leite de. *Ethnografia Portuguesa.* 8 vols. Lisbon, 1941–82.

————. *Tradições Populares Portugueses.* Lisbon, 1986. new ed.

Willems, Emílio. "On Portuguese Family Structure." *International Journal of Comparative Society* (Dharwar, India), 3, 1 (Sept. 1962): 65–79.

18. THE ARTS, ARCHITECTURE, URBAN PLANNING, MUSIC

Almeida, Rodrigo Vicente de. *História da Arte em Portugal. (Segundo Estudo) Documentos Inéditos.* Oporto, 1883.

Almeida D'Eça, Admiral Vicente M. *Castles of Portugal.* Lisbon, 1925.

Amaral, Francisco K. *Lisboa: Uma Cidade em Transformação.* Lisbon, 1969.

Azevedo, Carlos de and Chester Brummel. *Churches of Portugal.* New York: Scala Books, 1985.

Barreira, João (ed.). *Arte Portuguesa. As Decorativas.* 2 vols. Lisbon, n.d.

Barretto, Mascarenhas and George Dykes. *Fado: Lyrical Origins and Poetical Motivation.* Lisbon, 1977.

Branco, Luís de Freitas. *A Música em Portugal.* Lisbon, 1930.

Brito, Manuel Carlos de. *Opera in Portugal in the Eighteenth Century.* Cambridge, UK: Cambridge University Press, 1989.

Carlsen, Peter. "Historic Houses: Palácio Nacional de Queluz: A Former Portuguese Royal Palace." *Architectural Digest* (April 1981), 162–68.

Carvalho, Pinto de. *História de Fado.* Lisbon, 1903 and 1982 eds.

Chicó, Mário Tavares. *A Architectura Gótica em Portugal.* Lisbon, 1968.

França, José-Augusto. *A Arte em Portugal No Século XIX.* Lisbon, 1966.

———. *Lisboa Pombalina e o Illuminismo.* Lisbon, 1977. 2nd ed.

———. *A Reconstrução e a Arquitectura Pombalina.* Lisbon, 1978.

Gallop, Rodney. *Eight Portuguese Folksongs.* Oxford: Oxford University Press, 1936.

———. "The Fado (The Portuguese Song of Fate)." *Musical Quarterly,* XIX (1933): 199–213.

Kubler, George. *Portuguese Plain Architecture: Between Spices and Diamonds, 1521–1706.* Middletown, CT: Wesleyan University Press, 1972.

———. *Studies in Ancient American and European Art: The Collected Essays of George Kubler.* New Haven, CT: Yale University Press, 1985.

——— and Martin Soria. *Art and Architecture in Spain and Portugal.* Harmondsworth, UK: Penguin, 1959.

Lacerda, Aarão de. *História da Arte em Portugal.* 2 vols. Oporto, 1942–48.

Leão, Joaquim de Sousa. "Decorative Art, The Azulejo." In H. V. Livermore (ed.). *Portugal and Brazil: An Introduction*. Oxford: Oxford University Press, 1953.

Lopes Graça, Fernando. *A canção popular portuguesa*. Lisbon, 1953.

————. *A música portuguesa e os sus problemas: ensaios*. Lisbon, 1959.

Moita, Luís. *O fado: canção de vencidos*. Lisbon, 1936.

Picchio, Luciana Stegagno. *Storia del Teatro Portoghese*. Rome: Edizinio dell' Ateneo, 1964.

Queirós, José. *Cerâmica Portuguesa*. 2 vols. Lisbon, 1948. 2nd rev. ed.

Santos, Luís Reis. *Monuments of Portugal*. Lisbon, 1940.

Santos, Reinaldo dos. *A Escultura em Portugal*. 2 vols. Lisbon, 1948–50.

————. *História da Arte em Portugal*. Oporto, 1953.

Sasportes, José. *História da Dança em Portugal*. Lisbon, 1970.

Simões, J. M. dos Santos. *Azulejaria em Portugal no Século XVIII*. Lisbon, 1979.

————. "Azulejos in a Land of Many Colours." *Connoisseur* (London), CXXXVII, 551 (1956): 15–21.

Smith, Robert C. *The Art of Portugal, 1500–1800*. London, Weidenfeld and Nicholson, 1968.

————. "The Building of Mafra." *Apollo*, 97: 134 (April 1973), 360–67.

————. *A Talha em Portugal*. Lisbon, 1963.

Tannock, Michael. *Portuguese 20th Century Artists. A Biographical Dictionary*. Chichester, UK: Phillimore, 1978.

Taylor, René. "The Architecture of Port Wine." *The Architectural Review*, CXXIX, 772 (1961): 368–99.

Veiga de Oliveira, Ernesto. *Instrumentos musicais populares portugueses.* Lisbon, 1982.

Watson, Walter Crum. *Portuguese Architecture.* London: Constable, 1908.

Wohl, Hellmut. "Carlos Mardel and His Lisbon Architecture." *Apollo*, 97, 134 (April 1973): 350–59.

19. PORTUGUESE LITERATURE IN ENGLISH TRANSLATION: SELECTION

Alcaforado, Mariana. *The Letters of a Portuguese Nun (Mariana Alcaforado).* Trans. by Edgar Prestage. London: D. Nutt, 1893.

Andrade, Eugénio de. "White on White." Transl. by Alexis Levitin. *Quarterly Review of Literature. Poetry Series VIII.* Vol. 27. Princeton, NJ: 1987.

Andresen, Sophia de Mello Breyner. *Marine Rose. Selected Poems.* Transl. by Ruth Fainlight. Redding Ridge, CT: Swan Books, 1989.

Antunes, António Lobo. *An Explanation of the Birds.* Transl. by Richard Zenith. New York: Grove Weidenfeld, 1991.

———. *Fado Alexandrino.* Transl. by Gregory Rabassa. New York: Grove Weidenfeld, 1990.

———. *South of Nowhere.* Transl. by Elizabeth Lowe. New York: Random House, 1983.

Barreno, Maria Isabel, Maria Teresa Horta and Maria Velho da Costa. *The Three Marias: New Portuguese Letters.* Transl. by Helen R. Lane. New York: Doubleday, 1975.

Bell, Aubrey F. G. *Poems from the Portuguese (with the Portuguese text).* Transl. by A. Bell. Oxford, UK: Blackwell, 1913.

Camões, Luís de. *Camões. Some Poems Translated from the Portuguese by Jonathan Griffin.* London: Menard Press, 1976.

————. *The Lusiads.* Transl. by William C. Atkinson. Harmondsworth, UK: Penguin, 1952.

————. *The Lusiads of Luís de Camões.* Transl. by Leonard Bacon. New York: Hispanic Society of America, 1950.

Castro, José Maria Ferreira de. *Emigrants.* Transl. by Dorothy Ball. New York: Macmillan, 1962.

————. *Jungle.* Transl. by Charles Duff. New York: Viking, 1935.

————. *The Mission.* Transl. by Ann Stevens. London: Hamilton, 1963.

Dantas, Júlio. *The Cardinals' Collation.* Transl. by A. Saintsbury. London, 1962. 48th ed.

Dinis, Júlio. *The fidalgos of Casa Mourisca.* Transl. by Rosanna Dabney. Boston: D. Lothrop, 1891.

Garrett, Almeida. *Brother Luiz de Sousa.* [Play] Transl. by Edgar Prestage. London: Elkin Mathess, 1909.

Macedo, Helder (ed.). *Contemporary Portuguese Poetry: An Anthology in English.* Transl. by Helder Macedo et al. Manchester, UK: Carcanet New Press, 1978.

Mendes Pinto, Fernão. *The Travels of Mendes Pinto.* [Orig. title: *Peregrinação*] Transl. by Rebecca D. Catz, with Introduction and notes. Chicago, IL: University of Chicago Press, 1989.

Miguéis, José Rodrigues. *A Man Smiles at Death with Half a Face.* Transl. by George Monteiro. Hanover, NH: University Press of New England, 1991.

Monteiro, Luís De Sttau. *The Rules of the Game.* Transl. by Ann Stevens. London: Hamilton, 1965.

Namora, Fernando. *Field of Fate.* Transl. by Dorothy Ball. London: Macmillan, 1970.

————. *Mountain Doctor.* Transl. by Dorothy Ball. London: Macmillan, 1956.

Nemésio, Vitorino. *Inclement Weather over the Channel.* Transl. by Francisco Cota Fagundes. Providence, RI: Gavea-Brown, 1993.

Paço D'Arcos, Joaquim. *Memoirs of a Banknote.* Transl. by Robert Lyle. London, 1968.

Pessoa, Fernando. *The Book of Disquiet.* Transl. by Alfred MacAdams. New York: Pantheon, 1991.

————. *Fernando Pessoa: Selected Poems.* Transl. and ed. by Peter Rickard. Edinburgh, UK: Edinburgh University Press, 1991.

————. *Fernando Pessoa: Sixty Portuguese Poems.* Transl. and ed. by F. E. G. Quintanilha. Cardiff, Wales: University of Wales Press, 1971.

————. "The Mariner: A 'Static Drama' in One Act." In *Translation. Portugal.* Transl. by George Ritchie et al. *The Journal of Literary Translation.* Vol. XXV. New York: Translation Center, Columbia University, 1991, 38–56.

————. *Message. Bilingual Edition.* Transl. by Jonathan Griffin. London: Menard Press and King's College, 1992.

————. *Selected Poems: Fernando Pessoa.* Transl. by Jonathan Griffin. Harmondsworth, UK: Penguin, 1982. 2nd rev. ed.

Pires, José Cardoso. *Ballad of a Dog's Beach.* Transl. by Mary Fitton. London and Melbourne: J. M. Dent, 1986.

Queirós, José Maria Eça de. *The City and the Mountains.* Transl. by Roy Campbell. London: Max Reinhardt, 1955.

————. *Cousin Bazilio.* Transl. by Roy Campbell. London: Max Reinhardt, 1953.

————. *The Illustrious House of Ramires.* Transl. by Ann Stevens. London: Bodley Head, 1968.

————. *Letters from England.* Transl. by Ann Stevens. London: Bodley Head, 1970.

————. *The Maias.* Transl. by Patricia McGowan Pinheiro. London: Bodley Head, 1965.

————. *The Relic.* Transl. by Aubrey F. G. Bell. London: Max Reinhardt, 1954.

————. *The Sin of Father Amaro.* Transl. by Nan Flanagan. London: Max Reinhardt, 1962.

Quental, Antero de. *Sixty-four Sonnets.* Transl. by Edgar Prestage. London: David Nutt, 1894.

Redol, Alves. *The Man with Seven Names.* Transl. by L. L. Barrett. New York: Knopf, 1964.

Ribeiro, Aquilino. *When the Wolves Howl.* Transl. by Patricia McGowan Pinheiro. New York: Macmillan; London: Cape, 1963.

Santareno, Bernardo. *The Promise.* Transl. by Nelson H. Vieira. Providence, RI: Gavea-Brown, 1981.

Saramago, José. *Baltasar and Blimunda.* Transl. by Giovanni Pontiero. New York: Harcourt, Brace, 1987.

————. *The Stone Raft.* Transl. by Giovanni Pontiero. New York: Harcourt, Brace, 1991.

————. *The Year of the Death of Ricardo Reis.* Transl. by Giovanni Pontiero. New York: Harcourt, Brace, 1991.

Sena, Jorge de. *By the Rivers of Babylon and Other Stories.* New Brunswick, NJ and London: Rutgers University Press, 1989.

————. *The Poetry of Jorge de Sena: A Bilingual Selection.* Transl. by Frederick G. Williams et al. Santa Barbara, CA: Mudborn Press, 1980.

Vicente, Gil. *Four Plays of Gil Vicente, Edited from the Editio Princeps (1562).* Transl. and ed. by Aubrey F. G. Bell. Cambridge, UK: Cambridge University Press, 1920.

————. *Lyrics of Gil Vicente.* Transl. by Aubrey F. G. Bell. Oxford, UK: Oxford University Press, Hispanic Notes and Monographs, Portuguese Series 1, 1921.

Vieira, António. *Dust Thou Art.* Transl. by Rev. W. Anderson. London, 1882.

20. PORTUGUESE AND PORTUGUESE-AMERICAN COOKING AND CUISINE

Asselin, E. Donald. *A Portuguese-American Cookbook.* Rutland, VT: Charles E. Tuttle, 1966.

Bourne, Ursula. *Portuguese Cookery.* Harmondsworth, UK: Penguin, 1973.

Crato, Maria Helena Tavares. *Cozinha Portuguesa I, II.* Lisbon: Editorial Presença, 1978.

Dienhart, Miriam and Anne Emerson (eds.). *Cooking in Portugal.* Cascais: American Women of Lisbon, 1978.

Feibleman, Peter S. *The Cooking of Spain and Portugal.* New York: Time-Life Books; Foods of the World, 1969.

Koehler, Margaret H. *Recipes from the Portuguese of Provincetown.* Riverside, CT: Chatham Press, 1973.

Manjny, Maite. *The Home Book of Portuguese Cookery.* London: Faber & Faber, 1974.

Marques, Susan Lowndes. *Good Food from Spain and Portugal.* London: Muller, 1956.

Schmaeling, Tony. *The Cooking of Spain and Portugal.* Ware, UK: Omega, 1983.

Vieira, Édite. *The Taste of Portugal.* London: Robinson, 1989.

Wright, Carol. *Portuguese Food.* London: Dent, 1969.

———. *Self-catering in Portugal: Making the Most of Local Food and Drink.* London: Croom Helm, 1986.

21. GARDENS AND GARDENING OF PORTUGAL AND MADEIRA

Afonso, Simonetta Luz and Angela Deleforce. *Palace of Queluz—The Gardens.* Lisbon, 1989.

Araújo, Ilídio Alves de. *Arte Paisagista e Arte das Jardins em Portugal.* Lisbon, 1962.

Azeredo, Francisco de. *Casas Senhoriais Portuguesas.* Barcelos, 1986.

Binney, Marcus. *Country Manors of Portugal.* New York: Scala Books, 1987.

Bowe, Patrick and Nicolas Sapieha. *Gardens of Portugal.* New York: Scala Books and Harper and Row, 1989.

Cane, Florence du. *The Flowers and Gardens of Madeira.* London, 1924.

Cardoso, Pedro Homem and Helder Carita. *Da Grandeza das Jardins em Portugal.* Lisbon, 1987.

Costa, António da and Luís de O. Franquinho. *Madeira: Plantas e Floras.* Funchal, 1986.

Nichols, Rose Standish. *Spanish and Portuguese Gardens.* Boston: 1926.

Pereira, Arthur D. *Sintra and Its Farm Manors.* Sintra, 1983.

Sampaio, Gonçalo. *Flora Portuguesa.* Lisbon, 1946.

Sitwell, Sacheverell. *Portugal and Madeira.* London: Batsford, 1945.

Underwood, John and Pat Underwood. *Landscapes of Madeira.* London, 1980.

Vieira, Rui. *Flowers of Madeira.* Funchal, 1973.

22. EDUCATION, SCIENCE, HEALTH AND MEDICAL HISTORY

Albuquerque, Luís de. *Ciência e experiência nos Descobrimentos portugueses.* Lisbon, 1983.

————. *Estudos de História.* 3 vols. Coimbra, 1973–81.

————. *Para a História de Ciência em Portugal.* Lisbon, 1983.

————. *As Navegações E A Sua Projecção Na Ciência E Na Cultura.* Lisbon, 1987.

Baião, António. *Episódios Dramáticos da Inquisição Portuguesa.* 3 vols. Lisbon, 1936–55.

Cabreira, António. *Portugal nos mares e nas ciências.* Lisbon, 1929.

Carvalho, Rómulo de. *A Astronomia em Portugal (séc. xviii).* Lisbon, 1985.

Fernandes, Barahona. *Egas Moniz. Pioneiro de descobrimentos médicos.* Lisbon, 1983.

Gaitonde, P. D. *Portuguese Pioneers in India: Spotlight on Medicine.* London: Sangam Books, 1983.

Hanson, Carl A. "Portuguese Cosmology in the Late Seventeenth Century." In Benjamin F. Taggie and Richard W. Clement (eds.). *Iberia & the Mediterranean.* Warrensburg, MO: Central Missouri State University, 1989: 75–85.

Higgins, Michael H. and Charles F. S. de Winton. *Survey of Education in Portugal.* London, 1942.

Hirsch, Elizabeth Feist. *Damião de Góis: The Life and Thought of a Portuguese Humanist.* The Hague, 1967.

Lemos, Maximiano. *Arquivos de História da Medicina Portuguesa.* Several vols. Lisbon, 1886–1923.

264 / Bibliography

————. Vol. I. História da Medicina em Portugal. Doutrina e Instituições. Lisbon, 1899.

Mira, Matias Ferreira de. História da Medicina Portuguesa. Lisbon, 1948.

Orta, Garcia de. Colóquios dos Simples e Drogas e Cousas Medicinais da Índia. Ed. by Conde de Ficalho. 2 vols. Lisbon, 1891–95.

Osório, J. Pereira. História e Desenvolvimento da Ciência em Portugal. 2 vols. Lisbon, 1986–89.

Pina, Luís de. "A Ciência em Portugal (bosquejo Histórico)." In Secretariado Nacional da Informação (ed.). Portugal. Breviário Da Pátria Para Os Portugueses Ausentes. Lisbon, 1946: 277–301.

————. "As Ciências na História do Império Colonial Português-Séculos XV a XIX." Anais de Faculdade de Ciências do Porto (1939–40).

————. "Os Portugueses Mestres de Ciência e Metras no Estrangeiro." Actas do Congresso do Mundo Português. Lisbon, 1940.

————. "Uma prioridade portuguesa do século XVI. João de Barros e a Dactiloscópia Oriental." Arquivo da Repartição de Antropologia Criminal, IV (1936).

Richards, Robert A. C. (ed.). Guide to World Science: Volume 9: Spain and Portugal. Guernsey, UK: F. H. Books, 1974. 2nd ed.

Saraiva, António José. História da Cultura em Portugal. 3 vols. Lisbon, 1950–62.

————. "João de Barros." Dicionário de História de Portugal, I (1963): 307–308.

Silvestre Ribeiro, José. História dos Estabelecimentos Scientíficos, Literários e Artísticos de Portugal nos Successivos Reinados da Monarchia. 3 vols. Lisbon, 1871–83.

Veiga-Pires, J. A. and Ronald G. Grainger (eds.). Pioneers in Angiography: The Portuguese School of Angiography. Lancaster, UK and The Hague: MTP Press, 1982.

23. PORTUGUESE FEMINISM AND WOMEN'S STUDIES

Barreno, Maria Isabel, Maria Teresa Horta and Maria Velho da Costa. *Novas Cartas Portuguesas*. Lisbon, 1972.

————. *The Three Marias. New Portuguese Letters*. Transl. by Helen R. Lane. New York: Doubleday, 1975.

Goodwin, Mary. "Portuguese Feminism." *Portuguese Studies Newsletter,* 17 (Spring–Summer 1987): 12–13.

Lamas, Maria. *As Mulheres do Meu País*. Lisbon, 1948.

"Mulheres Portuguesas e Feminismo." *Análise Social* [special number on Portuguese Women and Feminism], 22 (1986): 92–93.

Osório, Ana de Castro. *As Mulheres Portuguesas*. Lisbon, 1905.

Sadlier, Darlene J. *The Question of How. Women Writers and New Portuguese Literature*. Westport, CT: Greenwood Press; Contributions in Women's Studies, No. 109; 1989.

Silva, Manuela. *The Employment of Women in Portugal*. Luxembourg: Office for Official Publications, European Communities, 1984.

Velho da Costa, Maria. *Maina Mendes*. Lisbon, 1974.

Vicente, Ana and Maria Reynolds de Souza. *Family Planning in Portugal*. Lisbon, 1984.

24. RELIGION AND CATHOLIC CHURCH

Almeida, Fortunato de. *História da Igreja em Portugal*. 6 vols. Coimbra, 1910–1924, and Oporto, 1967–1972.

Alonso, Joaquim Maria. *The Secret of Fátima: Fact and Legend*. Cambridge, MA: Ravengate Press, 1979.

Alves, José da Felicidade (ed.). *Católicos e política de Humberto Delgado à Marcello Caetano*. Lisbon, 1969.

Araújo, Miguel de (ed.). *Dicionário político; 1; Os Bispos e a revoluçao de Abril.* Lisbon, 1976.

Bishko, Charles Julian. *Spanish and Portuguese Monastic History 600–1300.* London, Variorum Reprints, 1984.

Blanshard, Paul. *Freedom and Catholic Power in Spain and Portugal.* Boston: Beacon Press, 1962.

Boxer, C. R. *The Church Militant and Iberian Expansion 1440–1770.* Baltimore, MD, and London: Johns Hopkins University Press, 1978.

Bruneau, Thomas C. "Church and State in Portugal: Crises of Cross and Sword." *Journal of Church and State,* XVIII (1976): 463–490.

Freire, José Geraldes. *Resistência Católico ao Salazarismo-Marcelismo.* Oporto, 1976.

Herculano, Alexandre. *History of the Origin and Establishment of the Inquisition in Portugal.* Transl. by John C. Banner. Stanford, CA: Stanford University Press, 1962.

IPOPE. *Estudo sobre liberdade e religião em Portugal.* Lisbon, 1973.

Johnston, Francis. *Fátima: The Great Sign.* Chulmleigh, UK: Augustine Publications, 1980.

Kondor, Fr. Louis. *Fátima in Lucia's Own Words: Sister Lucia's Memoirs.* Fatima: Postulation Center, 1976.

Lourenço, Joaquim Maria. *Situação jurídica da Igreja em Portugal.* Coimbra, 1943.

Mattoso, José. *Religião e Cultura na Idade Média Portuguesa.* Lisbon, 1982.

Miller, Samuel J. *Portugal and Rome c. 1748–1830: An Aspect of Catholic Enlightenment.* Rome: Universita Gregoriana Editrice, 1978.

Oliveira, Manuel de. *História eclesiástica de Portugal.* Lisbon, 1948.

Pattee, Richard. *Portugal and the Portuguese World.* Milwaukee, WI: Bruce, 1957.

Prestage, Edgar. *Portugal: A Pioneer of Christianity.* Lisbon, 1945.

Richard, Robert. *Études sur l'histoire morale et religieuse de Portugal.* Paris: Centro Cultural de Gulbenkian, 1970.

Robinson, Richard A. H. *Contemporary Portugal: A History.* London and Boston: Allen & Unwin, 1979.

———. "The Religious Question and Catholic Revival in Portugal, 1900–1930." *Journal of Contemporary History,* XII (1977): 345–362.

Rodrigues, R. P. Francisco. *História da Companhia de Jesus na Assistência de Portugal.* 7 vols. Lisbon, 1931–50.

Roth, Cecil. *A History of the Marranos.* Philadelphia: Jewish Publication Society of America, 1932.

25. AGRICULTURE, VITICULTURE AND FISHING

Allen, H. Warner. *The Wines of Portugal.* London: Michael Joseph, 1963.

Barros, Afonso de. *A reforma agrária em Portugal.* Oeiras, 1979.

Beamish, Huldine V. *The Hills of Alentjo.* London: Geoffrey Bles, 1958.

Bennett, Norman R. "The Golden Age of the Port Wine System, 1781–1807." *The International History Review,* XII (1990): 221–248.

Black, Richard. "The Myth of Subsistence: Market Production in the Small Farm Sector of Northern Portugal." *Iberian Studies,* 18 (1989): 25–41.

Bravo, Pedro and Duarte de Oliveira. *Vinhas e Vinhos De Portugal.* Lisbon, 1979.

————. *Viticulture Moderna.* Lisbon, 1974.

Cabral, Manuel V. "Agrarian Structures and Recent Movements in Portugal." *Journal of Peasant Studies,* 4, 5 (July 1978): 411–445.

Cardoso, José Carvalho. *A Agricultura Portuguesa.* Lisbon, 1973.

Carvalho, Bento de. *Guía Dos Vinhos Portugueses.* Lisbon, 1982.

Clarke, Robert. *Open Boat Whaling in the Azores: The History and Present Methods of a Relic Industry.* Cambridge: Cambridge University Press, 1954.

Cockburn, Ernest. *Port Wine and Oporto.* London: Wine & Spirit, 1949.

Coull, James. *The Fisheries of Europe.* London: G. Bell & Sons, 1972.

Croft-Cooke, Rupert. *Madeira.* London: Putnam, 1961.

————. *Port.* London: Putnam, 1957.

Delaforce, John. *The Factory House at Oporto.* London: Christie's Wine Publications, 1979 and later eds.

Fletcher, Wyndham. *Port: An Introduction to Its History and Delights.* London: Bernet, 1978.

Francis, A. D. *The Wine Trade.* London: Adams and Charles Black, 1972.

Freitas, Eduardo, João Ferreira de Almeida and Manuel Villaverde Cabral. *Modalidades de penetração do capitalismo na agricultura: estruturas agrárias em Portugal Continental, 1950–1970.* Lisbon, 1976.

Gonçalves, Francisco Esteves. *Portugal. A Wine Country.* Lisbon, 1984.

Gulbenkian Foundation. *Agrarian Reform.* Lisbon, 1981.

Malefakis, Edward. "Two Iberian Land Reforms Compared: Spain, 1931–1936 and Portugal, 1974–1978." In Gulbenkian Foundation, *Agrarian Reform.* Lisbon, 1981.

Moreira da Fonseca, A. *Port Wine: Notes on Its History, Production and Technology.* Oporto, 1981.

Oliveira Marques, A. H. de. *Introdução a história da agricultura em Portugal.* Lisbon, 1968.

Pato, Octávio. *O Vinho.* Lisbon, 1971.

Pearson, Scott R. *Portuguese Agriculture in Transition.* Ithaca, NY: Cornell University Press, 1987.

Postgate, Raymond. *Portuguese Wine.* London: Dent, 1969.

Read, Jan. *The Wines of Portugal.* London: Faber & Faber, 1982.

Robertson, George. *Port.* London: Faber & Faber, 1982 ed.

Rutledge, Ian. "Land Reform and the Portuguese Revolution." *Journal of Peasant Studies,* 5, 1 (Oct. 1977): 79–97.

Sanceau, Elaine. *The British Factory at Oporto.* Oporto, 1970.

Simon, Andre L. *Port.* London: Constable, 1934.

Smith, Diana. *Portugal and the Challenge of 1992. Special Report.* New York: Camões Center/RIIC, Columbia University, 1990.

Stanislawski, Dan. *Landscapes of Bacchus: The Vine in Portugal.* Austin, TX: University of Texas Press, 1970.

Unwin, Tim. "Farmers' Perceptions of Agrarian Change in Northwest Portugal." *Journal of Rural Studies,* 1, 4 (1985): 339–357.

Venables, Bernard. *Baleia! The Whalers of Azores.* London: Bodley Head, 1968.

World Bank. *Portugal. Agricultural Survey.* Washington, DC: World Bank, 1978.

26. ECONOMY, INDUSTRY AND DEVELOPMENT

Aiyer, Srivain and Shahid A. Chandry. *Portugal and the E.E.C.; Employment and Implications*. Lisbon, 1979.

Baklanoff, Eric N. "Changing Systems: The Portuguese Revolution and the Public Enterprise Sector." *ACES (Association of Comparative Economic Studies) Bulletin*, 26 (Summer–Fall 1984): 63–76.

————. *The Economic Transformation of Spain and Portugal*. New York: Praeger, 1978.

————. "Portugal's Political Economy: Old and New." In K. Maxwell and M. Haltzel (eds.). *Portugal: Ancient Country, Young Democracy*. Washington, DC: Wilson Center Press, 1990: 37–59.

Barbosa, Manuel P. *Growth, Migration and the Balance of Payments in a Small, Open Economy*. New York: Garland, 1984.

Braga de Macedo, Jorge and Simon Serfaty (eds.). *Portugal Since the Revolution: Economic and Political Perspectives*. Boulder, CO: Westview, 1981.

Carvalho, Camilo et al. *Sabotagem Económica: "Dossier" Banco Espírito Santo e Comercial de Lisboa*. Lisbon, 1975.

Cravinho, João. "The Portuguese Economy: Constraints and Opportunities." In K. Maxwell (ed.). *Portugal in the 1980s*. Westport, CT: Greenwood, 1986: 111–165.

Dornsbusch, Rudiger, Richard S. Eckhaus and Lane Taylor. "Analysis and Projection of Macroeconomic Conditions in Portugal." In L. S. Graham and H. M. Makler (eds.). *Contemporary Portugal*. Austin, TX: University of Texas Press, 1979: 299–330.

The Economist (London). "Coming Home: A Survey of Portugal." (May 28, 1988).

————. "The New Iberia: Not Quite Kissing Cousins" [Spain and Portugal]. (May 5, 1990): 21–24.

————. "On the Edge of Europe: A Survey of Portugal." (June 30, 1984): 3–27.

――――. *Quarterly Economic Review*. London: The Economist Intelligence Unit, 1974–present.

Fundação Calouste Gulbenkian and German Marshall Fund of the U.S. (eds.). *II Conferência Internacional sobre e Economia Portuguesa*. 2 vols. Lisbon, 1979.

Hudson, Mark. *Portugal to 1993. Investing in a European Future*. London: The Economist Intelligence Unit/Special Report No. 1157/EIU Economic Prospects Series, 1989.

International Labour Office (ILO). *Employment and Basic Needs in Portugal*. Geneva, ILO, 1979.

Kavalsky, Basil and Surendra Agarwal. *Portugal: Current and Prospective Economic Trends*. Washington, DC: World Bank, 1978.

Krugman, Paul and Jorge Braga de Macedo. "The Economic Consequences of the April 25th Revolution." *Economia*, III (1979): 455–483.

Lewis, John R. and Alan M. Williams. "The Sines Project: Portugal's Growth Centre or White Elephant?" *Town Planning Review*, 56, 3 (1985): 339–366.

Makler, Harry M. "The Consequences of the Survival and Revival of the Industrial Bourgeoisie." In L. S. Graham and D. L. Wheeler (eds.). *In Search of Modern Portugal*. Madison, WI: University of Wisconsin Press, 1983: 251–283.

Marques, A. *La Politique Economique Portugaise dans la Période de la Dictature (1926–1974)*. Doctoral thesis, 3rd cycle, University of Grenoble, France, 1980.

Martins, B. *Sociedades e grupos em Portugal*. Lisbon, 1973.

Murteira, Mário. "The Present Economic Situation: Its Origins and Prospects." In L. S. Graham and H. M. Makler (eds.). *Contemporary Portugal*. Austin, TX: University of Texas Press, 1979: 331–342.

OCED. *Economic Survey: Portugal: 1988*. Paris: OCED, 1988. [see also this series since 1978]

Pasquier, Albert. *L'Économie du Portugal: Données et Problémes de Son Expansion.* Paris: Librarie Generale de Droit, 1961.

Pereira da Moura, Francisco. *Para onde vai e economia portuguesa?* Lisbon, 1973.

Pintado, V. Xavier. *Structure and Growth of the Portuguese Economy.* Geneva: EFTA, 1964.

Pitta e Cunha, Paulo. "Portugal and the European Economic Community." In L. S. Graham and D. L. Wheeler (eds.). *In Search of Modern Portugal.* Madison, WI: University of Wisconsin Press, 1983: 321–338.

————. "The Portuguese Economic System and Accession to the European Community." In E. Sousa Ferreira and W. C. Opello, Jr. (eds.). *Conflict and Change in Portugal, 1974–1984.* Lisbon, 1985: 281–300.

Porto, Manuel. "Portugal: Twenty Years of Change." In Alan Williams (ed.). *Southern Europe Transformed.* London: Harper & Row, 1984: 84–112.

Schmitt, Hans O. *Economic Stabilisation and Growth in Portugal.* Washington, DC: International Monetary Fund, 1981.

Selgado de Matos, Luís. *Investimentos Estrangeiros em Portugal.* Lisbon, 1973 and later eds.

Smith, Diana. *Portugal and the Challenge of 1992.* New York: Camões Center, RIIC, Columbia University, 1989.

Tovias, Alfred. *Foreign Economic Relations of the Economic Community. The Impact of Spain and Portugal.* Boulder, CO: Reinner, 1990.

World Bank. *Portugal. Current and Prospective Economic Trends.* Washington, DC: World Bank, 1978 and to the present.

27. GOVERNMENT AND POLITICS SINCE 1974

Aguiar, Joaquim. "Hidden Fluidity in an Ultra-Stable Party System." In E. de Sousa Ferreira and W. C. Opello, Jr. (eds.).

Conflict and Change in Portugal, 1974–1984. Lisbon, 1985: 101–127.

Bruneau, Thomas C. and Alex Macleod. *Politics in Contemporary Portugal. Parties and the Consolidation of Democracy.* Boulder, CO: Rienner, 1986.

Coelho, Mário Baptista (ed.). *Portugal. O Sistema Política a Constitucional, 1974–87.* Lisbon, 1989.

Domingos, Emídio Da Veiga. *Portugal Político. Análise das Instituições.* Lisbon, 1989.

Goldey, David. "Elections and the Consolidation of Portuguese Democracy: 1974–1983." *Electoral Studies,* 2, 3 (1983): 229–240.

Graham, Lawrence S. "Institutionalizing Democracy: Governance in Post-1974 Portugal." In Ali Farazmand (ed.). *Handbook of Comparative and Development Public Administration.* New York: Dekker, 1991: 81–90.

——— and Douglas L. Wheeler (eds.). *In Search of Modern Portugal. The Revolution and Its Consequences.* Madison, WI: University of Wisconsin Press, 1983.

Gunther, Richard. "Spain and Portugal." In G. A. Dorfman and P.J. Duignan (eds.). *Politics in Western Europe.* Stanford, CA: Hoover Institution Press, 1988: 186–236.

Maxwell, Kenneth (ed.). *Portugal in the 1980s: Dilemmas of Democratic Consolidation.* Westport, CT: Greenwood, 1986.

Maxwell, Kenneth R. and Scott C. Monje (eds.). *Portugal: The Constitution and the Consolidation of Democracy, 1976–1989.* New York: Camoes Center, RIIC, Camoes Center Special Report No. 2, Columbia University, 1991.

Opello, Walter C., Jr. "Local Government and Political Culture in a Portuguese Rural County." *Comparative Politics,* 13 (April 1981): 271–289.

————. "The New Parliament in Portugal." *Legislative Studies Quarterly*, 3 (May 1978): 309–334.

————. "Portugal's Administrative Elite: Social Origins and Political Attitudes." *West European Politics*, 6 (Jan. 1983): 63–74.

————. *Portugal's Political Development. A Comparative Approach*. Boulder, CO: Westview, 1985.

Pinto Balsemão, Francisco. "The Constitution and Politics: Options for the Future." In K. Maxwell (ed.). *Portugal in the 1980s*. Westport, CT: Greenwood, 1986: 197–232.

Sartori, Giovanni. "Portugal." In Sartori. *Parties and Party Systems. Vol. 1*. Cambridge, UK: Cambridge University Press, 1976: 131–145.

Secretary of State for Mass Communications. *Constitution of the Portuguese Republic* [1976]. Lisbon, 1977.

28. CONTEMPORARY PORTUGAL SINCE THE APRIL 25, 1974 REVOLUTION

Aguiar, Joaquim. *A Ilusão do poder: Análise do Sistema Partidário, 1976–1982*. Lisbon, 1983.

Almeida, Diniz de. *Ascensão, Apogeu e Queda do MFA*. 2 vols. Lisbon, 1979.

————. *Orígens e Evolução do Movimento dos Capitães*. Lisbon, 1977.

Alves, Márcio Moreira. *Les Soldats Socialistes du Portugal*. Paris: Gallimard, 1975.

Antunes, José Freire. *Sá Carneiro: Um Meteoro Nos Anos Setenta*. Lisbon, 1982.

————. *O Segredo do 25 de Novembro*. Mem Martins, 1983.

Arouca, Manuel. *Os Filhos Da Costa Do Sol*. Mem Martins, 1989.

Audibert, Pierre and Daniel Brignon. *Portugal: Les nouveaux centurions*. Paris, 1974.

Baptista, Jacinto. *Caminhos para uma revolução*. Lisbon, 1975.

Barreto, António. *Memórias da Reforma Agrária*. Mem Martins, 1983.

Bermeo, Nancy Gina. "Worker Management in Industry: Reconciling Representative Government and Industrial Democracy in a Polarized Society." In L. S. Graham and D. L. Wheeler (eds.). *In Search of Modern Portugal*. Madison, WI: University of Wisconsin Press, 1983: 181–198.

————. *The Revolution within the Revolution: Workers' Control in Rural Portugal*. Princeton, NJ: Princeton University Press, 1986.

Braeckman, Colette. *Portugal: Révolution surveilée*. Brussels: Rossel, 1975.

Bruneau, Thomas C. *Politics and Nationhood. Post-Revolutionary Portugal*. New York: Praeger, 1984.

————. "Popular Support for Democracy in Post-revolutionary Portugal: Results from a Survey." In L. S. Graham and D. L. Wheeler (eds.). *In Search of Modern Portugal*. Madison, WI: University of Wisconsin Press, 1983: 21–42.

————. "Portugal Fifteen Years after the April Revolution." In *Field Staff Reports* (1989–90/ No. 1, Europe). Indianapolis, IN: Universities Field Staff International, 1990: 3–11.

———— and Alex Macleod. *Politics in Contemporary Portugal. Parties and the Consolidation of Democracy*. Boulder, CO: Rienner, 1986.

Carvalho, Ortelo Saraiva de. *Alvorada em Abril*. Lisbon, 1977.

————. *Cinco Meses Mudaram Portugal*. Lisbon, 1975.

Cid, Augusto. *PREC-Processo Revolucionário Eventualmente Chocante*. Viseu, 1977.

Cunhal, Álvaro. *A Revolução Portuguesa*. Lisbon, 1975.

Downs, Charles. "Comissões de Moradores and Urban Struggles in Revolutionary Portugal." In *International Journal of Urban and Regional Research*, 4 (186): 267–294.

————. *Revolution at the Grassroots: Community Organizations in the Portuguese Revolution.* Albany, NY: State University of New York Press, 1989.

Dufour, Jean-Marc. *Prague sur Tage.* Paris, 1975.

Durão Barroso, José. *Le systéme politique portugais face à l'intégration européenne.* Lisbon, 1983.

Eisfeld, Rainer. "Portugal and Western Europe." In K. Maxwell (ed.). *Portugal in the 1980s.* Westport, CT: Greenwood Press, 1986: 29–62.

————. "Portugal: What Role/What Future?" In K. Maxwell (ed.). *Portugal Ten Years after the Revolution.* New York: RIIC, Columbia University, 1984.

————. *Sozialistischer Pluralismus in Europa. Ansätze und Scheitern am Beispiel Portugal.* Cologne: Verlag Wissenchaft ünd Politik, 1985.

Faye, Jean-Pierre (ed.). *Portugal: The Revolution in the Labyrinth.* Nottingham, UK: Spokesman, 1976.

Ferreira, Hugo Gil and Michael W. Marshall. *Portugal's Revolution: Ten Years On.* Cambridge: Cambridge University Press, 1986.

Figueira, João Costa. *Cavaco Silva. Homem de Estado.* Lisbon, 1987.

Filoche, Gérard. *Printemps Portugais.* Paris: Editions Action, 1984.

Frémontier, Jacques. *Os Pontos nos ii.* Lisbon, 1976.

Fundação Calouste Gulbenkian. *25 de Abril—10 anos depois.* Lisbon, 1984.

Futscher Pereira, Bernardo. "Portugal and Spain." In K. Maxwell (ed.). *Portugal in the 1980s.* Westport, CT: Greenwood Press, 1986: 63–87.

Gama, Jaime. *Política Externa Portuguesa 1983–85. Ministério dos Negócios Estrangeiros.* Lisbon, 1986.

————. "Preface." In J. Calvet de Magalhães, A. de Vasconcelos and J. Ramos Silva. *Portugal: An Atlantic Paradox.* Lisbon, 1990: 9–11.

Gaspar, Jorge and Nuno Vitorino. "10 Anos de Democracia: reflexos na geografia política." In E. de Sousa Ferreira and W. C. Opello, Jr. (eds.). *Conflict and Change in Portugal 1974–1984/Conflitos e Mudanças em Portugal, 1974–1984.* Lisbon, 1985: 135–155.

————. *As Eleições De 25 De Abril: Geografia E Imagem Dos Partidos.* Lisbon, 1976.

———— et al. *As eleições para assembleia da república, 1979–1983: Estudos de geografia eleitoral.* Lisbon, 1984.

———— (eds.). *Portugal em mapas e em números.* Lisbon, 1981.

Giaccone, Fausto. *Una Storia Portoghese/Uma História Portuguesa.* Palermo: Randazzo Focus, 1987.

Gladdish, Ken. "Portugal: An Open Verdict." In Geoffrey Pridham (ed.). *Securing Democracy: Political Parties and Democratic Consolidation in Southern Europe.* London and New York: Routledge, 1990: 104–125.

Graham, Lawrence S. and Harry M. Makler (eds.). *The Decline and Collapse of an Authoritarian Order.* Beverly Hills, CA: Sage, 1975.

————. *Contemporary Portugal: The Revolution and Its Antecedents.* Austin, TX: University of Texas Press, 1979.

———— and Douglas L. Wheeler. *In Search of Modern Portugal: The Revolution and Its Consequences.* Madison, WI: University of Wisconsin Press, 1983.

Grayson, George W. "Portugal and the Armed Forces Movement." *Orbis,* XIX, 2 (Summer 1975): 335–378.

Green, Gil. *Portugal's Revolution.* New York: International, 1976.

Hammond, John L. *Building Popular Power. Workers' and Neighborhood Movements in the Portuguese Revolution.* New York: Monthly Review Press, 1988.

Harsgor, Michael. *Naissance d'un Nouveau Portugal*. Paris: Ed. du Seuil, 1975.

————. *Portugal in Revolution*. Washington, DC: CSIS and Sage, 1976.

Harvey, Robert. *Portugal, Birth of a Democracy*. London: Macmillan, 1978.

Insight Team of the Sunday [London] Times. *Insight on Portugal. The Year of the Captains*. London: Deutsch, 1975.

Janitschek, Hans. *Mario Soares. Portrait of a Hero*. London: Weidenfeld & Nicholson, 1985.

Keefe, Eugene K., et al. *Area Handbook for Portugal*. Washington, DC: Foreign Area Studies of American University, 1977. 1st ed.

Kramer, Jane. "A Reporter at Large: The Portuguese Revolution." *The New Yorker* (Dec. 15, 1975): 92–131.

Lauré, Jason and Ettagal Lauré. *Jovem Portugal. After the Revolution*. New York: Straus, Farrar and Giroux, 1977.

Livermore, H. V. *A New History of Portugal*. Cambridge, UK: Cambridge University Press, 1976.

Lourenço, Eduardo. *O Fascismo Nunca Existiu*. Lisbon, 1976.

————. "Identidade e Memória: o caso português." In E. de Sousa Ferreira and W. C. Opello, Jr. (eds.). *Conflict and Change in Portugal, 1974–1984*. Lisbon, 1985: 17–22.

————. *Os Militares e O Poder*. Lisbon, 1975.

Lucena, Manuel. "A herança de duas revoluções." In M. Baptista Coelho (ed.). *Portugal. O Sistema Político e Constitucional, 1974–87*. Lisbon, 1989: 505–555.

————. *Revolução e Instituições: A Extinção dos Grémios da Lavoura Alentejanos*. Mem Martins, 1984.

Macedo, Jorge Braga de and S. Serfaty. *Portugal Since the Revolution: Economic and Political Perspectives*. New York: Praeger, 1981.

Mailer, Phil. *Portugal: The Impossible Revolution.* London: Solidarity, 1977.

Manta, João Abel. *Cartoons/1969–1975.* Lisbon, 1975.

Maxwell, Kenneth. "The Communists and the Portuguese Revolution." *Dissent,* 27, 2 (Spring 1980): 194–206.

————. "The hidden revolution in Portugal." *The New York Review of Books* (April 17, 1975).

————. *Portugal in the 1980s. Dilemmas of Democratic Consolidation.* Westport, CT: Greenwood, 1986.

————. "Portugal under Pressure." *The New York Review of Books* (May 2, 1974).

————. "The Thorns of the Portuguese Revolution." *Foreign Affairs,* 54, 2 (Jan. 1976): 250–270.

———— (ed.). *Portugal Ten Years After the Revolution. Reports of Three Columbia University-Gulbenkian Workshops.* New York: Research Institute on International Change, Columbia University, 1984.

———— (ed.). *The Press and the Rebirth of Iberian Democracy.* Westport, CT: Greenwood, 1983.

———— and Michael H. Haltzel (eds.). *Portugal. Ancient Country, Young Democracy.* Washington, DC: Wilson Center Press, 1990.

Medeiros Ferreira, José. *Ensaio Histórico sobre a revolução do 25 de Abril.* Lisbon, 1983.

Medina, João (ed.). *Portugal De Abril. Do 25 Aos Nossos Dias.* In Medina. *História Contemporânea De Portugal.* Lisbon, 1985.

Merten, Peter. *Anarchismus ünd Arbeiterkampf in Portugal.* Hamburg: Libertare, 1981.

Miranda, Jorge. *Constituição e Democracia.* Lisbon, 1976.

————. *A Constituição de 1976.* Lisbon, 1978.

Morrison, Rodney J. *Portugal: Revolutionary Change in an Open Economy.* Boston: Auburn House, 1981.

Mujal-León, Eusebio. "The PCP [Portuguese Communist Party] and the Portuguese Revolution." *Problems of Communism,* 26 (Jan.–Feb. 1977): 21–41.

Neves, Mário. *Missão em Moscovo.* Lisbon, 1986.

Oliveira, César. *M. F. A. e Revolução Socialista.* Lisbon, 1975.

Opello, Walter C., Jr. *Portugal. From Monarchy to Pluralist Democracy.* Boulder, CO: Westview, 1991.

———. *Portugal's Political Development. A Comparative Approach.* Boulder, CO: Westview, 1985.

Pell, Senator Claiborne H. *Portugal (Including the Azores and Spain) in Search of New Directions. Report to the Committee on Foreign Relations, U.S. Senate.* Washington, DC: Government Printing Office, 1976.

Pilmott, Ben. "Socialism in Portugal: Was It a Revolution?" *Government and Opposition,* 7 (Summer 1977).

———. "Were the Soldiers Revolutionary? The Armed Forces Movement in Portugal, 1973–1976." *Iberian Studies,* 7, 1 (1978): 13–21.

——— and Jean Seaton. "Political Power and the Portuguese Media." In L. S. Graham and D. L. Wheeler (eds.). *In Search of Modern Portugal.* Madison, WI: University of Wisconsin Press, 1983: 43–57.

Porch, Douglas. *The Portuguese Armed Forces and the Revolution.* London: Croom Helm and Stanford: Hoover Institution Press, 1977.

Pouchin, Dominique. *Portugal, quelle révolution?* Paris, 1976.

Pulido Valente, Vasco. *Estudos Sobre a Crise Nacional.* Lisbon, 1980.

————. "E Viva Otelo!" In Pulido Valente, *O País das Maravilhas*. Lisbon, 1979: 451–454 [anthology of articles from weekly Lisbon paper, *Expresso*].

Rebelo de Sousa, Marcelo. *O Sistema de Governo Português antes e depois da Revisão Constitucional*. Lisbon, 1984. 3rd ed.

Rêgo, Raúl. *Militares, Clérigos e Paisanos*. Lisbon, 1981.

Robinson, Richard A. H. *Contemporary Portugal. A History*. London and Boston: Allen & Unwin, 1979.

Rodrigues, Avelino, Cesário Borga and Mário Cardoso. *O Movemento dos Capitães e o 25 de Abril*. Lisbon, 1974.

————. *Portugal Depois De Abril*. Lisbon, 1976.

Ruas, H. B. (ed.). *A Revolução das Flores*. Lisbon, 1975.

Rudel, Christian. *La Liberté couleur d'oeillet*. Paris: Fayard, 1980.

Sá Carneiro, Francisco. *Por Uma Social-Democracia Portuguesa*. Lisbon, 1975.

Sanches Osório, Helena. *Um Só Rosto. Uma Só Fé. Conversas Com Adelino Da Palma Carlos*. Lisbon, 1988.

Sanches Osório, J. *The Betrayal of the 25th of April in Portugal*. Madrid: Sedmay, 1975.

Schmitter, Philippe C. "An Introduction to Southern European Transitions from Authoritarian Rule: Italy, Greece, Portugal, Spain and Turkey." In G. O'Donnell, P. C. Schmitter and L. Whitehead (eds.). *Transitions from Authoritarian Rule*. Baltimore, MD: Johns Hopkins University Press, 1986: 3–10.

————. "Liberation by Golpe: Retrospective Thoughts on the Demise of Authoritarian Rule in Portugal." *Armed Forces and Society*, 2 (1974): 5–33.

Semprún, Jorge. *La Guerre Sociale au Portugal*. Paris: Champ Libre, 1975.

Silva, Fernando Dioga da. "Uma Administração Envelhecido." *Revista da Administraçao Pública,* 2 (Oct.–Dec. 1979).

Simões, Martinho (ed.). *Relatório Do 25 De Novembro. Texto Integral.* 2 vols. Lisbon, 1976.

Soares, Isabel (ed.). *Mário Soares. O homem e o político.* Lisbon, 1976.

Soares, Mário. *Democratização e Descolonização. Dez meses no Governo Provisório.* Lisbon, 1975.

Sobel, Lester A. (ed.). *Portuguese Revolution, 1974–1976.* New York: Facts on File, Inc., 1976.

Spínola, António de. *País Sem Rumo. Contributo para a História de uma Revolução.* Lisbon, 1978.

————. *Portugal e o Futuro.* Lisbon, 1974.

Stock, Maria José. *Os Partidos do Poder. Dez Anos Depois do "25 De Abril."* Évora, 1986.

Story, Jonathan. "Portugal's Revolution of Carnations. Patterns of Change and Continuity." *International Affairs,* 52 (July 1976): 417–434.

Sweezey, Paul. "Class Struggles in Portugal." *Monthly Review,* 27, 4 (Sept. 1975): 1–26.

Szulc, Tad. "Lisbon and Washington: Behind Portugal's Revolution." *Foreign Policy,* 21 (Winter 1975–76): 3–62.

Tavares de Almeida, António. *Balsemão: o retrato.* Lisbon, 1981.

"Vasco." *Desenhos Políticos.* Lisbon, 1974.

Vasconcelos, Álvaro. "Portugal in Atlantic-Mediterranean Security." In Douglas T. Stuart (ed.). *Politics and Security in the Southern Region of the Atlantic Alliance.* London: Macmillan, 1988: 117–136.

Wheeler, Douglas L. "Portugal's Crucial Test [election results, April 25, 1975, Constituent Assembly elections]." *The Christian Science Monitor* (April 7, 1975): 31.

————. "Survival Plus 5%: Portugal's Foreign Policy." *International Herald Tribune* (June 1, 1980).

————. "Will Portuguese Democracy Learn from History?" *Christian Science Monitor* (Sept. 18, 1978): 26.

Wiarda, Howard J. *Transcending Corporatism? The Portuguese Corporative System and the Revolution of 1974.* Columbia, SC: Institute of International Studies, University of South Carolina, 1976.

————. *The Transition to Democracy in Spain and Portugal.* Washington, DC: American Enterprise Institute for Public Policy Research, 1989.

Wise, Audrey. *Eyewitness in Revolutionary Portugal.* With a Preface by Judith Hart, MP. London: Spokesman, 1975.

APPENDIX A.
MONARCHS OF PORTUGAL (1140–1910)

Burgundian Dynasty
Afonso Henriques (Afonso I) (1140–1185)
Sancho I (1185–1211)
Afonso II (1211–1223)
Sancho II (1223–1246)
Afonso III (1246–1279)
Dinis (1279–1325)
Afonso IV (1325–1357)
Pedro I (1357–1367)
Fernando I (1367–1383)

Avis Dynasty
João I (1384–1433)
Duarte I (1433–1438)
Afonso V (1438–1481)
João II (1481–1495)
Manuel I (1495–1521)
João III (1521–1557)
Sebastião I (1557–1578)
Henrique (Cardinal-King) (1578–1580)

Phillipine (Spanish) Dynasty
Phillip [Filipe] I (Phillip II of Spain) (1580–1598)
Phillip II (Phillip III of Spain) (1598–1621)
Phillip III (Phillip IV of Spain) (1621–1640)

Braganza Dynasty
João IV (1640–1656)
Afonso VI (1656–1668)
Pedro II (Prince-Regent, 1668–83; King, 1683–1706)
João V (1706–1750)
José I (1750–1777)
Maria I (1777–1799)
João VI (Prince-Regent, 1799–1816; King, 1816–1826)
Pedro IV (1826–1834)
Maria II (1834–1853)

Pedro V (1853–1861)
Luís I (1861–1889)
Carlos I (1889–1908)
Manuel II (1908–1910)

APPENDIX B.
PRESIDENTS OF THE REPUBLIC
(1910–PRESENT)

First Republic (1910–1926)
    Teófilo Braga (1910–1911)
    Manuel de Arriaga (1911–1915)
    Teófilo Braga (1915)
    Bernardino Machado (1915–1917)
    Sidónio Pais (1917–1918)
    João do Canto e Castro (1918–1919)
    António José de Almeida (1919–1923)
    Manuel Teixeira Gomes (1923–1925)
    Bernardino Machado (1925–1926)

Estado Novo Dictatorship (Second Republic, 1926–1974)
    Óscar Carmona (1926–1951)
    Higino Craveiro Lopes (1951–1958)
    Américo Tomás (1958–1974)

Third Republic (1974–present)
    António de Spínola (May–September 1974)
    Francisco de Costa Gomes (September 1974–October 1976)
    Ramalho Eanes (1976–1981)
    Ramalho Eanes (1981–1986)
    Mário Soares (1986–1991)
    Mário Soares (1991–)

APPENDIX C.
PRIME MINISTERS SINCE 1932

Estado Novo Dictatorship (Second Republic, 1926–1974)
   António de Oliveira Salazar (1932–1968)
   Marcello Caetano (1968–1974)

Third Republic (1974–present)

Provisional Governments (1974–1976)
   1 Adelino de Palma Carlos (May–July 1974)
   2 Vasco Gonçalves (July 1974–September 1974)
   3 Vasco Gonçalves (September 1974–March 1975)
   4 Vasco Gonçalves (March 11–August 8, 1975)
   5 Vasco Gonçalves (August 8–September 19, 1975)
   6 Azevedo Pinheiro (September 19, 1975–July 1976)

Constitutional Governments (1976–present)
   1 Mário Soares (July 1976–January 1978)
   2 Mário Soares (January 1978–August 1978)
   3 Alfredo Nobre de Costa (August–November 1978)
   4 Carlos Mota Pinto (November 1978–July 1979)
   5 Maria Lurdes Pintassilgo (July 1979–January 1980)
   6 Francisco Sá Carneiro (January 1980–January 1981) [Sá Carneiro died in air crash Dec. 4, 1980]
   7 Francisco Pinto Balsemão (January 1981–September 1981)
   8 Francisco Pinto Balsemão (September 1981–June 1983)
   9 Mário Soares (June 1983–October 1985)
   10 Aníbal Cavaco Silva (October 1985–July 1987)
   11 Aníbal Cavaco Silva (July 1987–July 1991)
   12 Aníbal Cavaco Silva (July 1991–)

ABOUT THE AUTHOR

DOUGLAS L. WHEELER (A.B., Dartmouth College, M.A. and Ph.D., Boston University) is Professor of Modern History, University of New Hampshire, Durham, Research Associate, African Studies Center, Boston University and Affiliate, Center for International Affairs, Harvard University. He has been a visiting professor at Boston University, University College, Rhodesia (Zimbabwe), Morgan State College, and was Richard Welch Fellow in Advanced Research on the History of Intelligence at the Center for International Affairs, Harvard University (1984–85). In the 1980s he served as General Secretary of the SSPHS (Society for Spanish and Portuguese Historical Studies) and was one of the founders of the International Conference Group on Portugal (1972–) and since 1978 has been Coordinator of that academic association. He is Editor of the *Portuguese Studies Review,* a semi-annual academic journal. He is the author, co-author or co-editor of four other books on Portugal and Angola and is currently completing a history of Portugal during World War II and a history of 20th century spying. Among the periodicals he has published articles in are *Foreign Affairs, USA Today Magazine, International Herald Tribune,* and *The Christian Science Monitor.*